LIGHT FROM THE CAGE

25 Years in a Prison Classroom

JUDY PATTERSON WENZEL

FIFTH
AVENUE
PRESS

This book is dedicated to my brother
Eric William Patterson
(1954-2016),
who had unwavering faith in me,
and to
Christopher Constantine,
whose friendship and guidance
made all of this possible.

Fifth Avenue Press is a locally focused and publicly owned publishing imprint of the Ann Arbor District Library. It is dedicated to supporting the local writing community by promoting the production of original fiction, non-fiction and poetry written for children, teens and adults.

Printed in the United States of America

First Printing, 2017

ISBN: 978-1-947989-09-2 (Paperback)

Fifth Avenue Press

305 S Fifth Ave

Ann Arbor, MI 48104

fifthavenue.press

Contents

Prologue

JOURNEY

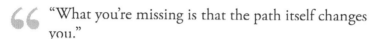 "What you're missing is that the path itself changes you."

—Julian Smith

"I JUST CAN'T BE the person I was anymore," Mr. Canner said as he walked into my classroom on the first day of a fall semester. "Is it okay to sit in the front row?" he asked.

"Sure, you will do fine!" I said.

A black man in his mid-fifties with white hair, he was the first student in the room. If he'd worn slacks and a jacket instead of prison khakis, he could have been mistaken for a professor. He had earnest eyes behind round glasses and an intent expression that exuded dignity and purpose.

He arranged notebooks and papers neatly as other students filed in to find seats in my classroom, shaped weirdly like a trapezoid. Our classroom ceiling was high, but there were only two small windows that looked out into the hall. I kept my door wide open on the first day to let the sun in from a tall window next to a door to the outside and to be as welcoming as possible to new students. I loved the first day of any new semester. My energy was high about meeting new students and seeing men who had been in my other classes. The wide, rather nervous smiles on my students added to the sense of expectancy.

"I haven't been in school for over 30 years," Mr. Canner whispered to me. "I feel like I've forgotten everything."

"It will be okay. Lots of people are nervous, but I can see that you want to work hard, which is the key."

"I will do my very best," was his response.

Immediately, he put his head down and went to work, his eyes on the prize, a high school diploma. Being in school and being so dedicated to success had already changed the path his life had taken. I felt admiration and awe watching students like this.

Not all of my students were this easy to work with. Mr. Slade gave me a half smile as he passed my desk. He settled his small body into his chair and promptly put his head on his folded arms. He was a black man in his early twenties. He was not very tall and was so thin that I wondered whether he was eating enough. On a few rare days, he paid attention and turned in good work, but even at the beginning of a semester, he couldn't seem to stay awake. Sleeping in class was not allowed.

"Are you feeling okay?" I asked as I gently nudged him during the first week, trying to get him to sit up. Nothing worked, so I suggested we talk quietly in hall.

"Can you tell me what's wrong?" I asked. "I'm concerned about you."

He shrugged, but refused to answer.

"Mr. Slade, I cannot help if I don't know what's wrong," I said.

Without looking at me, he mumbled, "My parents were both killed and I was there. I watched it."

I put my hand on his arm. "Oh, Mr. Slade. I am so sorry. What are you doing to take care of yourself?" I asked.

"I can't sleep very well and have a hard time getting up in the morning," he said, adding, "I sold some drugs to feed myself and ended up here."

I caught my breath. "Let's go back to class, and I will talk to people in the office," I said.

From his friendliness and from the thoughtful work he turned in, I suspected that a considerable person lived behind his wan smile and the soft, gentle greeting to me every morning. I was not trained to deal with trauma nor was he able to be in school, so he dropped out of the program. I hoped that people in the psychology department could help. He needed expert grief and trauma counseling and a consistent circle of loving people to help him want to start another day. Already, the path his young life had taken had changed him.

In the 25 years that I taught in this prison, I had all kinds of students, many as young as Mr. Slade and a few in their seventies and eighties. Their maturity levels spanned a wide spectrum, along with their school skills. I had men from all over the world and from many cultural groups across the country. The majority of them were young men in their twenties and thirties from the inner cities of the Midwest. I saw too many men who were profoundly traumatized like Mr. Slade, and I had students who suffered with mental disabilities far beyond my skill set.

I understood prison as a place of brokenness, with people separated from families, especially children. I saw men's lives put on hold for decades. I witnessed despair and grief, longing and loneliness. I also saw great courage and determination, good humor and great heart. It would take years for me to learn how and what to teach my students.

My path to prison came out of brokenness in my own life.

Moving is such a clear middle between the no longer and the not yet. The path began for me in one of my children's bedrooms as I lay down and let the tears come. The night before, after my Uncle Neil backed the moving truck up and it thudded against my old wraparound porch, family and friends had worked hard to move boxes onto the truck. When the job got done, he and my cousin Andy slammed the doors shut and headed south from Alpena in northeast

Michigan to Ann Arbor in the southeast. My dear, wise and wonderful friends Eddie and Rose invited me to stay overnight with them.

"I really want one more night in my house, and I don't really care if I sleep on the floor," I told them.

"Good idea," Eddie said. "Get up in the morning and move through all the rooms. Say good-bye to each one. Then come over and we'll have breakfast ready."

I loved my old house. I moved through it in the morning, the memories of raising my two daughters, Cynthia and Natalia, and my two sons, Seth and Stefan, in its gracious and sunlit old rooms overtaking me with all the jumbled-up feelings of joy, pain, change and loss. Cynthia and Natalia were headed off to college; Seth and Stefan would be caught between parents in two towns. I was feeling empty about my family and about what it meant to be moving away from the security of family rituals and a wondrous neighborhood in which to raise kids, steadfast friends and too many joyous milestones to count. After a good cry in the last bedroom, I went over to breakfast, hugged my friends through a tearful good-bye, got in my car and headed south. I would soon start a summer session at the University of Michigan.

The years leading up to the yellow moving truck had been rugged. I had finally signed divorce papers a few months before, after three long, painful years. Divorce hit me with what felt like an earthquake, the underground plates of my family's foundations rumbling and moving, forcing old, familiar forms into rubble on the surface. My family felt uprooted and forever changed. Almost everything, family, friends and finances felt profoundly different. My divorce now final, I needed a job. After several years of re-imagining my life, I knew I first needed to leave town and go back to school.

I had been *Mom* for many years, loving it. I knew how lucky I was to be happy and contented at home with just the right amount of part-time teaching. But, the yellow truck brought the reality of my empty nest in the near future. My children and I would be in three different towns now, some things about that a natural progression of events as they graduated and left for college, but I had no idea how to create new family shapes. As I drove south, I was sleep-deprived and shaky, feeling unmoored and nervous about an unknown future. If anyone had told me I was headed for a job in prison, I would have been thoroughly shocked.

I was 40, late to be starting a new career. As I left Alpena and drove south along Lake Huron, it sparkled in the sun like a sheet of tin foil. I was thinking: *What will I do without the lake? What will I do without my friends and family close by? Can I really do this?*

I did know I wanted to continue in education. My own educational history was rich and diverse after attending three different high schools and several colleges and universities, earning a degree from Wayne State University in Detroit. But, all of that jumping around didn't give me any confidence about being a student, and mediocre grades reflected my lack of self-esteem as a student. Like many women in the 1960s, I had earned a degree in elementary education. As the oldest of many cousins and siblings, I hadn't even considered another path. Wanting both a career and a family, teaching younger children seemed to fit. For a while it did, but as more of my children arrived, I made a decision to stay home and teach part-time. After many happy, balanced years with classes in the evenings with adults, I had a checkered career to put on a résumé: teaching fifth and sixth grades, along with classes in childbirth education and some tutoring of pregnant teens. I worked with two terminally ill children, both difficult teaching assignments, but I will treasure forever what they and their families taught me about love and courage.

In the last three years in Alpena, I started to substitute teach, primarily in high school classes where the need was greatest. I had many pleasant days, but the students were not mine, and it did not feel rewarding. After several years, I'd had it with the insecurity and low pay of substituting. I had a few years of teaching adults working on high school diplomas, my favorite classes. I ached for my own full-time classroom. The substituting gave me a huge gift, however. I now knew I needed to teach at the secondary level. On the few days that I could actually teach a lesson, students stayed right with me in the discussions, asking questions and offering comments. Connections to them and to the subjects thrilled me, and I realized that though I loved younger children, I didn't have the skills or talent to teach them well. I felt my adult students' excitement about having a second chance, and when they brought their life experiences into the class discussions, there was greater depth and understanding about the subjects at hand. They inspired me with the courage and determination it took to finally finish high school.

After almost 20 years away, courses at the University of Michigan to shore up an English major and earn secondary certification provided some humbling moments, and it took a few weeks to get in the swing of things. This experience would be useful later to discuss with my own returning students. I see now that I was in the process of a huge identity shift during that time. I was still *Mom*, but my children were forging their own paths.

My group of prospective English teachers visited some high school classrooms, and I pictured myself in places like that. After finishing my classes in the summer, I began to look for a job. It kept me awake at night as Labor Day got closer and my own classroom had not materialized. I needed as much work as I could get, so gritting my teeth, I stopped at a neighboring school district to put my name on its substitute list.

"Have you checked across the hall in Community Education? They are looking for teachers for the high school program in the prison," a secretary asked.

It was September 1986. I was hired on the spot, part-time at the prison, and I filled in with other high school completion classes during the first year. Milan Federal Correctional Institution and the town of Milan are seven miles south of Ann Arbor, a perfect commute. I was thrilled with the prospect of a full-time job teaching adults.

I DON'T REMEMBER THINKING about prisons or prisoners before I walked into this place. We had only a county jail in Alpena, and I paid little attention to it. I can remember jokes about prisoners, but I'd heard no stories about anyone who'd been incarcerated—nor had I met anyone who had done time. It was as if people behind bars did not exist. When word got out that I was going to prison to teach, I heard a whole lot of disparaging chatter. "Aren't you afraid?" people asked all the time. I heard the usual conversational banter about the *slammer*, the *pen* and I began to pick up the labels for people behind bars: *thugs*, *crooks*, *gangsters*, *convicts*, *hoodlums* and *jailbirds*.

"They're the scum of the earth," one person said.

It wasn't that I didn't have difficult students. I did. I met some unsavory characters who seemed to need time to think things over. People needed to be accountable to the people they'd hurt, but punitive policies and long sentences made the hard, inner work of becoming accountable harder. But, when given a chance to finish high school in a nurturing environment, so many men did well, grew up and changed their attitudes about school. Essentially, they changed their identities from *felon* to *successful student*. They began to envision a future, both in prison and when released. Education changed them. It helped them become *accountable to themselves* and enabled them to envision a future that was far better for them and their families.

Along with disparaging comments, many other people listened to the stories I told and began to get a more realistic picture of who was behind bars. Within just a few years, I could see that my classroom experiences needed to be shared. Several students and people on the outside suggested I write a book, so I began to collect special student papers, notes and reflections about what was happening in my classes.

I am not surprised when people have negative views of who lives behind the prison fence. It is human to fear people we don't know. And, there's the *fence*, a potent symbol saying the people inside need to stay there. With the security, which comes first in every facility, and the difficulty of ever getting inside to know people, it is not surprising that negative attitudes about the people inside persist. Though I experienced just one of thousands of jails and prisons in the country, I knew hundreds of men. My hope is that this book will add to a different conversation and enlarge the understanding of who our incarcerated citizens are—and what they can give the world. I have changed their names to protect them.

I knew nothing when I walked in the door in the first few semesters. I did not know when I first arrived how delightful surprise, along with profound shock about realities so different from my own, would come all the time. At first, this adventure was about needing a job, but from the first mention of these students, a little match scratched at my heart. I had no idea what to expect of the place or of my students, going in like a blind person. Though it would take many years to recognize it, I was starting out on a *pilgrimage*, a sacred journey. It was a journey toward wholeness, for my students as they discovered the goodness and beauty within them, and for me as I discovered, along with the brokenness, richness, beauty and courage within prison walls.

I say now that a short walk across a hall changed my life when I first accepted the job. I was so lucky to meet people whose backgrounds and experiences were so radically different from my own. I didn't have any idea what this journey would be like, but it gave me the access to people I never would have known otherwise. I didn't know how to teach them, but we struggled and learned together. For 25 years, being in my classroom was a journey about experiencing the beauty and humanity in the men I taught, a journey filled with breathtaking moments, laughter and joy, struggle, pain and triumph.

My students laid such complete grace upon my heart. My hope is that they lay some grace upon your heart, too.

I. MAPS

"THIS PROGRAM IS the only one that provides a high school completion program beyond passing the GED test in the whole country, and we are proud of it," my boss told me. I had no ideas about the institution, what it looked like inside, how it operated or how its culture affected its function. I knew nothing about the constraints of prison life, how overcrowding affected daily life or what it was like to be locked up for decades. I could not imagine being separated from family members, especially children, for decades.

I soon learned that the high school completion program was popular, and like other adult students I had taught in Alpena, most of these men were eager to work hard and succeed. I loved it immediately. I loved the freedom to design my own classes.

Like any teacher, I had my share of problem students, and I failed to reach some of them. But I loved being part of giving these men, most of whom came from inner-city schools, many more opportunities. Their experiences of haphazard attendance and poor performances in the programs "on the street" as they would say, often created an eagerness to set some new goals and succeed. Almost to a man, they were delighted and grateful for the chance to graduate from high school.

My boss called one morning and said, "We have a new class in Michigan history. The class will meet on Tuesdays and Thursdays, and you can start tonight if you wish."

My knowledge of my state's history was a bit sketchy, to say the least. That was the least of my problems. I had no prison training and I wasn't even sure where to park. Most importantly, I had no idea who the people were who I would be privileged to teach, their complicated lives, their enormous needs and their fierce desires to make their lives better. I did not know my students would be my teachers. I did remember my own nervousness and insecurities as a returning student after four semesters at the University of Michigan. It was the mid-1980s as I set off that early evening on this great adventure. Michigan's topography is interesting, so I decided to stop at a gas station and pick up some Michigan maps. It did not take long to get in trouble.

WHERE IN THE WORLD AM I?

Maps in hand, I gave myself some extra time and started driving south to the Milan Correctional Institution. I was nervous, not knowing what in the world to expect. I followed signs to the institution, parked in what seemed like the right place, and walked down the long sidewalk toward the front door. As I got closer, I had a better idea of the fence, really a double fence. A grassy no man's land lay between the two, the razor wire looping along the formidable barriers that surrounded everything except the front entrance and office areas. The razor wire gave me the shivers. I was startled to see a sign near the front door that warned: DO NOT ENTER BEYOND THIS POINT. I decided that did not include me. The lobby was empty except for a heavily glassed-in "house" on a diagonal in the corner. A small slot operated as a place to talk into so that I could get someone's attention.

"Hello," I called.

"Stay right there," a woman's voice answered. "I will come around."

In a few minutes, she appeared. Dressed in a blue and gray uniform, she was tiny and thin, not matching her authoritarian, clipped voice. "Where are you going?" she asked.

"To the education area," I answered.

"Oh. Okay," she answered. "Open the grilles," she said into the radio in her hand. "I will give her a ride."

"I'm confused," I said. "What does that mean?"

A motorized, grilled metal door slid sideways as we both walked through first one door and then another one like it.

"A ride means I escort you down there," she answered, as we walked down the hall together. I had an eerie feeling as the second door slid closed. The woman walked a little in front of me and did not seem interested in any conversation. As we walked down the hall, I saw bars on the windows and a lot of gray paint. Everything looked spotlessly clean. When we got to the education area, she unlocked a regular door and I stepped through as she disappeared. I found myself standing in a lobby with high ceilings and many doors to classrooms and offices. I found a short, business-like woman who showed me to my classroom. She was neither interested in knowing my name nor in answering a couple of my questions about breaks or when I should get ready to go.

"The inmates will be coming when there's a move," she told me.

Everything and everyone seemed sort of military.

The classroom had a wall of windows, which did not open. A large heavy mesh-like device covered it like a cage, but the windows were large and let in a lot of light. There were several long tables and a blackboard in the front. I soon learned that the men could move between buildings only when an announcement was made on the loudspeaker, and I understood that the glass house in the lobby was Control, a communications center for the whole place. I watched from the hall outside my room as about 50 men walked in resolutely, turning in several directions. I didn't feel afraid, but I was nervous about meeting my students, the old insecurities bubbling up. Plus, I wasn't exactly prepared to teach for several hours about—road maps.

I had no idea who or what kind of behavior to expect, but when I saw my seven students come down the hall to meet me, I noticed that everyone wore khaki clothing. They also wore disarming smiles —all of them.

"I'm Mrs. Wenzel," I said and smiled back at them while shaking their hands at the door.

The men filed in and took their seats.

"My English not too good. I'm from Mexico," one man told me.

Another man shook my hand and said his English wasn't too good either.

"I'm from Mexico, too," said another man, folding his hands and bowing a little. "Very nice to meet you, teacher."

A slight, dark-haired man with a heavy Brooklyn accent seemed the most at ease as he watched all these introductions. He put his hand out, declaring, "I'm Tony Bandoni and I can help with anything you need."

The only materials were a few old Michigan history textbooks I'd put on the tables. They did not help much as the Mexican men could barely speak English, let alone read it. Three other men were quiet, and I had a hard time getting them to talk. They looked nervous and unsure of themselves. I wondered how we would spend almost 3 hours talking about maps. As the men unfolded them, I pointed out all the Indian names and together we concluded that Indians had settled in Michigan first, and then when white people came, they used many of the Indian names. The Great Lakes define much of Michigan, so we learned what most Michigan students learn: the acronym HOMES, for Huron, Ontario, Michigan, Erie and Superior. The men looked at the colored photographs of lakes and rivers in Michigan on the maps, one Mexican man exclaiming, "Wow! Very pretty!"

I pulled a large map of the United States down and asked them to find Michigan. The Mexican men were very confused—they had no idea where Michigan was or where they were. I would soon learn that inmates are often flown in on what they call "Con Air" as they are first incarcerated or transferred to other facilities. None of this had anything to do with being in school, and they were not given a geography lesson on either the airplane or the bus from the airport.

They all *loved* the maps though, poring over them, pointing out the lakes they had learned and chatting among themselves. They were amazed at all the water. Eager to please, I said they could borrow them until the next class. The men were still smiling as they left, and everyone had been so pleasant and cooperative. As I put things away and walked down the hall to the office, I concluded that really—things had gone quite nicely.

Standing in the federal office waiting for another "ride," the same woman I'd seen earlier noticed my last remaining road map, clipped neatly to my clipboard.

"What are you doing with that road map?" she asked accusingly.

I was about to learn some vital prison lingo.

"These are *contraband*," she continued. "Don't you see these could be used as *escape routes*?" I felt a dunce cap slip over my face as she called Control.

"Students in Milan High School have Michigan road maps, and these students need to be searched immediately," she said into her radio. "I will bring you a list of them in a few minutes."

Sheepishly, I walked through the halls with her to the grilles and the outside. "You need to think about what you bring in here," she said. "These people are always thinking about ways to escape!"

I wanted to escape, too, and was so relieved to be outside and heading for my car. With my hands still shaking, I drove home and wondered if I'd just had the shortest teaching job in history. I felt silly. Why hadn't I thought about escape routes? My students had all been so nice and cooperative, and I worried that they would be punished, having no idea what that might be.

I approached the place warily five days later, still concerned about my men. Mercifully, the map problem had blown over, and the woman in the office didn't mention it. I was immensely relieved. My students did tell me that their maps had been taken away. This experience defined the next several years. I had so much to learn.

My Michigan history students continued to be on time, do their work and smile a lot. We did no more work with maps, but Tony Bandoni was the first man in the room when I returned after the escape route episode.

"Don't you worry about those maps, Miz Winslow. Your friend Tony's gonna be right here to help you," he assured me.

Mr. Bandoni, with his friendly smile and high energy, continued to be the first one in the room for the rest of the semester, very eager to help other students and eager to help me figure the place out. I was surprised to have students who spoke so little English, and I hadn't even heard of teaching English as a Second Language. It was the first of many times when I was winging it. I was realizing that my qualifications were frozen in my résumé and meant almost nothing when working with a student. We practiced pronouncing English words, reading a little and learning vocabulary words, but I felt inadequate. We soon developed a routine, the men worked hard and helped each other. No one gave me a minute's worth of trouble.

The first night was a rocky start, and I see now that I should never have been allowed to go near the place without at least some information. Security tightened over the years, and that would never happen now. I was thinking: *Maybe I could do this.* My hourly salary was a little more than two-thirds of what I could have made "on the streets," as my students called the outside world. We were required to teach 120 hours for a whole credit class and 60 hours for a half credit. If I missed any days, these were added on at the end of the semester. The program, run by the local school district, did not have any paid leave, but I did have a health care plan and time toward retirement. I had word from the director that additional classes would be available, which made me start daydreaming again. I would be presented with some very difficult students in the future and somehow understood that the Michigan history men were an exceptional group. They were so kind and happy. Helpful. Cooperative. And, every week as they left the room to go back to their units, they said, "Thank you, teacher, so much." Who wouldn't like students like these? It hadn't occurred to me that my students would be so polite and grateful.

Word was getting out that I had a job in a prison. The chatter from people continued like this: "Why should those guys get an education when there's not enough money for K-12?" "They're all sociopaths." "Aren't you afraid of the murderers?"

The comments reflected an attitude that people behind bars deserved nothing. An older woman, a professor, warned, "At your age, you have little time to build an important career. You should not waste your time on people like this."

I remember feeling like I'd been hit in the stomach and realized just how potent negative attitudes about prisoners were.

But, from that first night and meeting those lovely men, things felt *right*. It didn't once occur to me to be afraid of my students, and that little scratch at my heart when I first heard about it was growing into a glow. My next job was to try and get my bearings, learn about and get used to the institution itself.

———

Michigan is an interesting state geographically. I think—the *most* interesting. I live in the southeast corner in Ann Arbor, a college town with many parks and gentle little hills that slice through town. Traveling south toward Michigan's only federal prison, the terrain levels out. The prison compound, covering about 350 acres, sits in the middle of flat, rich farmland. Built in the 1930s, it houses about 1,600 men. There is little to see from the prison windows.

I was quickly learning three pieces of important information: how fast word travels inside prison walls, the warning from my program director to address all students as *Mister* _____, while I was *Mrs. Wenzel*, and that I needed to learn the prison jargon. (I gave up having my name pronounced correctly after a while. From the first class, I became *Miz Winslow* to many of my students). So far, all the new words and phrases like *call-out* and *counts* had done little except confuse me.

I so badly wanted a map of the place to get my bearings, but in those first months, I saw very little of the rest of the prison, called the *compound*, but I did become familiar with our area, called the *Complex*. In addition to the gym with connecting weight rooms and the library area, there were six larger classrooms and four smaller ones with two educational offices that opened to the lobby. The Complex also held religious services, which included chaplains' offices and a large room used for gatherings by all religious groups.

During the evening, the Complex was a good place for inmates to be. After the doors were unlocked, some men went around the corner and through the doors to the gym. Later during a break, when I walked down the other hall leading off the lobby, I saw the prison's library. I learned that the library was a popular place to be in the evenings, and many of the men had rushed forward in order to use one of the 10 typewriters available. Men relaxed and read on comfortable chairs in the library, which had a tall row of windows to the outside. They talked in small groups. Every federal correctional institution (FCI) is required to have a law library. I would later learn that men were busy all day working on their legal cases or helping other men work on theirs.

Prisons have rules and procedures unlike any outside of the fence. Some of my first lessons were about the need to be patient and flexible about interruptions and cancellations. There is a long history of inmates escaping in fog, so instead of the usual Michigan snow days, we had *fog days* when the men were locked down until the fog cleared and the restriction lifted. I was hearing that sometimes by mid-morning the day would turn beautifully sunny, but if the restriction went on early, classes were canceled for the day. It was sometimes difficult to finish the fall semester on time if we had too many fog days or were sent home for other security reasons, or if the administration needed our area for meetings and programs and did not want the men there.

Right away, I learned about "the hole," the segregated part of the compound where men were put when they broke a rule. Time in the hole might be just a day or two, but sometimes men spent months there for more serious offenses like fighting.

Prisons count their inmates regularly every day. My Michigan history men needed to get to their bunks for a *stand-up count* about 8 p.m., so they left class in a hurry. I learned that if someone wasn't where they were supposed to be, then there would be an additional count—often in the middle of a class. Teachers could get sent home immediately if there were emergencies like not having a count clear or needing to lock the men down when there were fights or other such altercations. I had little trouble in my first years in night classes with these interruptions, but it was good to be warned. Every teacher had to create an efficient system for getting appropriate work made up. Other security procedures became part of the job: many sets of fingerprints, annual security forms to fill out, annual in-service and training sessions, and a continually changing list of contraband items.

I would soon be issued two *chits*, small, round brass discs with my name on them that on arrival I would exchange for a body alarm and a set of keys to open my classroom door and filing cabinets. An identification badge was issued every day, but I wouldn't qualify for an unescorted pass, allowing me to move freely around the compound, for several years. Those were the rules, and they applied to all contract staff.

The jarring cacophony of noise never let up. Every time I went into the place, I had to adjust to an alternate universe. No country club, the place did not exactly hang out a welcome sign. Inmates need to work hard to find quiet and peaceful places, and I had to get used to doors slamming and the loudspeaker blaring all day long. Radios, carried by all federal staff, crackled with static, and radio messages were heard by anyone within earshot. A bunch of keys hung from large rings that clipped onto staff belts, the rattling keys an ever-present reminder of where we were. When I got ready to leave after an evening class and had gathered my things, locked everything behind me and walked down the hall with an escort, I had an eerie feeling when the grilles would grind open for me, allowing me to walk out into the autumn night. The fence looked ugly, the razor wire menacing. I could hear the cars on the freeway, all going somewhere else. Railroad tracks ran along the back fence, the train's whistle trailing mournfully into the air.

I was learning the rhythms and some of the language of the prison and a little about the high school program, but because I taught only at night for the first semester, I had almost no contact with my own co-workers. Instruction for taking the GED high school equivalency test was offered as a federal educational program, and if an inmate had not passed the GED test or did not have his high school diploma, federal rules required him to be in a federal class at his level until he passed the test or to be in our high school program for 240 hours. GED instruction certainly had its place for men who were

18

close to going home and did not have time to graduate, who were not interested in taking high school classes or who wanted both a diploma and a GED certificate. Both a GED certificate and a high school diploma are helpful gateways to colleges, especially at the community college level and helpful on job applications.

Our high school completion program, under the umbrella of community and adult education in the local school district, was created in 1977. At its strongest point, the program had 30 teachers, more than half of them teaching in the evenings and on weekends. At one time the high school program had 11 full-time teachers and 11 part-time teachers. Offering more in-depth instruction than GED classes, our high school program had classes in science, math, social studies, English and the humanities, art, computers, English as a Second Language, Spanish, French, accounting and business classes. We offered vocational programming, like auto repair and welding, conflict resolution, upholstery, film and video studies and food preparation. We offered pre-release classes for support and guidance about going home. Science teachers were able to teach courses like astronomy and the biology of cancer, winning praise from students.

It had never occurred to me that I would not be able to graduate from high school. As I got to know my students, I was learning that a high school diploma is a milestone accomplishment for many people on the margins of American society. For men who were incarcerated sometimes for decades, bored behind bars and worried about their future when they are released, going to school in prison was a very good idea. Being in school was not as easy as it appeared to be, but these students were immensely grateful for the opportunity—and said so all the time.

The institution felt heavy, harsh and hard, weighed down by the negative forces of oppression and punishment. The grass is green outside, but essentially, the buildings are devoid of comfort and hospitality. The place is filled with cold, metal doors and very few other colors besides gray and beige. And yet, the students I was meeting had a lightness about them, a laughing, smiling, eager joy about being in school. I was feeling lighter, the pain in "my other life," as a friend called it, was fading away. I was feeling nurtured by these lovely people.

Embedded in the American Dream is the idea that huge potential lies within all of us. Most people want purpose in their lives and to be of use, and these men were no different. They wanted to be doing something healthy and worthwhile while they were locked up, and they wanted to plan a better future for themselves and their families.

CLASS IN A FACTORY

After two semesters of teaching at night, I wanted to teach more classes, and since I was *certified* K-12, I could teach basic skills. I soon discovered that I wasn't very *qualified*. As soon as a man enrolled in the program, he was given a standardized test that measured reading, language and math skills. The first students I knew were in their thirties and older, so they had been out of school for at least a decade. Often, test scores were low and skills were rusty. Our high school program always offered classes in Adult Basic Education (ABE) for men to learn and review the basics up to a ninth-grade level.

After the first year, I was offered a class teaching ABE, but with a big catch. There were no more available rooms in the Complex, so my class would meet in the large building that housed a metal factory. UNICOR or Prison Industries was a part of a government-owned national network of factories established in 1934. Also, we would share a small room with a GED class, taught by one of the teachers on the federal staff. Sharing a room with another class did not sound wonderful, but I needed more hours and was eager to get my foot in the door to a more full-time schedule. For me, it would prove to be a class that I privately called: Developing Patience. And, I would also meet one of my favorite characters that fall.

The "region," the next level up in the Bureau of Prisons, dictated a lot of rules for contract staff. With a badge that required that a federal staff member had to accompany me everywhere, I felt restrained. I always needed a *ride,* as we called it. Two teachers who were part of the federal staff worked in this area, one teaching GED and the other teaching a welding class, and they were assigned to escort me. I would wait in the lobby until one of them arrived, and then both of us would walk across the inside yard and wait by the entrance until a factory supervisor would come along with the large key to let everyone in. Standing in the middle of about 30 inmate factory workers waiting with us in the cold and the rain, I remember thinking and laughing to myself more than once: *How did I get here with all of these people?*

The factory was noisy, dark and drab. It was hard to talk and be heard on the first floor. Metal mesh stairs led to a second floor that contained our classroom, a glassed-in area in the back corner. The ceilings in the factory were high, and I remember seeing a lot of birds flying around above us. A few men reported that they fed the birds. The classroom had bright lights, three large tables, some book shelves on our side in the back of the room. There was no divider between the two teaching areas. It was not ideal, but at least my class size was manageable with about 10 or 12, some who started later in the semester and some who left early. I remember wondering in the early weeks if it was possible to feel any more isolated from the rest of the program, from the rest of the prison and from the world outside the fence.

Teaching in the daytime required learning new rules and proce-dures. I think the body alarms we were required to wear were to make us feel safer, but I found mine, which was about 8-by-3-by-2 and weighed about 3 pounds, to be a huge annoyance. I came in every morning, stood in a "key line," threw my chits in the slot in Control, slipped my body alarm and badge in a black leather pouch on my belt and snapped on a set of keys. My alarm bumped on my body all day long. I needed to test my alarm at 8:30 every morning. So, I would pick up the phone, call Control, announce that I needed to test my alarm—and then wait in a queue for as long as 10 or 15 minutes. I quickly learned to get over my annoyance and have some work to do while I waited. My students and I all had to learn to share the room with the other class, which meant we learned to ignore them. I didn't want to disturb men on the other side of the room, so we had few discussions. I was usually working with only one student at a time and occasionally with a couple of students together.

One day the button on the top of my alarm caught on the

underside of the table and started to buzz. I was clueless as to what was happening, but in a few minutes, about 12 staff members rushed through the outside door and then into our room, there to make sure I was okay. I was embarrassed by all the attention, but when the staff filed out, my students assured me that this happened all the time. Almost all contract staff experienced a false alarm. I can remember several more false alarms of my own, but in 25 years, I did not need to push the button even once because I felt threatened by an inmate.

I was eager to settle down and start teaching, and I had to learn that teaching ABE was all about the ABE test. "Teaching to the test" was never a method I believed in, so I was trying to drum up my own enthusiasm in the first few weeks. That got easier as I got to know my students as individuals, sitting with them and asking them questions about their school experiences. Most of my students were pleasant and cooperative, but none of them seemed to have much momentum. I was discovering that many students who returned as adults were afraid of taking tests, remembering how they failed them over and over in their earlier school years. That class was my first introduction to students with very low reading abilities, almost no writing skills and who were downright terrified of math. I was comfortable teaching basic math and language. Teaching reading scared me. I have such admiration for people who know how to do it and do it well. I made several phone calls to my aunt, who helped with her long career teaching reading, but I was still separated from my fellow teachers. I felt professionally alone and unskilled.

But meeting new people was exciting. I'd never talked to anyone who was Native American, and was delighted to see the two Native American students in my UNICOR ABE class. Mr. Runs Like the Wind was probably in his fifties, tall and thin with small, round glasses and his gray hair pulled back in a ponytail. He embodied a quiet dignity as he walked slowly with his head held high. He was so quiet that I wondered if he even spoke English.

One day I sat down beside him and asked, "How is school going for you?"

"All I want is to pass the language test and not have to be here," he answered quietly. "I'm sick of failing it all the time, and I don't care about all this stuff, but math's okay."

"Why don't you think about telling me where you're from, and I will write it down," I suggested. I had the silly idea that maybe we could learn some comma rules as I wrote.

The next day, we moved to a quiet corner of the room. "Do you live on a reservation?" I asked as I got paper ready.

"Ya, it's out West," he said.

"Why don't you tell me what the land is like?" I suggested.

He barely answered my questions, trying to be very polite, but mumbling and looking down at the table. He seemed to be upset by the whole conversation, so I put my hand on his arm and said, "This is hard for you, isn't it?"

"I just miss my horse," he said softly.

I liked being in the presence of this solemn, courteous man, and I thought about what he could teach me. With a few more questions, he looked at me and said, "You are not the problem. I just don't want to be here. It's just too hard. I'm keeping track of my hours, but I'm not up to 240 yet." He didn't ever pass the language test and finally reached the required number of hours to drop out. I wondered how different his school experience would have been if he had been in regular academic classes.

My other Native American student was in his twenties, with long brown hair that he kept out of his face with a headband. When he came in, he sat as far away from other students as he could. When I sat down with him, he ignored me. I persisted and asked, "How can I help?"

"I hate these tests, but I want to pass them, and all I want is more worksheets," he said. His name was Johnny Kills a Bear. Another set of scores came back.

"Mr. Kills a Bear, your scores didn't quite make it, but you've improved. Is there someone who could help you outside of class?" By then I'd learned that there were men in almost every unit who were eager to help our students. Mr. Kills a Bear scoffed at the idea.

Sweeping his hand over the table, he said, "I don't care about none of this stuff. I just want to get out of here. I worry about my family every day, and I just want to get out of here."

I said, "I'm just so sorry." His behavior became more understandable. He went to the hole one day and did not return before the semester was over. Though an ABE class did not provide the rich discussions I would be privileged to hear in history classes, Mr. Runs Like the Wind and Mr. Kills a Bear did give me a sense of their reticence and shyness that I would encounter in many native students.

The majority of this group worked at whatever I gave them, but our extreme disconnection from the rest of the program did not allow them to see all the other students taking high school classes and get excited about moving on to higher level material. All they wanted was to pass the darn test and get out. Exacerbating these attitudes was a lack of continuity because we rarely had a complete week of school. Some weeks we would miss as many as three days. I could wake up at home to a bright sunny morning, drive to work and hit a thick, soupy wall of fog. The men would be locked-down in their units until the restriction was lifted. Even if it cleared up in the next hour, our program would cancel the day. So, I would turn around and drive home, and we would need to make the day up at the end of the semester. Adding to the problem was arriving in the lobby and not seeing either of my escorts. I would stand in the key line and wait on the side, trying to be patient, and neither one would show up. This happened over and over, and I would again drive home. I asked them to call me at home, but usually they did not know what their schedules would be if they were called to another area or a meeting. I looked forward to Fridays when escorts would take me to the Complex, where my colleagues gathered in one of the smaller classrooms for a potluck lunch. I could talk to them, compare notes, gather up more materials and feel like I was part of something.

Things were about to change. ABE students could be enrolled after the beginning of a semester, since it was a more individualized course. One morning in October, Mr. T-Bone arrived, making such an immediate impression on all of us in the room that he might as well have come into the room accompanied by a brass band. He was African American and in his late fifties or early sixties, always wearing a blue knit cap that sat jauntily on his forehead.

From the very first day, he approached the teacher on the other side of the room (who almost never interacted with us), grabbed his hat in his fist and made a little bow. "Good *mornin'*, sir! I hope you are having a nice day!" he would say, and then move over into our area.

The other teacher ignored him, not responding to his greetings at all.

He greeted me like I was a member of the royal family with wide smiles and more bows. "Oh my, my, I am sure glad to meet *you*, and I certainly am glad to be here. I can read my name and I can read 'Stop' on a sign, but that's about all. You and I are gonna have a real good time in here!" he said, as he circled the room, shaking hands with his classmates and engaging them about where they were from. After a September of feeling discouraged by our isolation and unsure of how to proceed with my students, T-Bone's entrance felt like being sprinkled with magic dust. Without being impolite, he talked to other students in the room and gradually pulled us together as a group. If we needed to define charm in a human form, here he was. He insisted we all call him T-Bone.

He settled right down to work, and several of his classmates volunteered to help him. Wanting to get to know him, I asked if he would like to tell me a short story that I would write down, then see if he could read it. "Well yes! You need to have one of my famous recipes!" he answered, as he began with the title, "Mr. T-Bone's World-Famous Bar-B-Q Sauce Not to be Fed to Children Under 10." Then came a long list of ingredients, some repeated for a yield large enough to feed about 50 people. He dictated and I copied; we worked on a few words to learn, and then he copied them, slowly and painstakingly, in his own handwriting. I added a copy to my own recipe collection. I found a workbook of short paragraphs with a controlled vocabulary, T-Bone much preferring the lesson called "Having a Date" to one titled "Going to Jail." Tempting as it was, I could not spend all of my time with him, but he was just the catalyst we needed to get into groups for discussions. He worked steadily through the morning, rarely taking a break, but he did like company while he worked. Mr. Runs Like the Wind quietly moved to T-Bone's table, and after one of T-Bone's unique and funny remarks, I looked over to see Mr. Runs Like the Wind wearing a huge smile and shaking with laughter, but not making any noise at all.

One day, carefully scripting out a line of upper case letters, T-Bone, without looking up from his paper, asked, "Ma'am, you divorced or he die?"

"Mr. T-Bone," I admonished. "You know you're not supposed to ask me questions like that."

Again, without looking up from his letters, he said quietly, "You divorced, you tell us where he is and we go git 'im."

Everything we did delighted him. Every day he arrived in a sunny mood. Every single day, he greeted the staff member on the other side of the room in the same way. One of his classmates asked, "Why are you so nice to him? He never even answers you."

T-Bone replied, "Aw, that don't cost me nothin'. Besides, I ain't gonna let no one else tell me what kind of man I'm gonna be." T-Bone's insistence on kindness and friendliness went beyond most people's standards. In such a harsh place imbued with negative interactions, courtesy and civility made our days go far better.

Over the course of the semester, T-Bone was making steady progress with reading, telling me often how grateful he was to be there. On the last day before Christmas break, I brought in some colored paper for paper chains. All of the men would have made them long enough to stretch from one end of the compound to the other they were so delighted with them. Even Mr. Runs Like the Wind was participating and smiling. Everyone took a long piece of chain back to their unit.

T-Bone called me over and said quietly, "Now you just listen careful. I made you a little something and put it in your bag, but you need to just walk on outta here and don't even look until you get home. Don't bring it back in here neither. The warden's got one just like it 'cept his is green."

When I got home, and opened my brown bag, tears sprang up in my eyes. There was his gift, an orange and white striped hat with a large orange tassel on top. I discovered later he had crocheted it himself.

I did not expect to learn so much from my students when I began this adventure. I think that if someone would have asked me about people who had absolutely no reading skills at all and what they were like, I would have imagined a sort of blank slate, someone who didn't know anything. T-Bone proved how wrongheaded that thinking was. He was a master of hospitality and group dynamics. He treated everyone as if they were special to him. It was no surprise to me that he had landed in jail. How in the world do people support themselves without being able to read in today's complicated world? What simply knocked me over as I stood back and watched him was how he pulled us together, pulled in the shy people, was warm and welcoming to everyone. And he worked his head off. Many of our students were below a third-grade reading level, but very few had to begin with the alphabet. I can still see T-bone laboring over how to form his R's and S's, and yet, he filled our room with wisdom and grace as he interacted with fellow students and staff in this harsh place. In his presence, we all felt charmed, warmed and welcomed. I so often think about his statement about not letting anyone else's behavior determine his and have tried to apply it to my own life. I was back in my factory classroom after the Christmas break, but Mr. T-Bone was not. I heard that he'd been transferred to another institution. We all missed him terribly, and I hoped that he would find another classroom.

"WHERE'S THE BLACK STUFF?"

My factory students and T-Bone had me hooked, and I began to imagine other classes. The prison atmosphere was so beige, gray and bleak. Some of the men had access to small transistor radios, but there was no art, no music and few books of literature in the very small library collection. They also had a lot of free time. Before the first semester at the prison was over, I approached my boss. "I have an idea for a class in humanities to look at art, music and literature. Could I teach one at night next semester?" I asked.

"Sounds good," he said.

I spent the Christmas break happily preparing as many interactive and interesting activities as I could. I planned lessons in art history with a special emphasis on the impressionist period; I wanted my students to learn about classical music and its instruments. I thought we'd read a few classic plays like *Antigone* and Shakespeare's *Othello*, and I wanted them to know the basics of Greek philosophy. It seemed like a pretty good standard outline for any high school humanities class. I worked hard on the course outline and gathered materials.

The class filled quickly with about 15 men. My new group had gone to early chow, so they were all waiting outside of Room 1 in the Complex, eager and ready to go. The class met from 5-8:30 p.m., and I was learning how to make the hours go quickly by doing the really tough lessons first, and then ending with a short film or a hands-on activity like grouping paintings according to artists on large tables. Night school can be hard on everyone after a busy day, but every one of them continued to be waiting for me when I got there. I was enjoying this class immensely and felt comfortable and confident. I was about to learn my most important lesson— and learn it painfully.

The teacher who used the room during the day graciously offered some storage space for my books, cassette tapes and pictures. Being able to teach what I loved was one of my favorite parts of this job, and the men caught my enthusiasm. There were two white men, and the rest were African American. Two men stand out from that group. Mr. Smith was a black man about 30 years old, 5-foot-10, thin and wiry and charismatic. He could not wait to get his hands on whatever material I brought in, and he slid into a kind of self-appointed leadership role, organizing tables, materials and his fellow students. He was well-liked. No one seemed to mind his new role, and I appreciated his friendly support. Mr. Hawks, the second man would teach me a most important lesson.

Mr. Hawks was a total contrast to Mr. Smith and his generous brand of hospitality. Ten years older than Mr. Smith, black, thin and not very tall, Mr. Hawks had a dignity about him, dressing neatly and walking with good posture. But, he looked sour, never smiling. He rarely interacted with the group. He would not respond to any greetings from me and headed for the back corner of the back row. I sensed he was unhappy as he mumbled to people around him when a new lesson was introduced. He said little for weeks and did his assignments, but he also continued to sulk. He did not contribute to discussions, even though I could see from his written work that he was a very competent student. He stood out from the other students who were enthusiastic and cooperative.

As the weeks went on, I began to feel rattled by him, feeling insecure and unsure of myself. He began to read magazines in the back row, and I wondered why he had even signed up. He made me nervous, and I did not know what to do. One night as I introduced a new topic, he raised his hand and asked in an impatient tone, "Mrs. Wenzel, where's the *black* stuff? All we're learning in here is about the white man's art and music. Don't you *like* what black people have done?" Then he got up and walked out of the room.

I was relieved to see him go because I had no idea how to respond. I felt like I'd been punched in the stomach, my comfort and security all gone. Stumbling through to the end of class, I drove home feeling confused, upset and filled with questions about where to go from there. *Where did I think I was? Hadn't I looked out at them for half the semester and seen who they were—mostly black men? Why hadn't I thought to have at least some lessons on black art, music, literature and drama? How could I be so blind and insensitive?*

All I could think about was my carefully crafted lessons for the whole semester, which seemed to be working well. I was so busy teaching in so many places that I did not see how I could possibly rewrite the course outline for the last half of the semester. Overshadowing that was the fact that I didn't *know* anything about black music, art or literature, had never had a class in it, had no materials, and certainly no confidence. The textbooks in my classroom had almost nothing about African Americans. I felt overwhelmed and dreaded the next class.

Fortunately, I had a weekend to think it over, and I decided to be honest with the men, apologize and ask for their help. Now, years later, I see the situation far more clearly. There is a tendency for white people to feel like their history and culture is "normal," therefore most important. A Eurocentric focus was the norm in the mid-1980s. I looked carefully at all the textbooks that were available in Room 1 for anything that reflected any diversity at all and realized they were useless. It was a revelation. The standard American literature textbook of the day had not one story that was written by a person of color. All I knew were some African-American spirituals, so I did get some cassette tapes from my local library and brought them in. The men loved them, and it shocked me how many of my black students had not heard them. My local library helped with some tapes by black classical musicians like Jessye Norman and Leontyne Price, and the men liked listening. I also discovered Gordon Parks, the wonderful black photographer, and men loved leafing through his moving photographs. I had so much more to learn.

Mr. Hawks stayed quiet in class, but he relaxed and began to greet me when he came into the room. He began to smile at me, which mattered a lot. He seemed satisfied that at least I was trying. When my boss showed up unannounced one night, several of my students said, "This class needs to be offered again!" We finished the class on a positive note, but I had a mountain to climb. That was when I knew where I was. I had to pull myself out of my own comfortable, white-centered reality. It would take years and many more mistakes to begin to get it right, but I know now what a favor Mr. Hawks had done for me. I taught humanities again the next semester with more balanced and diverse lessons, but a huge trek up the mountain would be my reality for years.

My old map about what this country looked like, the one I'd grown up with that told a single story about white people only, had suddenly and dramatically changed. I thought about my sheltered, white-focused education and wondered how I would have reacted in school if all I learned was about other people and nothing was about people like me. A bigger understanding about who we are as a country began to grow. I saw that all students, whomever and wherever, need to know about *all* of us. When I looked very carefully at textbooks and materials that presented everything from a white perspective, I began to understand the divisions between our various groups. The divisions felt like wide chasms filled with misunderstandings, misinterpretations and misinformation. We know so little about each other. I now added another huge element to the curriculum my students would need: They needed to know about *their* people, *their* culture and *their* humanity. But, this was at the end of the 1980s and educational materials about anyone who wasn't white were sparse. I worried about how in the world I would find adequate materials—and the time I would need to adequately prepare.

BOUNDARY COUNTRY

When a full-time staff member resigned the next fall, I moved into Room 1 in the Complex, back where I had taught Michigan History. I did not miss UNICOR. I was delighted to have my own classroom and finally be able to teach English and social studies. The lessons I learned in the humanities class would continue in other classes, but they would be far more complex and painful. I still didn't really know what I was doing and still feeling inadequate.

Being there for eight hours every day in my second year and having men in each class for two hours opened opportunities to know my students well, but I also had to learn to observe all the boundaries the prison imposed in its many rules and restrictions. I needed to develop vigilance and patience about the restrictions placed on my students—and on me. I needed to be careful about the student-teacher relationship. I needed to be aware of and compassionate about their genuine pressures and worries.

As contract staff teachers, we had to attend annual staff in-services. Some years a captain or a lieutenant would be there with warnings about how dangerous inmates were, and they would show us hand-made weapons placed in the cutout pages of a book. I could see that they were trying to protect us, but by then, I always felt safe with my students. This kind of talk lined up with the perceptions and warnings I was hearing when I told anyone where I worked.

"You be careful!" I heard from several people. The authorities warned us that inmates were very manipulative. I did need to be aware of and address any inappropriate or dishonest behavior, but I learned that manipulative behavior—like a litany of excuses about not having school work done—was a common response to feeling and being powerless as an inmate and to feeling insecure about being back in school.

My stress always came from the institution itself. I had one eye over my shoulder all the time to make sure I was following the institution's rules. Any suspicion of impropriety was grounds enough to be watched more carefully by federal staff. Such suspicion, which could have raised red flags, leading to potential problems for me, my students and my program, was far more terrifying than any inmate and could have cost me my job. Being incarcerated places psychological stress on people, and many men that I taught were emotionally needy. Keeping a professional boundary between my students and me was critical. I never wanted a student to misunderstand our relationship. At the same time, I needed to be authentic and warm. It was a fine balance, but the older I got, the easier it became.

In an early class that year, a student handed in an assignment and a letter to me, telling me how pretty I was, how much he liked me and how much he liked the class. I was new, green and unaware of how the place operated. So, I turned it in, and the man was immediately transferred to another institution. I felt terrible. I think it was a kind and innocent gesture, and realized later that a talk in the hall would have cleared the whole thing up.

As annoying as the rules and restrictions could be, I knew I didn't have even a vague idea of what it felt like to be locked up. I saw only the surface challenges my students faced and knew only what a few of them experienced and were willing to share. I would learn to rely on one remarkable student for insight and information. He would eventually become my mentor, a teaching guide and a lifelong friend.

One day in my second full-time year, as the fall semester was about three weeks along, one of the teachers who taught basic skills in our program brought me a new student, introducing us in the hall during a break. With a smile she said, "This man passed all of his tests on the first try, and it is very obvious he needs the challenge of this class. So, in walked the most phenomenal student I have ever had. I called him by his last name when he was my student, but he became "Mr. C" to everyone after he graduated and became a program aide.

Mr. C was about 5-foot-10, thin and walked with a regal bearing, his black, red, yellow and green Rasta hat covering his dreadlocks. He never walked quickly; he strolled slowly from place to place. The teachers joked and said, "If there was a fire, Mr. C would walk *slowly* out." He had a deliberate, intense kind of attention to whatever was happening and to whomever he spoke. He had measured, careful responses to what was being said, and would say quietly, "One question," and then proceed to zoom in on the issues that were being discussed. His comments were always to the point and well thought out. If his assignments were any indication of his hunger for school, turning in sometimes as many as 18 pages (many more than any other student) would make the point. Reading and especially writing would become the way Mr. C made sense of where he was and how to process it. He made an impression on all of his teachers, signing up for as many classes as he could, but he did tell me in those early weeks that he was struggling with feeling down and out of energy.

Like many men, he felt down and depressed when he arrived in the facility. His friend Mr. Lott, who was also from Jamaica, gently coaxed him into thinking about getting into the high school program. Mr. C told me that he had looked into my room a couple of times and loved hearing music and seeing fresh flowers. "I could see that this room was different and unlike the rest of the prison," he noted.

From the first day, Mr. C provided a model for other men to see how to move from being a good student to a great one. I needed one more student in a newly created class on cultures one semester and we couldn't seem to find one. Mr. Lando, one of our star students, had not registered at all that semester, telling people in the office that he needed to work and earn some money. One of the students offered to try and talk him into it. When Mr. Lando heard that Mr. C was enrolled, he said, "Okay. You've got me. If Mr. C's there, I can't turn it down."

It was Mr. C who pointed out the idea of a prison being a place of *boundaries*. "Mrs. Wenzel, it is harsh and cold in here, believe me.

Everything is different. The fence separates us from everything that's familiar and comfortable," he said.

As I watched and listened, and as I read what they were writing for class, I was learning a little about what it means to be locked up and cut off from the rest of the world. I was learning that being incarcerated is about loss and grieving all that is left behind—from family to freedom to the small comforts of being home.

As I was leaving one day, visitors were being buzzed out. I followed a young boy of about 9 or 10. After exchanging keys for chits with people in Control, I heard choking sounds as I approached the main doors to the outside. The boy was leaning his head against the building, taking big gulps of air in an attempt to stop crying, but tears were streaming out of his eyes. It looked like he had managed to look brave during the visit, but once away from whomever he was visiting, the dam broke. He was trying, but he could not stop crying. The image of the tears streaming down his round, brown face and the sounds of his sobs stayed with me. I wondered as I drove home: *How many thousands and thousands of children in this country are growing up without their fathers—and mothers? What must it feel like for fathers to leave their children in the visiting room?* I ached when I thought about the loss and grief incarceration imposes on so many families.

Especially for men whose families did not live within comfortable driving distances or for men whose families simply could not afford to visit, the fence creates a formidable boundary. Many of the men I knew well expressed their worry and sadness about losing contact with family, especially with young and vulnerable children. I knew too many men who had not had a single person visit during their entire incarceration.

Of the many fathers I taught, Mr. Basha stands out. A particularly difficult student in one of my early government classes, Mr. Basha arrived just a little bit late every day, crossing in front of me to get to the far edge of the room. Before long he would stroll out to get a drink of water. I was green, so new at the game that I did not know how to handle the situation. He was black, Muslim, of medium height and stocky. It seemed he wanted control, and argued with me about the rules all the time. Though he knew that I needed to address them as Mister _____, he wanted to be called Hazir, his first name, and argued about it several times a week. I finally compromised with Mr. Hazir. He talked a lot about his religion, and he despised anything to do with the government, interrupting me all through the class to remind me of what an evil system we lived under. He argued about the validity of assignments and the subjects being discussed. Our relationship was getting worse, with more interruptions and arguments, so I thought that if I knew his crime, it might help me understand him. I looked it up in the federal office file. That was the last time I ever made that huge mistake. I didn't think his was a terrible crime, but knowing it did nothing for our already fragile relationship. I was learning to look for the goodness in my students, to see them as students and not *felons* or *criminals*. Knowing what they'd done to be there made that harder. When I looked in his file, I felt like I'd crossed a boundary. This information was none of my business. Knowing his crime was not part of my job.

I finally asked to talk to Mr. Basha in the hall, trying to be friendly and work at some mutual solution. In a rare, disclosing moment, he said, "Mrs. Wenzel, I don't mean to disrespect you, but I have five kids and I worry about them every day all day."

I felt another emotional hit and thought: *How do they endure being away from their kids?* Eventually, he became more cooperative, and did the good work he was very capable of, but I could feel his anger and his tenuous control of it every day of that semester. The subjects of being convicted for drug offenses and the long sentences under mandatory minimum sentencing laws came up all the time, pointing to the reality that many men would not be home to have any time at all with their children as they were growing up.

———

One semester with a group of delightful students, I asked my friend Amy, a Presbyterian campus minister, to visit us. She and I decided she would talk about the philosophy of education, wanting them to discuss why they were in school, what they planned to do with their education and the difference between making a living or making a life. We put everyone in a circle. The discussion went extremely well as she was able to engage them easily and they were eager to share their thoughts and feelings about how much they appreciated being back in school, how differently they experienced it as adults and how humbled they felt about how much they didn't know. A few discussed their fears about being able to get a job when they were released. The men loved her.

When the class was over, she said, "Okay, I want you to line up so I can give you all a big hug."

One man quietly moved to the back of the line for a second turn. Nervously, I watched the hall through my small windows, not wanting anyone to see the "hugging line." No one specifically said that we could not touch the men, but there were so many warnings about getting too close to them that I worried about a small thing like a hug being misconstrued. Amy called that night.

"I managed to get to my car, and then I broke down and cried in the parking lot. They were all so nice, and I hated the thought of them spending so much time there!" she said.

I tried to be very careful, but I did eventually learn that sometimes touch was necessary in order to comfort someone. I learned to "bump into them," as I moved between desks, squeezing a shoulder or touching an arm as I went by. I touched their hands when I was working with them at their desks. They would line up to shake my hand as they left on the last day of a semester, but they would also hug me. It would have been a rude affront to not hug them back, so I would let them. No one ever said anything, and I thought I could defend it if they did.

There were almost no boundaries that gave men any privacy. Older housing units off the inside yard were different from the buildings built later, which resembled a rather sterile college dorm. I had only one tour of a unit, which was one big room about the size of a gymnasium with "cubes," places for two "bunkies" to sleep and share storage space. The "walls" that separated cubes were about five feet high, and the area held lockers and drawers for clothes and a small set of bunks. The whole area for two people had barely enough room to turn around in. Generally, new inmates were placed in the older dorms first and then later moved out to three larger dorms that were built to the side of the original building. I was told that rooms there were a bit bigger. The first "tour" made me uncomfortable. Another teacher once requested a tour of the entire compound, but I remembered how voyeuristic I felt on the first one, and I didn't want to repeat it. I thought I would intrude on what little privacy and space they called their own. It was good to see that men could move around the compound with some degree of space.

Space has a lot to do with freedom. I thought about my freedom when I walked out the front doors of the prison building. I thought about how I could go for a walk in my neighborhood, cross-country ski through the woods, drive home on back roads and notice the beauty of the countryside or get on a plane and travel.

This brings to mind an image of a new inmate who was taking a class in the Complex. For several days, he paced up and down the hall between my room and the library. He went up and back, up and back for hours, reminding me of a newly caged animal. Bigger and taller men complained about their bunks being too narrow and too short. They would mention how much they missed soaking in a bathtub. They missed their cars, the food they were used to from home, and being able to wear nice clothes. They missed being able to talk on the phone without worrying that the authorities were listening in. Any freedom they did have could be taken away if they broke the rules.

Prisons have prisons within them, most often called *the hole*. As contract staff, teachers were not allowed in the place, but I did know that men were locked up all the time in individual cells, except for an hour every day to exercise. The hole, or D-Block, was the segregated unit where men were sent as disciplinary action and sometimes for their own protection. The hole was also called *seg*, the *dog house*, the *bucket*, the *can* or the *Hilton*. Federal staff often referred to it as the *SHU* for segregated housing unit.

Sometimes men would send teachers notes about homework. Mr. Maher, a young, tall black man, said little and did all of his work on time. He spent months in the hole, and in response to my note saying that I just could not send enough assignments and he had missed too much time to receive any credit, he wrote this: "I feel like I'm going crazy in the hole. It's easy to do. Your sanity just starts slipping away from you and works on your unconscious. Now I know why they come around every half hour to check on you. This is a high-stress environment. When I get out, I can't wait to get back to the gym. I feel so stiff and unhealthy."

I tried to work with prison rules, but it was hard and frustrating to have them in the hole. They could not make the work up adequately if they missed too many days, and students were invariably upset if they got too far behind. I did not ask why they were in the hole. Like the offenses they committed, it was none of my business.

The definition of freedom is a slippery one; it seems like Americans have been working on it for centuries. I hear all kinds of chatter about our basic freedoms and rights, especially as established in the Bill of Rights. But, there is also freedom *from* the difficult realities on the outside: hunger, homelessness and, for some of my students, freedom from some stresses and violence in the outside world. There were men I knew who had lived on the streets or in their cars and expressed some appreciation for having food, clothing, and housing, calling it "three hots and a cot," though they didn't go overboard in their gratitude. I never stopped being amazed by men saying that sometimes they felt freer inside prison than they had on the outside, indicating the kind of traumatic and chaotic lives they had been living.

I was finding many boundaries between my life experience and theirs. We had news one day that a staff member had lost her father, who died from old age.

One of my younger students, who had grown up in the inner city, asked, "Do they know who shot him?"

I never got used to the amount of violence my students had witnessed and experienced. I can still see the ugly knife scars down their faces, hear the stories of gun battles, surgery and the bullets remaining in their bodies. News of death was omnipresent. It was not at all unusual for them to hear of family members who had been gunned down in the streets.

I knew Mr. Spence well, one of the men who came in with a friendly smile every day. He was older, in his forties, African American, always neatly dressed and very polite. All of his work got his maximum attention, resulting in his excellent grades. He graduated, was released and went home to his mother, who he told us was desperate to have him around again. A few months later, we heard that he'd been shot and killed. The air would change with news like that. It would feel heavy and dark and, in the middle of a busy teaching day, I felt like I couldn't wade through it to process such a loss. I could have found—and often heard—a heart-wrenching story about street violence every week, but I was sheltered from what happened inside the prison. I knew there were occasional stabbings, fights and other violence among the men. It buzzed in the background as I would pick up small pieces of it, but I did not hear it directly. It was clear that any violence that I did not witness was none of my business. The men were reluctant to share it, too.

I was becoming more and more aware of how different my life had been from the lives of so many of my students. I've never experienced any personal violence and trauma, but in many cases, I needed information about their difficult backgrounds to understand their behavior as students. Leaving the prison every day seemed like moving from one universe to another, the prison fence a visible boundary between people whose lives had been and were so hard—and my own, which so often seemed serene and easy in comparison.

———

Sometimes during the first week of a new semester, I directed my students to imagine our classroom was an outline map of the United States and had them stand in a spot in the room approximately where their home was. I gave up when I had students from other countries. There were days when we looked like a United Nations with men from places like: Mexico, Puerto Rico, Jamaica, Haiti, Trinidad, Venezuela, Colombia, Poland, India, Iran, China and Vietnam. I had two brothers who were Turkish Kurds and a couple of Palestinians.

In the 1990s, I knew many men from all over Africa. Like legions of immigrants, most of these men were lured to the States by the American Dream and came here for all kinds of reasons and in all sorts of ways. Some came to the United States as students, like a wonderfully generous gentleman who often lectured in my history class about his life and culture in Africa. He had applied to Alabama State University from Nigeria, because he thought the one at the top of the list had to be the best school in the country. Most others came for better work opportunities. A very funny man from Jamaica came as a stowaway on a ship.

Their diversity showed up in how they'd made a living too. We had truck drivers and a few pilots. I met a man who designed and made kites for a living. Many had been auto mechanics and barbers. Some had not only cooked for a living, but were first-rate cooks in jail—no easy trick with only a microwave in their units. I knew welders, carpenters, teachers, accountants, fishermen, ranchers and mountain men who had lived off the grid in the wilderness. Many of my younger students had never held an actual paying job. A few came from affluent families. Many more came from abject poverty. They came from homeless shelters, had lived in barrios and ghettos, wealthy suburbs and Indian reservations. They came from small towns and occasionally from remote villages.

When it was a medium-security-level facility in the early years that I was there, students were older, typically in their thirties and forties. Many of the men I knew then had moved down in security levels after many years. Later when we were a *low*, a minimum-security level, the men were most often in their twenties and early thirties. I had students over 60. One man was in his eighties. (He took not one of my assignments seriously).

This institution's second language was Spanish, but I also heard French, Arabic, Russian, Polish, German, Chinese, Vietnamese and Jamaican patois. Our students spoke the language of their streets, and in all accents and dialects. By federal law, any religious hat is allowed, and so some Muslim men wore their kufis and occasionally the Jewish men would be seen wearing yarmulkes. The Rastafarians, most often from Jamaica, wore their black, red, green and gold hats.

One fall I gave an entry test to a Spanish-speaking student the first week of class. I had never seen him before and he dutifully answered the basic questions in one sentence or one-word answers. When I asked him what difficulties he had because he did not speak English, he answered with some surprise. "Oh, teacher, it isn't English that's the problem. I find that being here and being gay is what's hard!"

The inmates were straight, gay, bisexual and transgender. My students dealt with being incarcerated much as they dealt with life in general. Some chronically complained about everything, rarely smiling. Others brought sunshine into every place they entered. Many were stand-up comics. *Most* of them were likable and winsome. Particularly distasteful personalities were rare.

For such a small space, they created quite a colorful, fascinating map. So much diversity provided us more solutions to problems. We were learning that when we share who we are, what we love and what we can do to make life meaningful and fun, we create community. Boundaries began to disappear. I did not expect that at all.

RAGAMUFFIN SOLDIERS

In British-influenced parts of the world, like Jamaica, a ragamuffin is a person who follows reggae music. The term also suggests a poor street kid, which many of my students were as children. My childhood could hardly have been more different, which was an idyllic time in the 1950s—the images of Currier and Ives or Norman Rockwell's Saturday Evening Post covers not a far stretch. We lived right on Lake Huron in the beautiful small town of Rogers City. Mothers in the neighborhood put potluck picnics together on the shore where the lake had hard, wavy sand in the water and gentle dunes of sugary sand on the beach. We made beach bonfires, roasted hot dogs and marshmallows and watched the stars. We regarded 30 neighbors' yards as our own and played all sorts of imaginary games in the woods on the next block. We were at home all over town. We heeded clear instructions to stay away from the lake without adults, but my mother did not worry if I disappeared for several hours. I don't remember any discussion of crime—at all. I don't remember locks on our doors. We felt free and totally safe everywhere.

In the summers, we spent a lot of time at my grandparents' nearby farm. Gramma made us clear and dry the dishes and hang clothes on the line. Any boy cousins helped Grampa in the fields and the barn. We gathered eggs and watched in fascinated horror when a chicken she had just beheaded would still flop around on the grass. We picked vegetables from her huge garden, then had to help her with meals for as many as fifteen people. All of the food tasted homey and wonderful. When our work was done, we could grab the knotted end of a rope secured to the peak of the barn and swing across the hay mow to fall into its itch and scratch. We sat with our uncles and tried to milk the cows. Gramma gathered us around when she sat on her porch in the evenings, the lightning bugs winking in the dark. The farm is still in the family, our own Place on the Planet, giving a large family roots and connection to the earth and each other.

I see now that I had been grounded and given a predictable pattern of place. Growing up with a strong sense of family and community, I knew friendliness and safety, learned to trust people. I learned to move around in the world with ease. My grandmother taught me balance, leading to an understanding that walking and hiking in the natural world was what I needed in order to balance a long day in a windowless prison classroom and the frustrations of having to wait for an escort or someone with keys to unlock the doors.

As lovely and nurturing as it was, growing up in a remote, northern small town had its limitations. Except for a couple of families, we were insulated from the realities of poverty. Everyone I knew was white. Isolated and insulated, I was innocent of the darker American forces of racism and widespread poverty. I had some student teaching experience with young children in Detroit, but I wasn't there long enough to hear any personal stories that explained the realities of an inner city's impoverished neighborhoods.

I took education for granted, and even though I attended three different high schools, because my family emigrated to northern Quebec, it never occurred to me that I might not graduate from high school or not go on to college. I saw a secure economic future ahead of me with a good job and a husband who would provide well, because that is all I had ever known. I envisioned living in a nice house and being able to send my children to college. I took privileges like having parents who would help with college, trips to visit them and loans for down payments on mortgages for granted. I had little knowledge of how the labor of African Americans contributed to the economic security of white people. When I was divorced at 40, I had some economic stress, but I was always aware of the large and loving safety net my family provided.

The men I knew in prison received news of deaths of family members all the time, and they would talk about how hard it was not to be able to support their families and attend the funerals. Prisons affords no privacy. Without it, grieving is difficult. Mr. Willis sat in the back row of an English class, put his head down, did his work, but said very little. He was a young black man with very short hair, a shy smile and a gap between his front teeth. All I knew about his background was that he had grown up in the inner city. I was learning to create a peaceful, serene atmosphere, and if they agreed, I played music when they were working at their desks. Some men requested what they called "space music," the new-age music that soothes so well. I had some soft music playing one day and heard someone breathing differently. When I looked out at the group, I noticed Mr. Willis leaning his head against the back wall. He was trying to keep some composure by taking in some big breaths, and his face was wet with tears. I motioned him out in the hall, put my hand on his arm and asked if I could help.

"No one can do anything, Mrs. Wenzel," he said. "My grandmother died right after I got locked up, and I've never cried since then. She raised me. I'm worried now that I won't be able to stop." I think that the losses had all added up, and the music had finally brought his defenses down.

"You can go back to your unit now if that would help," I said, breaking the rules.

Our friend Amy, who had become a frequent visitor, had told us, "Rules are made to serve people, but when people serve rules, we lose a chunk of our humanity." I quietly gathered his things while he waited in the hall, deciding that I would explain if he were caught out of bounds. I wondered what the unit would be like—and what an acceptable outlet for people's grief would be in this place. Would he be able to flop down on his bunk and just cry? Would he have any privacy at all? Men would tell me that they would hear men, especially new inmates, cry at night. Thinking I couldn't hug him frustrated me, and his lonely grief tugged at my heart.

It seemed like we heard about family deaths every week. Mr. C lost a beloved aunt, and had a very hard time gathering enough energy for class for several weeks. Students' sisters, brothers and parents died. One of the chaplains told me once, "The hardest thing I've ever had to do in this place was to tell a father that his 8-year old son had died in an accident—just months before the man was scheduled to be released."

At age 12, Mr. Chase, a young black man, was pushed out of the house during the winter time. A temporary arrangement with a friend was just that, and he ended up on the streets, stealing food and sleeping under bridges. Eventually, he sold some drugs for food, ending up in prison.

Also at age 12, Mr. Messer had two parents with severe drug addictions and was in charge of several younger siblings. "As long as I didn't ask for anything or get in their way, my parents didn't beat me up. Coming up was full-time drugs and part-time school," he said.

Many men talked about how drugs had infested their neighborhoods and their lives. They talked wistfully about how different their families, schools and neighborhoods would have been without drugs and addictions. I had Mr. Conley for a basic language class. He was in his forties and walked with a dignified bearing. He smiled wanly every morning, greeting everyone warmly in our small class, but sadness hovered around him like a gray cloud. He hardly talked at all, and he did very little work. On an occasional good day, he could whiz through any material I gave him, but most of the time he seemed out of energy for anything. Through some writing, he finally opened up and one day we talked in a quiet corner.

"I'm so sorry I'm not working very hard, but I can't seem to get it together. We found out that my wife had MS, and I sold some drugs so that she could take her medicine. That was real stupid, and now she's locked up too and my mom has the kids. My mom isn't well and everything just feels hopeless," he said.

Unresolved grief and depression wafted thickly through the air in the place. When the public thinks of people who are locked away from us, I don't think they understand the ugly experiences these people have endured. I sure didn't. I did not think about the loss and grief, which were so apparent as soon as I got to know them. The system was not set up with ongoing grief groups. The men were lucky if they could find a friend, a chaplain or a psychologist who could listen and be helpful. I needed to understand the sorrow they were feeling—and its depths. I needed to listen well. I also needed to be careful. I was not their grief counselor. I was their teacher. If I took in too many sad stories, the sorrow drained what seemed like my very limited amount of energy, and I got too tired after long, 8-hour teaching days. I had to work on a careful balance all the time, and I often failed. There were days when all the sorrow would weigh too heavily, and I would think I just couldn't do it. Then, there were men who got me up in the morning.

When I first had Mr. Elliott in class, he made me want to pound my head against the wall. He was very polite, soft spoken and kind —always. But, getting to class every day and getting any work done? Just not part of his program. He spent a lot of time talking with me and the director in the office, but if he saw his school problems in the same way that we did, he had no solutions. I can still see him sitting there respectfully but quietly shrugging his shoulders.

I had him for at least four semesters. Duration was such a help in getting to know men well—and so hard when they were difficult. Gradually, after not earning credit one semester, Mr. Elliott started doing some work. Attendance continued to be a problem, and he learned to do just enough to get by.

I watched him carefully, looking for ways to interest him, because I sensed that underneath all of his apparent apathy, there was a considerable person. I felt a kindness and compassion in him from the way he interacted with people. He listened so well. I knew that he'd had a very troubled childhood, especially with his father, but he had never shared any details. There was a quiet centeredness in him, too. He would come alive in class when deeper subjects were discussed. At the time I had him, I was getting a little four-page meditation flyer in the mail with excerpts and quotes, so I brought one in for him. He pored over it and asked me if he could have them when I was finished with them. I was beginning to see how serious he was, how these subjects resonated with him. When he could write about profound subjects like sorrow, integrity, civility and the way we all can live together, when he could think about "soul work" and how to live his life, he started working hard. Anything he regarded as superficial or frivolous (that was stuff like spelling, sentence structure, matching subjects and verbs) was a total waste of time. Very gradually, he got his act together and graduated.

What I now see is that Mr. Elliott understood wholeness better than anyone I knew—inside prison or out. He understood that all human beings have dark, painful experiences—and that much light comes from them. He wrote, *"Sorrow is better than laughter because the heart is made better. Those who do not let sorrow do its work, trivialize it and try to explain it away, remain shallow and indifferent. They never understand themselves or others very well. In fact, I think before we can become good citizens, we must learn about sorrow. It can uncover hidden depths in ourselves. Sorrow causes us to think earnestly about ourselves. It makes us ponder our motives, our intentions, our interests. We get to know ourselves as never before. Grieving also helps us see God as we've never seen him. Sorrow is my fuel."*

I think about him often—and what he taught me. I realize that great wisdom can come out of brokenness.

Most teachers would like to reach every student and succeed in teaching them. I was no different, but there were men who simply had too many emotional and psychological problems to be able to handle school very well. Some, like Mr. Conley, were too distracted by their family problems on the outside. Amid so much pain and suffering, my students often needed more compassion than I could summon up in a day, and I often wondered how some got going in the morning. I saw that, for so many of my students, there was no such thing as childhood innocence, and the effects of trauma and loss followed them into adulthood. I was meeting so many kinds of people I'd never met before and bumping uncomfortably into my own naïveté as I heard and read my students' stories. Like any teacher, I had my share of really bad days. But, I felt so lucky to be working with these men. They were widening and deepening my life.

"They play—they have to pay. They need to be punished!" I heard from people outside the fence more than a few times.

I was seeing people who had been damaged and traumatized by death, murder, violence, hunger, homelessness and betrayal. I was seeing brokenness and grief in people almost every week. I continued to wonder how being punished helps people who are hurting so badly.

My own losses of my marriage, being away from old friends, my children leaving home and growing up were dissipating. I was learning, as I got to know them better, how compassionate my students were. As I got to know them, I looked forward to seeing them, especially after winter and summer breaks. Hurting people are often healers, and being in their presence I felt myself being mended. They asked how I was doing and worried when I looked tired. They were fun and cheerful a lot of the time. Almost all of them worked hard. I certainly didn't expect to find role models in this unlikely place, but I was humbled and inspired by their courage to keep working to make their lives better. Robert Frost's words made total sense behind the fence, "Before I build a wall, I'd ask what I was walling in and what I was walling out."

Mr. C once signed a letter from "A ragamuffin soldier in the depths of hell." Sometimes that said it all.

EVERYBODY NEEDS BEAUTY

"Everybody needs beauty as well as bread, places to play in and pray in, where nature may heal and give strength to body and soul."

—John Muir, American author and naturalist

As a nation, we do not incarcerate people with the idea that they need to be *healed*. Punished—for sure. Rehabilitated—well, hopefully with some educational and drug treatment programs. To be healed would require that we acknowledge the brokenness—the hurt, the damage and the suffering that so many people behind bars have endured. I don't see myself as a healer necessarily, but while teaching, I did see that connecting to nature and beauty in any way provided rich possibilities for learning, growth and renewal.

Prisons are barren spots on the landscape, but this one at least had a yard in the back of the compound intended as a space for sports and recreation. Over the years and depending on who the warden was, some flowers would appear along walkways. Other than that, the landscape was fairly monochromatic. Prisons aren't designed to be beautiful, but I knew in the first weeks how quickly the men responded to a black spiritual, to a bouquet of tulips, to photographs by Gordon Parks and the poetry of Langston Hughes. Literature is filled with stories and poems about nature, and it seemed like a neutral subject to add to a course outline. Again, I was about to realize the gaps between my experiences growing up and theirs.

The majority of my students came from the inner cities of the Midwest: Detroit, Flint, Saginaw and Grand Rapids in Michigan, Chicago, Cleveland and St. Louis. They talked about moving around a lot and attending many schools. I heard stories of overcrowded housing projects and dangerous neighborhoods. I heard their fears

53

about being in the woods or about being out of their comfort zones outside of the city.

One fall Mr. Vallente appeared—new to me and to the program. He didn't just walk in—he swaggered, refusing to acknowledge my greeting. When he sat down, he turned slightly away from me. I tried to be firm but welcoming in the first few days and humor usually worked. It fell flat with him, and he interrupted me several times as I tried to get the class going. With his hair buzzed to almost no hair at all, he was about 5-foot-5 with a slight build. He said he was born in Puerto Rico but had lived in New York City since he was very young. From that first day, he transmitted a coiled-up energy. He wore small round, rimless glasses and kept his prison khakis neatly washed and crisply ironed. His demeanor reflected dignity and keen intelligence. Right away, I knew he wanted to learn. He loved language, crafting sentences like a careful carpenter. He read whatever he could and was not shy about sharing ideas. He wanted to be in school, but he was clearly uncomfortable too. If he had to join a group, he placed his chair just far enough away that he wouldn't have to interact with the other students.

I hadn't anticipated any resistance to assignments that included themes about the natural world. The assignment was to respond to, or describe, something about the outdoors. I listed all kinds of possibilities—discussing a nature poem, responding to a photo or a painting, remembering an experience of being outside. Mr. Vallente wasn't completely cooperative about other assignments, needing to argue about the merits or methods to them, but he loved to write and always did a good job. This assignment put us on a collision course. He flat out refused to do it. It was hard when one student balked like that—hard on me and hard on the other men.

"I don't know nothin' about this. I grew up in *concrete!*" he declared. "I can't remember any trees, and I never played in any parks. I never been in the woods, and I never got close to a lake or the ocean. I ain't never been swimming."

Foolishly, I suggested that he look at the stars.

"What are you talkin' about, Miz Wenzel? They lock us down

before it even gets dark and we can't see nothin' from our cubes anyway." When I asked if he could write about growing up in concrete, he refused. I was struck by how different his childhood had been from mine, and I didn't know quite what to do with the assignment—or my feelings of loss for him. His behavior wasn't making anything easier. We finally compromised on another assignment, and I wondered how many of my other students were this cut off from nature.

Mr. Vallente finally settled down enough so that I didn't need to talk to him all the time, and with continued hard work, he earned enough credits to graduate. What got him through was not only his desire to get his high school diploma, but his need to put his good mind to work. He was transferred to another institution before the graduation ceremony and declared he was happy to miss it. "No one's going to come and see me anyway," he said.

Mr. Dexter was at the opposite end of the spectrum in regard to experience with nature. Unlike most of my black students, he had grown up, not in a city, but deep in the mountain hollers of Appalachia. African American and in his mid-forties, he was not shy about telling us that he could neither read nor write.

"At least now I can go to school," he said. "It is something I have always wanted to do."

It did not take long to notice severe dyslexia as he turned letters around like Scrabble pieces on a board. His other teachers and I had seldom seen such determination, however, and that along with intelligence, intense curiosity and an easy way with people, made him progress rapidly. After several years of very hard work learning to read, his reading teacher wanted him to move into a high school class. She would miss him, she admitted, but also reported that he would ground and focus any group he was in. He enrolled in a basic English class.

He told us about the poverty, but his smile would widen when he spun tales of growing up in his beloved mountains, describing the wildness, the freedom and the simplicity he'd known. I often wondered how much that particular place had formed him, how much of the balance and wisdom that made him who he was in middle age had been gained there. Perhaps his maturity and focus on overcoming his reading problems were a direct correlation to his enthusiasm and contagious joy when talking about his mountain home. I felt warmed when he walked into the room. His courage and determination rubbed off on me.

In my early years, we had a lot of men from Jamaica. Mr. Newman bounced in one day with a huge smile and a deep bass voice. He was a black man in his twenties, about 5-foot-7, with a bald head and unending eagerness. From the first day, I could count on him to keep the classroom as clean and well-ordered as possible. He was the first person in the room for class and proceeded to arrange the desks in perfect rows. He washed the board and the top of my desk. He picked up any stray pieces of paper that were on the floor. When I complimented him, he said proudly, "My grand-mudder taught me to be clean all the time."

He was constant motion. I often opened my door to let some sun in from a big window in the hall, but Mr. Newman would slip out of his seat and out in the hall when he needed to be sitting still. He did all of his work and often told me how much he *loved* school. His wide smile, his willingness to help and his very deep voice helped him work his way into people's hearts.

Mr. Newman's unit officer talked to Mr. C about his talent for trouble. He didn't fight with anyone, he just couldn't seem to stay put and was too often out of bounds—not where the computer said he should be.

"Let me have him," Mr. C said.

So, Mr. Newman moved to the outer dorms and became Mr. C's bunkie. Mr. C reported that their cube was as spotless as possible after the cleaning that happened every Saturday morning. When it was done, Mr. Newman arranged some chairs outside in the hall, saying, "This is my front porch," as he invited other men to sit down and chat. That was against the rules, but his hospitable personality would not be squashed.

I found it hard not to worry about him. He had a chronic

kidney disease and was taken out to an area hospital on a regular basis for treatment and tests.

With a wicked grin he would inform me, "I know a lot of pretty nurses there."

After one short hospital stay, he walked down the hall to my door, then motioned me out in the hall. "Yesterday was my birthday, Mrs. Wenzel, and those nurses all came around my chair and sang to me. They had a cake too," he said. Totally charmed, I told him now nice that was.

"No, see they were all so pretty and I was wearing a *dress!*" he said, referring to his hospital gown.

All of us, his teachers, his unit officers and Mr. C, looked for projects that would keep him focused and out of trouble. When there was a staff member willing to take on a garden program, the inmates eagerly enrolled. Mr. Newman's unit officer came up with the idea of keeping him busy outside digging and planting. Mr. Newman quickly discovered his green thumb and talked a lot about *his* plants. Mr. C reported that he would stand guard by his vegetables in case anyone "messed wid 'em." He then worked on a way to get me out to see them.

"You just gotta see, Miz Wenzel! They're amazing," he said.

I wish now that I had somehow made that happen. I had a feeling that he felt some ownership of his vegetable plants. Gardening can be so satisfying when we watch things grow and thrive, and the process seemed to fit Mr. Newman's nurturing, caring personality. His vegetables grounded him in a way that nothing else could.

Eventually Mr. Newman was too sick to maintain his garden and had to give it up. Mr. C took over for him—with no previous experience at all. For many summers, the garden absorbed Mr. C, and he eagerly participated in an organic gardening class the institution offered.

"Working in the earth puts me in another realm altogether," he reported. "I find peace there that is not like anything else I do around here."

When his sentence was completed, Mr. Newman was released back to Jamaica, and occasionally Mr. C would get word of, or from, him. Mr. C came in one Monday morning and I knew immediately that something was wrong. His face was drawn and he looked like he hadn't slept in days. We got class started and he motioned me out in the hall.

"I got word over the weekend that Newman died of his disease," he said.

The news hit me physically with a lump forming in my throat. I got through the day feeling totally distracted. When I got home, I let the tears come. I still think about him when I see a well-ordered garden or I hear someone with a deep, resonant voice in a thick Jamaican accent. He had burrowed into my heart.

I felt brokenness all over the place, men who had grown up in unimaginably impoverished conditions, men who were cut off from families and cut off from the rest of the world, men like Mr. Newman who were chronically sick. I was getting to know men who needed treatment for mental health issues that were getting in the way of their succeeding in school. I was shocked by how many men had grown up without fathers. It was difficult to think about how many of them were fathers themselves, this damaging cycle continuing. On many days, I felt overwhelmed by sickness and sadness.

On the first day of school one September, Mr. Winter marched in, put his hands on my desk, leaned over and pressed this question, "Do you know how I can find my father?" That was our first interaction, and he startled me. He was a young, tall, thin black man. I was aware of how many students did not have nor even know their fathers very well, but this was the first time anyone had suggested I might know how to find someone. I have no idea why he asked me. I knew that if I tried to help that it would be breaking institutional rules.

"Gosh, sir, I don't see how I could help you with that," I replied. I felt an ache for him.

From the first day, Mr. Winter was a tough one, the kind of student who made me think that when I saw him I needed the day off. He had disruptions down to a science, so we had many chats in the hall and trips to the office, where the staff would talk to him and send him back. He settled down enough to pass the class, but it took time and energy to keep him focused. His massive problems, which seemed to stem from abandonment issues, made him difficult for other students as well. He resisted group activities with a lot of fussing and complaining.

I came back in January with a package of paperwhite bulbs and a box of pebbles I'd received for Christmas. Paperwhites, a kind of narcissus, are often found at Christmas as small bulbs. When I looked at my class list, there was Mr. Winter's name. I had to figure out a way to make the coming semester better than the last—and I remembered my paperwhites. On a whim, I decided to enlist his help. I asked him if he would mind taking care of them for me— watering them every day. I doubted this man had experienced seeds in a cup as so many young children have. He was very intrigued by the idea that all that was needed was some pebbles and water. I explained that they had all they needed in the bulb itself. He took right over, announcing to the class, "These are *my* flowers, and I don't wanna see anyone messin' with 'em."

Paperwhites grow very fast, and he watched the new sprouts with incredulity, measuring them every day. He came early to change the water, and brought a friend down to see. When the little white narcissus-looking flowers blossomed, he was even more amazed and marveled at how sweet they smelled. It was a sad day when we had to throw them away. Again I saw a sense of ownership and the joy of nurturing something that grows and thrives so successfully. Mr. Winter calmed down that semester, and I think being in charge of his flowers helped.

———

My Native American students, in spite of most of them being initially very shy and hard to get to know, had much more to say about the whole subject of nature. In my early years before a federal correctional institution was built in Colorado, Native Americans were about 6% of this institution's population. Many of my students were from reservations in South Dakota: Pine Ridge, Rosebud and Cheyenne River, but we also had men from Cherokee tribes in the Southeast and from several tribes in southwestern states. Some of them used their wonderful tribal surnames: *Red Feather, Takes a Knife* and *Black Crow.* It was a good day for them when they could write about nature. Their art reflected their connections to nature also. My native students identified with the land like no other group. Land was *home* and *culture,* embodying their history, their language and their stories. They talked about Mother Earth providing water, air, shelter and food. At times, the way they talked about the land they loved felt like another language, compelling and memorable.

———

As I walked through the halls one day in the spring carrying some daffodils, an inmate I didn't know stopped me to say, "Oh my! Daffodils! Thank you so much—I haven't seen one for years." The more beauty in nature that we see, the more it carves a place within us, teaching awe, humility and grace.

I had a white man in his thirties who had grown up in northern Michigan, hunting and fishing. *"We need a fundamental idea of beauty in order to survive,"* he wrote.

When spring came and the yard opened, most inmates could not wait to be outside, but it was a long time inside during the winter months. I heard students talk about how they honed the ability to remember, to conjure up something they loved when they needed it. Mr. Andrews told us about going on a field trip to a pumpkin patch when he was in grade school, writing about the straight rows, the green grass and the pumpkins, organized from smallest to largest.

"There was nothing but punkins wherever you looked," he said. "I never seen anything so beautiful in my whole life. I think about that." I asked him how many times he had been out of Detroit, and he said that was the only time.

One time as I was participating in a weekly meditative group at my church, we had an environmental assignment to go outside and find something in nature that "allured" us. We were then to come back and write about how that item was like us. A bit nervously, I decided to try a version of the activity in an English class. I gathered leaves, flowers, pine cones and branches in my neighborhood, brought them to class and put them on a large table. I told my students to look carefully, then choose something that really appealed to them. I also told them to carefully describe the item they had chosen. They seemed to be intrigued. I had expected some negative comparisons, but that never occurred in all the classes that I did this activity. I got these responses:

"I am like this pine because we are both strong and long-lasting. We are beautiful through certain eyes. We are both tall and determined to keep growing."

"I think change in a person is like how this leaf changes colors. I can feel myself taking more responsibility now."

"The stem in my leaf holds the whole thing together—just like I need to be the strong one in my family."

"This is what a human being really is, a whole universe in his or her interior. Like flowers and leaves that change, every person has the gift and the power to turn his interior into beauty, peace, kindness, humor and love."

Mr. Stanley lived and breathed sports. I could hear him arguing authoritatively with someone sitting next to him about statistics or the trade of a player. He was not the easiest of students for me to connect to and get along with. He seemed reluctant about everything having to do with school and a tad grumpy most of the time. He wasn't uncooperative, he just didn't think he knew anything: except for sports.

One fall morning, wanting to forge a better connection with him, I mentioned the winner of the World Series game the night before. This guy was honest and straightforward. He played no teacher-pleasing games. My question stopped him dead in his tracks as he turned around and came back to my desk.

"You know what, Miz Winslow? You musta heard sompin' on the radio 'bout that cuz I know you and there just ain't no way yer sittin' in front of T.V. watchin' some baseball game. No way. Wadja hear anyway?"

He had me. "I was just trying to make conversation," I mumbled.

"You gotta stay way far away from sports. You know lotsa things, but you *sure* don't know sports."

Mr. Stanley rarely smiled, but when he did, it was quick—like a streak of lightning and that's all you were getting. He settled down after all those pronouncements, flashed one of his fleeting grins and started on a worksheet.

The day I laid out the nature assignment, I knew there would be trouble. Reluctantly, he picked up a tiny pink flower, shaking his dreadlocks on the way back to his seat.

"Miz Winslow, I don't know what you're talkin' about. This looks like any ole flower to me and now you're tellin' me that I need to be *like* this li'l thing?" he asked, holding it up between his thumb and forefinger. "I don't know what you're up to today, but I just can't do this!"

I went back to sit beside him in an attempt to settle him down. The last thing he wanted was to disappoint me, but firmly believed that I had *lost it* on this one. I told him that the flower's name was cosmos and that its color was fuchsia.

"If you say so," Mr. Stanley allowed, gray-green eyes sliding toward the ceiling. With lots of sighs, he began to describe the strong color, the delicate shape, the fragile stem. That took a while and class was over.

"I dunno," he replied when I asked him to do the second part for homework. "I'll try. You know me. I always try."

He did try and off he went, shuffling down the hall, shoulders stooped and rounded. His clothes hung right off him so that his shoes walked on the cuffs of his pants. The little flower stuck out of his back pocket. I had no great hopes and some disquiet, judging that he didn't have a very good self-image. When he returned in the morning, the flower had shriveled and faded, but he had a contented look on his face. He wanted me to read what he had written,

"My sense of responsibility to myself and my family is strong and vibrant, like the color of this flower. I think of all the things I should and should not do. Then I try to change for the better. My awareness of giving freeheartedly is sweet. As well as when I play basketball.

"Hatred is small in me. There is enough of that going around. And, most of the time, it is for nothing. It is also delicate because most people take not hating as soft and weak. I think two ways about being in jail. I don't like it, but I am becoming a better person."

II. WHAT WE MAY BE

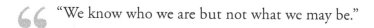 "We know who we are but not what we may be."

—William Shakespeare
Hamlet

"We should not judge people by their peak of
excellence; but by the distance they have traveled from
the point where they started."

—Henry Ward Beecher

WHEN I INVITED visitors as guest speakers into the prison, they
were stamped on the hand with an almost invisible ink. Being in the
middle of the grilles, the two barred doors that slid sideways to
open, was intimidating even when visitors left as they had to put
their hands under a sensor so that the invisible ink would show up.
Because security was the institution's main concern, they had to

know who was an inmate and who was a visitor. One of my students had an identical twin, and when his twin tried to leave one night after a visit, he could not. Someone had forgotten to stamp his hand, and he was delayed for hours. The inner shame that many inmates felt was like an invisible stamp. Prison reinforces the idea that *felon* means *bad person* all the time. I thought about the twin who was not incarcerated and just how much easier his life must be without such a negative label attached to him. I heard a few men say that they could not tell people at home that they were incarcerated—especially aging parents and small children. I have no idea what explanations they gave for their absences, but being in jail carries shame and stigma, guilt and regret. My students worried about their families and didn't want to add to the difficulties at home.

Prisons are identity thieves. Inmates were assigned a number and all of them had to dress alike in boring khaki clothing. Added to that were their internal identifying "hats." They couldn't be part of our program unless they had dropped out of high school—or like some—had never even attended one, so they were *dropouts*. A few would write down that they felt like *losers*. I wanted them to take those hats off, but in my first few years, I had few ideas and even fewer skills to help them do that.

When they enrolled in school, new students could not imagine what they could be, but I did begin to see that a solid, positive identity was critical to being a successful student. I was learning, slowly. I was learning that listening and watching were more important than talking. What were the keys to finding their hidden strength and confidence? How do I make them work hard and then build the framework around which real growth could take place?

"WHO'S GEORGE WASHINGTON?"

By the early 1990s, having my own classroom and storage closet helped enormously. A more predictable schedule helped, and I did not miss teaching a class that taught to a test. I was more used to the institution and could relax a little more, but I always felt the stress of making sure we were following the rules. In a few instances, it created panic for me, especially if I felt intimidated by the staff person, like the day when a lieutenant appeared at my door and ordered me out in the hall. The men froze. My knees shook. What he wanted was any information about some of my program's materials that had disappeared.

At that point, still in my early years of teaching academic subjects, I also allowed myself to get hoodwinked. When I assigned reading and writing in social studies and English classes, my students had resistance honed to a fine art: "I don't know how," "My bunkie's too noisy," "I never did this before," and always "I can't find my notebook." On and on. It felt like pushing a tractor uphill. All of that reinforced my ideas that they were not very capable, and I often felt overwhelmed by 15-18 students who couldn't or wouldn't read and most who struggled to write a simple paragraph. My students came in carrying a lot of baggage. Dropping out of school leaves huge holes in one's skills and knowledge. When a man asked me who George Washington was and another angrily challenged the idea that ole George couldn't ride his horse to England, I wanted to run out the door.

I did not have adequate materials in the first years. The program's history books were outdated and were almost all about white people. I could easily have felt overwhelmed by so many levels of competency in one class. Even really good students lose skills when they spend too many years away. I had that experience myself when I returned to college at age 40.

I wore labels too and felt them acutely. I felt so *white*, and I was still making a lot of mistakes. I hadn't yet learned how much my white, institutional privileges dominated my perceptions. I hadn't yet learned that the more privilege I experienced, the less I saw and understood it. One of my worst lessons in an early American history class illustrates the point.

A friend had loaned me a book about the origins and meanings of surnames, and it seemed like a good ice breaker and fun activity to do in the first week of my English class. My students got right into it and dutifully wrote the information down. They were cooperative and engaged. Many were African Americans, yet the majority of them looked up names like Miller, Smith, Young, Lewis, Jackson, Scott, Jones, Douglas and MacLeish—not sounding exactly African like Daboiku, Mafanya or Olapade. They started a banter around the room with information like the connection between occupation and names—Smith was a blacksmith, Miller was a miller and so on.

"My name is from Scotland!" somebody sang out.

"Mine's Irish," said another.

Then I heard a voice say, "I can tell you where my name came from. It came from a *slave master*, that's where it came from!" Though some of the people freed from slavery used their occupation as a surname, many used the last names of their slaveholders.

I remember blushing, shaking and wanting to disappear, wondering how I could have been so stupidly insensitive. I apologized and we got through the class. This was the early 1990s, and I had not heard the term *white privilege*, but it was a good example of my white blindness. It not only reflected my lack of thoughtful preparation, but it reflected how, as a white person, I typically don't give much thought to how differently people of color think and feel about their backgrounds. It reflected the isolation I experienced growing up in all-white communities. Like most painful lessons, this one was good for me. I was learning how important identity issues were and what role they would play in the courses I taught. It was another wake-up call to the pervasiveness of the dominant white American story.

The first few days of any semester proved crucial to how the weeks would unfold. I went in a day or two early to make sure my room had colorful posters, calendars, interesting charts and some fresh flowers. I loved looking out at a new group. Some of them were men I knew well, others were brand-new students, back in school after many years away. The new people often looked nervous, but almost all of them exuded fresh-start attitudes. A buzz of expectancy and hope hung in the air.

The first few days looked like "halo time." For a couple of days, men in most groups came in on time and simply glowed, their halos shining brightly. Then, reality set in. They had very different past school experiences, both good and bad. They were all over the place in responsibility and maturity levels. Most of my students at that point were in their late twenties and thirties, but with the War on Drugs kicking into high gear in the 1990s, we were seeing younger and younger men. Often a class would have men who were reading below eighth-grade proficiency and men with enough knowledge and skills that they could have handled classes on a graduate level. Some men had never been to high school; others had dropped out in their senior year and needed only a credit or two to graduate. Some were model students from the very first day and occasionally, someone would make life miserable from the beginning of the course until the last blessed day.

I could use the basic skills test to get a general idea of where students were, but generally they were useless and showed nothing about intelligence or ability level. The test could not measure their task commitment, their motivation nor their total delight about being in school—nor could it measure their lack of confidence in themselves nor their levels of fear and stress about taking tests. It took me years to create my own materials in order to boost the reading abilities for men who fell below a ninth-grade competency level, while also presenting enough challenge for men who could have handled college or graduate school.

I had to get to know my students better, and it helped me to ask them *why* they were coming back to school. Mr. Otis was a young black man, small and slight, with perfect manners and an impeccable appearance every day. He was not a strong student, but he certainly made up for it in enthusiasm.

During a chat about his progress one day, he said, "Miz Wenzel, this is like a dream come true. I gotta tell you about how I decided to do this. I was over here in Education last year when Milan High School was getting ready for graduation, and I saw all those guys in those red caps and gowns through the window. I gotta tell you that I went into the bathroom and I just cried I wanted it so bad for myself. It was that day that I decided to sign up even if I was real scared." He was a delightful, cooperative, hard-working student.

Each man had his own motives for signing up.

Mr. Palermo was working on a valentine letter one day, writing it over and over to make it perfect.

"I'm trying to get my woman back," he explained. "She's educated, and I'm not."

Mr. Piper was a middle-aged Native American student who was confident about his academic skills, eager to lead the class in any activity and a daily participant in discussions. When he enrolled he told me, "I spent most of my nights drinking and just being out of control when I was out there, and this is now a big part of trying to straighten my life out."

In spite of going to three different high schools, it never occurred to me that I wouldn't graduate. One of the first things to tug at my heart was the reality of how important a high school diploma is when you don't have one. I learned to listen to why students enrolled in the program when they could have simply gotten their GED.

Mr. Spivey, a white man in his mid-thirties, entered the room with his hand out and a need to know everyone. "I am so excited to be able to graduate!" he announced. "And my mom will be so proud!" Well-spoken and, unlike so many other students, he had an ease with any material I gave him. I figured out why after a few weeks.

"Mr. Spivey, how much high school have you had?" I asked him quietly one day.

"Oh, I was bored and just took my GED so I could go on to college!" he answered.

"How much college have you had?" I asked.

"Oh, I have a bachelor's degree and a master's degree in communications," he said in a matter-of-fact manner.

The early 1990s was a time when the institution had more older men, and these students were all in their thirties and forties. Students were talking one day about graduation and how glad they were to be getting through high school. I had many men over the years with college credit after passing the GED, but I think Mr. Spivey was the only one with a graduate degree. He was a conversation starter, and his enthusiasm for his high school diploma sparked many discussions.

Confidence was everything. If they thought they could do the work, then they usually could. If men were afraid and doubted their ability to succeed, many of them had a slow start. I checked in with them after a few weeks, asking them to write how they thought they were doing in class. I read many comments like these: "I let everyone down." "I'm no good." "I don't know if I can stay strong." "I want to graduate, but I don't think I can do this." Embarrassment could be a hurdle or a motivator.

This note from Mr. Carmel appeared on my desk early in a new semester:

Dear Teacher,

I like your teaching and I enjoy your class. I want to remind you that I can't participate as much as I would like to because of my lack of education. As you know, I only went to third grade. I'm hoping to learn as the class goes along. I also want you to know that sometimes I feel closed in like I'm inside a Vienna sausage.

He was from Puerto Rico, and as soon as I got to know him, I was astounded to learn that he had been in school until he was only about 8. It wasn't his skill level that mattered. How he perceived himself would determine his success. I had him for several years, and he would become my resident philosopher, putting wise little notes at the end of all of his assignments. He was a small, slight man who rarely talked, but lent a sense of seriousness to the group with his quiet demeanor, his kind face and his total focus on doing the best work he possibly could. In the notes that accompanied his assignments, he would apologize for not doing well or not knowing something, but the apologies gradually lessened and then disappeared. I wondered if his reference to feeling like he was inside a sausage had to do with how hard it was for him to talk in front of the group. He was not alone in fearing that.

Eventually, I learned to tell my students in the first week of a semester that many of their schools had failed them, and that this program was their chance to work hard and make it right. If they'd come from inner-city schools, they reported realities like 40 to 50 kids in one class. One man said he dropped out of school because there were too many broken windows and he was tired of being cold all day.

"It didn't seem like anyone cared about us at all," was not an uncommon statement.

Asking the right questions and listening carefully helped make the connection between their identities—how they saw themselves, how much they internalized the harmful labels they brought into prison with them—to the confidence they needed to become capable students doing their best work. More than one man said his worst mistake was not the crime he committed, but dropping out of school. "If I stayed and graduated, I'd have a job and not be here," they said.

I didn't have the language back then, but now I know we, my students and I, needed to be in right relationship: a healthy relationship with good boundaries that we could all respect. The idea of respect came up a lot. One morning, after I had an unescorted pass, I was walking down the hall and a student I did not know was waiting to get into the Complex. I said good morning, unlocked the door, smiled at him and said, "After you, Sir." He looked shocked. When we were both through and the door was locked again, he said he needed to tell me something.

"No one has ever treated me like that," he said. I looked puzzled and didn't know what he meant. "Letting me through the door first and calling me 'Sir' means you respect me," he added.

It seemed like such an insignificant gesture on my part, but the encounter stayed with me. A lot of the men I knew talked about how it felt to be *dis*respected. If they hadn't heard what our program was like, many of them were suspicious and wary about how they'd be treated. I had figured out the simple truth that if I treated people with respect, I got it back. Every day I knew that simple courtesies made the whole day so much better. Courtesy and respect were connected, but there was more to respect than surface civility.

After listening to the richness of their comments for a few semesters—and realizing the amount of free time they had, I knew that I was not treating these men with the full consideration and respect they deserved. I was simply not making them work hard enough. It took me a while to look beyond all their well-oiled resistance and understand that what they needed, more than anything, was as much challenging work as I could give them. I had to toughen up and not listen to their litany of excuses. I was hurting them. As their teacher, I had to face and undo my own stereotypes that they were not very capable. I didn't think they were capable—and I think now—neither did they.

We talked a lot about self-esteem, and they agreed it was not my job to give it to them. They agreed that work done well gave them large measures of confidence and energy to keep going. They needed to try, scary as it was. They wanted school success, they just didn't know what that looked like. I was learning to say, "If you've heard that I'm strict and that my classes are hard work, the rumor's true. I have high expectations for you because you deserve them and *I care*."

If only it had been this easy. The problem of expectations was that my idea of good and hard work was miles apart from theirs. If they'd dropped out of school and never been accountable to a boss in a job, a fair number of them did not know what *any* kind of hard work was. More powerful than any of that, however, was that they had very little idea of their talents, abilities, intelligence and wisdom. Rarely did they even know what they were interested in.

Explaining assignments, I would say, "When I ask you to write two pages about a topic or if I ask for your comments, please know that I will not be impressed with three sentences."

"What if a couple of sentences pretty well wraps it up?" was the inevitable response.

They had to experience just how much was in their hearts and minds about so many new ideas and subjects, but it was a long, hard road for many of them. They had little experience with writing, and had to learn to do that too. I gritted my teeth some days and counted to 10 when they fussed.

Even in later years as I was still struggling to stay on the line between encouraging them and holding them responsible for their own learning, Mr. C would pull me aside and say over and over, "I love it when they fall apart. They not only need to develop confidence, but some of them think they know everything. They also need to develop humility. *Let them fail."*

He encouraged me to jump right into the material on the first day, setting the stage for how things would go. "Show them how little they know. Put it all right up there on the board. They can handle it," he said. Most men were fine, but some were wide-eyed with fear.

"I just can't do this," they would tell me on the way out the door.

Mr. Berry, a black man in his late thirties, had a mustache and a perpetual scowl on his face. Sitting in the very back of the room, he fussed loudly when I handed an early paper back with a note saying that I knew he had more to say than his two sentences, but that I would give him a chance to add to it. "You just don't understand, Miz Wenzel—I don't know any more than that," he said. But after I let him talk it through with me, he handed in a much better paper.

After a few painful weeks of gaining some traction and confidence, he wrote me a note that said:

Dear Mrs. Wenzel,

Thank you for what you have to teach me. I know that I gave you a hard time in class. You remind me of my mother. She is not with us anymore. Thank you for being hard on me and making me learn things I didn't know so good.

L. Berry

Like many students in every kind of school, most of the men I taught hated and feared tests, and they had to take a lot of them. The Bureau of Prisons administered them, and the state not only required a set of standardized tests for basic skills as men were enrolled, but our program's funding was dependent on showing progress with another set at the end of the year. I spent a lot of time trying to make my own tests worthwhile. I did not want to make things too easy and not challenge them. In my history and civics classes, I told them that testing scores almost always improved with experience, but it was still hard when I had to give a paper back with a low or failing grade.

The loving cooperation in a testing situation between two young black men in their early thirties still warms me when I think of them. Mr. Holt was well over 6-foot and stocky. He smiled a lot and always asked how I was when he came in the room. He was friendly to all other students too. He sat in the front row and called me over in the first week. "I never even once passed a test," he said quietly. It was painful to give him the first test back with a failing grade and watch him hang his head.

Mr. Esch, a young man I knew well, worked very hard and earned straight-A's in everything. Any group was lucky to be in his bouncy, cheerful presence. When I discovered that Mr. Holt and Mr. Esch knew each other and were in the same unit, I pulled Mr. Esch aside to see if he would help. His face lit up. "You know I would do anything for you, Mrs. Wenzel, and you know how much I want to be a teacher," he said.

I organized the next test so that they could study over the weekend. I gave every group a day to review before a test, which they used to organize their material and figure out what they needed to study. Creating three questions by themselves, they came forward to ask the whole group. I listened carefully to make sure they understood each question, but they had to plan how the day would go. I had fun watching who took charge and how they did it, and I loved hearing them discuss the material, knowing how much they were learning by talking about it. I suggested that Mr. Esch help prepare Mr. Holt ahead of the review so that he could participate. I liked having a podium to put books and papers on, and it helped them to use it and feel more professional. As Mr. Holt left the room, he said, "I'm feeling better and Esch is going to help me all weekend!"

Mr. Holt worked hard and carefully, but still had a wild, fearful look in his eyes when he turned his test in on Monday. "I dunno about this," he had said.

It was such a joy to give back good grades. Mr. Holt came in the day I promised tests back, still with huge round eyes and a worried face. He got a C+. His face broke into a huge smile when he high-fived his friendly tutor. Then he looked at me, still wide-eyed, motioning me over.

"I don't get it," he said.

"If you can go from a failing grade to a C+, I think you can get a B or better next time," I said.

"No, Mrs. Wenzel—that's not it. What I don't understand is how did you *know I* could do it?"

I often think about Mr. Esch. I knew he was there for selling drugs, but many states deny teaching certification to people with criminal records for drug crimes. He told me that he loved little kids and would love to teach in the lower elementary grades. What a good teacher he would have been!

There were other challenges for students and for me about being in school inside of the institution. Work details sometimes trumped school, and the men were on call-out for appointments and visits. Men had to figure out their individual priorities and schedules. The jobs in UNICOR paid the most, so men who needed to send money home wanted to work there. For most of my years there, the pay started at $0.11/hour and the highest pay grade was $1.25/hour. Several of my native students told me how important it was to their families to have the money they earned. Going to school created a conflict for some of these men. Men shopped in the commissary, and they had to go when they were on the list. Sometimes that would interfere with being in school. I had to get used to being interrupted all the time, but I can't claim I was a good sport about it. I could see that men were caught in the system too. I had to admire their patience.

———

Mr. C was a student in those early years, and I was watching and listening to him very closely. One Friday he dropped a packet of pages on my desk with a note asking me to read it carefully. I was on a constant look-out for new, diverse material, but I wasn't finding much. The other problem was that we couldn't buy many new materials. I bought things myself, but I resented spending too much of my own money. Mr. C's package had five pages about how limiting the history textbooks were with their Eurocentric focus and how important it was with a group of predominantly black and native men to include *their* history. He pointed out that information about African and Native Americans was often in a box or in the margins.

"These people already feel boxed in and at the margins," he wrote.

It felt like another punch. It was not a great weekend as I tried to figure out what to do, but I did start collecting the right materials. When I read Howard Zinn's *The People's History of the United States*, things improved dramatically as I planned lessons around some of his chapters. Gradually, over the next 10 to 15 years, educational materials improved and represented all kinds of people. The catalog for social studies had more and more textbooks, plays, biographies and audio-visual materials about African Americans, Hispanic Americans, Native Americans, Asian Americans and women. The program started to loosen up funds for better materials.

With so much of their daily lives decided for them: schedules, work assignments, who they lived *with* and in what unit they lived, it was easy for the men to feel powerless. Just being incarcerated and knowing there was no way to get out made them feel like they had no control over their lives. I was learning to address their sense of powerlessness by giving them a lot of decisions to make. I had to find the balance between help and encouragement—and helping too much.

An African-American superintendent of schools came in as a guest one day. I told him to talk about whatever he wanted, so he gave us his educational journey, and he engaged the students by asking them questions about being in school.

When it was time to leave, he pulled me aside with a piece of wise advice, a teaching *gem* I sorely needed. He said, "You can be very helpful and encouraging, but don't put yourself in the position of wanting it more than they do."

One of the hard lessons I had to learn was to realize that coddling and cajoling, taking any responsibility away from my students was patronizing, and it assumed that they couldn't follow directions, get work done well or in on time by themselves. It assumed that I was in charge of how hard they wanted to work. I was also learning to be clear about what everyone's job was. I talked to them about how much I loved my job, what a privilege it was to work with them and how much I always learned. But, I said that chasing them for assignments was *not* part of my job. I told them that my job was to create as many opportunities for them to learn and succeed as I could. Eventually, I posted a monthly calendar for each class with assignments due on whatever day.

I put a point system in place, and I took a point away for every day that an assignment was late. Assignments, tests and projects were worth one hundred points for the semester. If they earned fewer than

60 points, they could not get credit. How many points they earned was up to them. I said I was there to help, but that they were adults and these decisions were up to them. Things settled way down without the arguments and fussing when I finally had a workable plan—and I knew what my job was and what it was not.

I had so much more to learn about them and how to teach them, but men in all of my classes kept me going and made me laugh. In the first week of any semester in history, I usually spent a few days getting them comfortable with the background of the West, making sure they knew how to identify centuries, the culture clashes between Europeans and Native Americans and background to the arguments with England. I did a quick time line, making it as clear and interesting as I could, followed by a research project and a few statements about what they had learned that would stick with them. I got these conclusions:

"Columbus is no hero in my book. He was a low-budget explorer who got lost," Mr. Bell wrote.

"The Black Death was no joke. The disease was carried by fleas on the rats that came from Asia. They killed millions of people from 1347-1350. It is amazing to me that fleas could do that. I was shocked. I also learned never to mess with no rats," Mr. Houck said.

MANNING UP

I wish I'd had a class in college called *Classroom Management in a Men's Prison*. On too many days, I was walking around like a blind person wielding a white cane. Gradually, I was figuring it out, but there were many days when I yearned for my car and the road home. Once again, if I listened carefully enough, many answers came from the students themselves.

Many answers with critical help and focus came from Mr. C, both as a student and then as my classroom aide. He graduated in 1994 after taking every class the program offered—and being the recipient of our one and only Student of the Year award. I didn't see him the next semester, missing his wise counsel. I decided to ask him to be my "tutor," my classroom aide. He agreed, and it was the best decision I made in my many years there. He moved into his role immediately with his good listening and observing—and his centered calm affected all of us all day. I would have been a far less effective teacher without his daily presence and guidance.

Mr. Jensen was a tall, good-looking and friendly black man in his twenties, and his early assignments indicated how capable he was. But, his back-row behavior put spit and polish on horsing around. He talked, joked, moved around the room, made smart-aleck comments and then looked around to make sure his buddies approved. His eighth-grade classroom antics matched the year he dropped out. I could often see this kind of connection, but this kind of behavior had to go—for him or for the rest of the students in the room.

The process of how to become men, give up their teenage behaviors and become responsible adults was helped enormously by learning how to become competent students. Though most of the men I taught had respectful manners, some needed to learn the basics of coming to class on time, listening and responding respectfully and turning in their best work on time. They needed to learn to respond to greetings, not interrupt, and not get up and stroll out of class when they felt like it.

One man insisted on leaving early for lunch in the first week. When I talked to him about it, he said, "I'm just not feelin' it."

They could make my ears ring. Sometimes I wasn't feelin' it either.

I saw adolescent behavior and I saw some that was childlike. Mr. Madden was another young black man with a sweet smile. He rarely had his work done on time and rarely followed directions. In the first weeks as a new student to me, he would come in just a little bit late in the morning, greet me with a big grin, then lean over my desk and whisper, "That's a real pretty dress, Miz Winslow." One day, coming in a little later than usual, he *winked*. His comments bordered on downright silly, and then he would check in with his back-row buddies, talk out of turn and not pay attention. I tried talking to him in the hall a couple of times, but he didn't seem to get it. Finally, I detailed his behavior in writing, told him he would lose points if he continued to be late and wrote that I thought he could do much better while in class. I asked him to read it over, then sign it and bring it back the next day.

He read it soberly, gave me some furtive looks and left the room with his head down. The next morning, he asked to speak to me in the hall. "Miz Winslow, you hurt me *bad*! Reading all them things on that paper made me not even sleep last night. Miz Winslow, I don't wanna be bad. You just gotta give me another chance!" he pleaded.

I worked with him, realizing he really didn't have the first clue what good behavior looked like. Happy to have his seat changed to a place directly in front of me, he would often ask, "Am I doin' okay?"

This kind of childlike simplicity frustrated and puzzled me. I wondered if Mr. Madden had been to school at all—and if he had, what kind of classrooms he'd been in. I had to be careful. I was not anyone's mother, and I didn't want to treat them like they were in eighth grade or lower. I heard many men use the terms "man up" and "mirror up." Both were useful ideas. I knew they wanted to act like men, and I could see that if I acted like a mirror and carefully spelled out what kind of behavior I was seeing, many men were surprised. School was a good place to learn what grown men looked like.

It was so easy for men to feel powerless on the compound, so issues of control came up all the time. A few students clearly articulated that there just wasn't any way they were doing things they didn't want to do. I had to find a way to become an immovable wall to their resistance—and to remove any power issues between us. I had many students who talked about how boring their schools had been and so they dropped out. Typically, they welcomed a challenge. Most of them were eager and polite, but occasionally I had enough large egos and arrogance to fill the room to the ceiling. Some would act as if they knew it all, and anything I said was beneath their level of expertise. But, I was learning to see a lot of bravado that covered up their feelings of failure and inadequacies.

Prison is a hard place to fit into, and new students sometimes put teachers in the same category as corrections officers. None of the men wanted to be perceived as weak or soft. Inmates had to learn how to deal with the rules and the people who had the control over their prison life. It wasn't easy to be subjugated or treated with disrespect by anyone. By the mid-1990s with a group of many more younger men, I had figured out a system that would work in my classroom. We all needed structure and clear expectations for how things should go, and because they were adults, they needed a sense of ownership about the rules.

In the first week, to give them a chance to speak up, we all talked together about what kind of atmosphere we wanted in the classroom while someone took notes. After we decided what the rules should be, I always asked if there were things they didn't like about the program's rules. Few offered any opinions at all. We all agreed they should sign a contract, and I stressed the idea of coming to class on time so that they didn't interrupt the rest of us. I told them that if they came back from break too late, they could find the door locked.

Some students agreed with the rules on paper, but I had the sense that some of them thought "she doesn't really mean *me*."

Mr. Lyman was a new student, a small black man with a head full of dreadlocks and an in-your-face attitude. He talked when I talked, and acted like everything I said was beneath his level of intelligence.

"This stuff is bullshit!" he announced one day from the back row.

He made me nervous and uncomfortable. I talked to him in the hall and asked him what he was doing in school if he thought so little of the program.

"I just want to graduate," he said, sneering.

"You can't just burst things out or use inappropriate language," I said. "And if you do it again, I will have to ask you to leave."

So then, he would sit in the back of the room and read other books. One day he read a magazine. Men like this made the day a lot longer. I tried to take a friendly route, not wanting to discourage him so soon, but he was determined to do things his way and kept strolling in late from break. I warned him that the next time he did it, he would face a locked door. It didn't take long. The next day, with everyone else back and ready to work, I locked the door. When he got there, he banged on the door and yelled at me to open it. The rest of the group hated that level of disruption, and as I tried to ignore him, I could see people glance at each other and fidget. Most students wanted me to be treated with respect, and they looked embarrassed. When Mr. Lyman failed to get my attention—or my keys in the door—he moved on to pounding on the windows. Before I had a chance to call the federal office, an officer noticed him and promptly put him in the hole. He returned subdued and followed rules more carefully, but he never lost his sullen, angry attitude.

I had no small number of emotionally needy students, and Mr. Lyman was one of them. They were people who tried to get any attention they could. I was learning that it did not really matter if the attention was positive or negative as long as someone was validating the fact that they were there. When I had to deal with a student like Mr. Lyman, Mr. C reminded me that if I had problems with him, it was almost certain that other teachers, his bunkie and his boss did too. "Do not take his behavior personally. This is not about you," Mr. C would caution.

I was learning to take myself out of it, stay calm and simply ask them why they would go back on their word, their word being the signature on the contract. That put their behavior between them and the rules and not between them and me. They needed to be accountable to the rules they'd agreed to, but they also needed to be accountable to *themselves* and learn to behave maturely. One of my big frustrations was students who were eager to be in school, capable of doing well but still dealing with their old angers and damage. So often, a few semesters in school would change their behaviors and attitudes dramatically, so when they were transferred to other prisons before they graduated, it was hard to have seen them make such good progress and then not have a chance to earn their diplomas.

Evaluations carry great weight in a prison setting. What is written down, even by teachers, can affect even the good time they earn for a shorter sentence. Teachers crafted evaluations for three, six and nine weeks, so that people in the office could track how students were doing. Questionable behavior or lack of progress needed to be in writing. The three- and nine-week papers were yellow, and the six-week papers were purple. There were places for us to check: *Always, Sometimes,* and *Rarely* about classroom performance and behaviors. Another way to provide some self-reflection was to have the men evaluate themselves first and write down their comments in the place provided, providing a mirror for them and vital information for me. There were men in almost every group who proved very hard on themselves. If someone had handed everything in on time, he would still check *Sometimes.* "I'm not doing so good in this class," he would say in the comment section. It flagged his confidence level for me, even if his work was satisfactory. I found almost all of them to be honest when they looked at themselves. Other comments were these:

"I'm not smart." "I never did good in school." "I feel like I don't know nothin'."

One purple sheet looked like this:

Teacher comments: You are a capable student, but you are losing points for late assignments and not working very hard. If you don't stay focused, you are in danger of not earning any credit.

Student comments: *I think Mrs. Wenzel is a good teacher. She also looks real nice every day. She shows a lot of love for her work. I think if I just had my notebook, everything would be just perfect.*

This student had a distance to travel.

I had to be clear and fair about grading. Rarely could I mark on a curve—it just wasn't fair with so many ability levels in one class. I had to try and find the line between making sure the student was motivated and yet not let him get away with not working hard enough. I talked a lot about *effort*, wanting their best work. It meant that I needed to watch them carefully.

Realizing that chasing them for assignments was a bad idea, I posted assignments on calendars for every class. Many men had never paid attention to calendars, so sometimes it took losing points for late papers to learn. Mr. C explained his relationship to calendars and said that if he kept track of time too carefully, it went by too slowly. That helped me understand. Often students were disorganized, especially about what needed to be done and when, but in time they learned.

I used the halfway point in the semester to spend one-on-one time with each student. I counted the points they had given themselves and then matched my total with theirs. With larger classes, it was the only way I could get to know them individually, ask about future plans and chat about how things were going. It was a time to encourage the idea of going to college when they were released and to provide extra materials and assignments for men who were working harder than everyone else. It became a favorite time for me.

Occasionally someone who was not doing his work and creating some classroom upset would refuse to evaluate himself. "That's *your* job!" he would say. My response was simple, "This is up to you Sir, but you need to know that these evaluations go in your file and I will simply write down that you refused to do it or sign it." That got their attention—and results.

Even some very bright students needed to be shown that they could do far better, by learning what hard work and focus looked like. Learning to write well proved difficult for almost everyone. I had a sign on the wall that said, "That which is written without effort is read without pleasure." This did not keep them awake at night. Editing and rewriting was new to them, so I finally decided I would accept no papers without at least one draft attached to them. A student in one English class labeled it a "ruff draft." Another labeled his last one "finally draft." Somehow both labels caught on, and most of the class used them. They knew the correct spelling. They were pulling my leg. It worked. I laughed.

I found that creative assignments could motivate them to work harder. If I gave them ideas like writing a play or illustrating, graphing, charting, mapping, they got into it quickly and produced wonderful work. Others were giddy about the chance to be in school and could not get enough work. If I asked for two pages, they might hand in six.

———

Many of my students equated manliness with not being disrespected, and often that meant that they valued guns and were willing to be violent. Violence is endemic to many neighborhoods. I had a hard time listening to the talk about guns.

One man related how he had taught his 7- and 9-year-old children to shoot. "They gotta know to stay alive!" he argued.

That kind of information gave me the shivers.

My colleague had a physician in as a guest one day. The doctor asked if anyone was walking around with bullets in their bodies. Seventy-five percent of the group said they were. Their casual references to the guns and violence in their lives unnerved me, pointing again to the wide differences in our backgrounds.

There were many times when I needed to fade and get out of the way. Mr. Howell was the kind of student whose dignified presence set the tone for the rest of the group. A black man about 30, he walked slowly, smiled a lot, and paid close attention to what was being discussed. He stayed quiet in most discussions, but when he did speak up, we all listened carefully. A very thoughtful person, he said this in a discussion about nonviolence one day: "Guns have become an extension of our manhood. We need to rethink what it means to be a man."

We talked a lot about nonviolence in both history and civics classes, always engendering lively discussions. Most men said that they'd heard of Dr. Martin Luther King Jr.'s nonviolent strategies, but I found that very few men really understood how these strategies could be used in their own lives. The idea of standing up for one's own carefully thought out principles and values was not familiar to many of them. I told them it wasn't familiar to many of us out in the world either. I was heartened to see that men did not dismiss nonviolence immediately, instead wrestled with what they had experienced on the streets about being respected and what it meant to stand up for their values—and for others.

Mr. Tanner grew up in the impoverished black neighborhoods of Washington, D.C. He was a tall and lanky black man with a long, serious face. He was a good student but said very little from the back row, so I didn't know him well.

As we were discussing nonviolence one day, he shouted out, "Mrs. Wenzel, you just don't know!"

Other men were startled and turned around to look. I squirmed, but managed to ask him questions.

"Mr. Tanner, tell me what I don't know," I said.

"You don't know what it means to live in a neighborhood where there are so many guns. All we have is our respect," he answered.

"But, what if an innocent person gets hurt and you are to blame?" I asked. "Do you always know who's an enemy and who is not?"

"It's about sticking to your own neighborhood," he said. "But I see what you mean if someone doesn't know."

He looked very uncomfortable and I knew it was a hard thing to talk about. But, I realized he was right. What did I know about growing up in the kind of neighborhoods many of my students had endured? I felt humbled. It seemed like I could never really know what it was like to be in his skin, but it seemed like admitting my own inexperience needed to be verbalized. I wish now I had talked more about my own advantages because of my whiteness.

To his credit, he continued to wrestle with the whole idea of nonviolence, writing about it in assignments and once in a while saying things like, "I don't go for that turning the other cheek stuff."

It took a while to explain and show them that nonviolence was not passive. Movies like *Gandhi* and learning about the events of the civil rights movement helped.

On an assignment in history to write a letter to anyone in the past, Mr. Tanner wrote to John Brown: *"Sir, if you hadn't massacred the people in Kansas, I think you would have far more respect today. That one incident really damaged your reputation."*

My students also struggled with the weight of their ancestors' painful history and the continuing disparities in policies such as the sentencing guidelines that resulted in so many young black men in prison. These kinds of issues were an ongoing difficulty within so many of the classes I taught. So many subjects in history classes such as the conquest of North America and its cost to native peoples, slavery and segregation, and restrictions on civil and voting rights triggered their anger. None of this was hard to understand, especially as they sat in a federal prison, many of them enduring long sentences for nonviolent drug offenses—and earning what they considered slave wages at eleven cents an hour.

I had to be careful to let them vent their pain and frustration, but not allow them to argue disrespectfully in class by interrupting each other or putting anyone down. Mr. Peer was new to the program when he took my history class. He was in his thirties, a black man with few school skills and a lot of anger. I explained early in the course that I did not want to whitewash anything and that we would be talking about the hard, painful issues.

One day, out of nowhere, he burst out, "Mrs. Wenzel, you think slavery was just fine, don't you?"

Stunned, I told him, "Of course not."

A few days later, I heard that he was spreading the rumor around the compound that I thought slavery was "benign." It got back to me, and it hurt. I felt betrayed, angry and worried as I worked hard to uphold my reputation as a fair and balanced teacher. Mr. Peer and I had a talk in the hall. I tried to be calm.

"Mr. Peer, could you please give me an example of telling my students that I think slavery is fine? What did I say to give you that impression?" I asked.

"I can't really remember exactly, but you acted like you thought that," he said.

"Mr. Peer, I work very hard to be clear, and if this gets around the compound, it will not only damage my reputation as a fair and balanced teacher, but it will harm Milan High School too," I said.

"I guess I didn't hear it quite right," he mumbled. "And I'm sorry."

But, I was still struggling. He continued to make me nervous. I didn't think he really understood the damage he could do, and I secretly hoped he would drop the class. I was on edge, never knowing what to expect from him, and I had a hard time helping him.

Then one day, I played *Missa Gaia*, Paul Winter's *Earth Mass* as my students worked on a research project. The music is lovely, filled with saxophones, drums and voices along with the sounds of wolves and whales.

Mr. Peer was in the back row with his head back and his eyes closed. Annoyed, I went back to wake him up. He sat up and said, "I'm sorry Miz Winslow, but I am not sleeping. I *loves* this music. It just gets me right here." His fist hit his chest. "It just takes me somewhere else," he added.

My heart softened. People are so layered and complex. I needed to find what was good in him, too.

The atmosphere in my room was often contentious and difficult. Mr. C helped a lot by helping to elevate the discussion into a societal frame, saying that from his cultural distance as a Jamaican, he noticed the discomfort in discussions about race in the United States. He was almost always willing to talk to students who were upset—and upsetting—one-on-one outside of class. We muddled through. As hard as these discussions were, I knew I should not avoid them, and I counted on the many men who were more experienced and mature to set examples as they talked about the old, painful issues with wisdom and sensitivity.

———

Teachers don't like to fail with students, and I failed with enough students that it bothered me. Mr. Thayler kept signing up for not just my classes but others in the program. His basic skill levels were lower than fourth grade, and he would start to do work, get some help from me or someone else in the room—and then start to wander around the room, talking to people and generally being disruptive by going in and out of the room. He just could not seem to focus on the task at hand. I could—and did—send him down to another room which served as a study hall with very competent help from other inmates, but he did not ever do enough work to pass the class and earn credit. Many of our students had degrees of ADD, Attention Deficit Disorder, and they found it hard to focus. Mr. Thayler was very hard to reach—even to talk to, as he couldn't seem to sit still long enough for a simple conversation. Being in and out of the hole and missing many classes did not help. He tried classes with other teachers without success and eventually dropped out of the program.

Mr. Nash was chronically late for class, not doing his work and talking when other people, including me, were talking. I asked to speak to him in the hall, wondering if he could tell me what was going on. "You just don't get how dysfunctional we all are, Mrs. Wenzel," he responded.

His comment stuck with me, and I wondered how much, for some of them, the awareness about their dysfunction seeps into their identity. They carried huge burdens on their shoulders: unresolved grief about more losses than I could imagine or count, worries about their families, especially their children on the outside, old damage and terrible trauma they had endured.

Mr. Buhl, a man in his sixties talked openly about his post-traumatic stress disorder (PTSD) after being at war in Vietnam.

"A lot of time I just feel out of control, like I can't really make good decisions," he said. "I get all anxious and can't think straight. Sometimes I do things that are not good, and then I feel real bad."

Observing my students carefully, it was not hard to suspect that many of them had unresolved and continuing PTSD behaviors, and it seemed like their anxieties and their traumas had affected their ideas of who they were, replacing healthy self-esteem with anger and resentment that were difficult to give up. Or, they simply shut down.

It's a big job to give up the old ideas of being tough on the streets and to recover the more gentle parts of their identities. Like we all do, these men had to sift through the parts of their identities that were useful and those that were not. It's scary and painful to give up ideas and habits that have landed them in prison and no longer impress people.

In his fifties, Mr. Palmer was more introspective, sensitive and charming, a total joy to have in any group. Asked to speak at the end of a semester in an all-student assembly, he said, "I thought I knew how to be a man, but in school I learned to be a gentleman." Tears flooded my eyes.

My students told me, in person and in writing, how hard it was to feel like a man out on the streets without a job, and how hard it was to feel like a man inside prison walls with so little control of their lives. I saw how hard it was for them to process what they had lost. It is not just loved ones that are lost—but respect, dignity and dreams. Many men who occupied my classroom were barely out of adolescence, both in age and maturity level, and would express the loss of childhood innocence they never had. They experienced the same identity issues that everyone does, but got loaded up with extra baggage behind the prison fence. They used all available energy to forge an identity that they thought would work.

Mr. C would tell me, "Hang in there with them. Growing up and becoming men is all a process. Be patient. They want to graduate, and they'll get there."

When the days dragged, when I dragged, when too many students had too many problems, I felt like my energy was running out completely. Mr. C gave me constant, gentle prodding about good self-care at home.

HOUSE OF SIXTY FATHERS

In 1956, Meindert DeJong wrote a children's book called *House of Sixty Fathers*, winning a Newberry award that year. It spins out a tale about a small boy in war-torn China, who accidentally floats away on his sampan. On the river, he helps rescue an American airman and is then taken into the airman's barracks where he is nurtured and aided by his sixty new fathers. Television and other societal messages have put across the idea that prisoners learn only about how to be better criminals behind bars. Like many stereotypes, there are elements of truth to this claim, but what I saw was a house of sixty fathers in prison. Mr. C and I needed a lot of extra help. It came in older men reaching out to younger ones to calm them down, help them out and shake them up. I saw them encourage, cajole, nurture and rescue.

Two older gentlemen, Mr. Dexter and Mr. Holder, were role models of gentleness, calm and compassion not only for younger men but for me, too. Mr. Dexter was the black man who had grown up in his beloved Appalachian hollers and struggled with dyslexia. His example of enthusiasm and hard work stirred the whole class to greater effort, including me. Day by day and year by year, he worked tirelessly without losing focus or energy. Modest by nature and not needing any attention beyond what he needed academically, he was an asset in any class. I walked by him in the hall one day beside a much younger and far taller white student, who was dealing with a lot of problems in school.

"C'mon man. You and I gotta go for a little walk and have a talk here. I'm a little worried about you," he said gently, as he hooked his arm up and around the younger man's shoulders. The younger man was just one of the students he encouraged and nurtured.

Early in another semester's English class, I took a stack of writing assignments home and discovered that two of them were identical.

Word for word. Cheating always upset me. I had just that week explained how I felt about it. I told all of my classes, "I teach *honorable* men. Cheating is never okay—under any circumstances." We went on to discuss how we needed to trust each other and how a semester was not enough time to win my trust back. Though these two students were new to me, it was obvious that they were good friends, and I decided to talk to them together. I asked them to come out in the hall.

"Why would you guys think this was okay?" I asked, putting the papers side by side.

Mr. Tait, tall, thin and looking very vulnerable, panicked and pleaded his case. "I'm SO sorry, Miz Wenzel," he said earnestly. "Can I write it all over again? I'll even do it on another subject and give it to you tomorrow morning. I won't ever do this again!"

Mr. Wilkins, short and stocky, lifted his chin and announced, "There ain't no way I'm gonna do this over. This is *your* fault. You told us we could work together and we did. I was just doin' what you told me. I'm goin' down to the office to talk about it." As he stomped down the hall, he turned and threatened, "Maybe I'll drop your class!"

I was thinking, *oh please do.* He slipped back into class looking somewhat smug. I asked to speak to him before lunch, wanting to tell him that if he did it over again, I would give him partial credit and let it go. I knew how few school skills they had, and ideas they have about what is proper behavior did not always match mine. But, with his chin up, he refused to talk to me.

Mr. Tait was true to his word, turning in a good paper the next day. I braced myself for another confrontation with Mr. Wilkins.

"I ain't droppin' cause I want to graduate and that lady in the office says I have to have this credit, but I ain't doin' that paper over—no way," he said defiantly. "All I want to do is pass, so just give me a zero."

Men like this tired me out, and I saw long weeks ahead. Later I challenged them with a quiz that required some hard thinking. Mr. Wilkins took one look and folded his thick arms across his chest.

"I ain't doin' that cuz it's too hard. I didn't mind doin' that other sheet, but I ain't doin' this."

"That's fine," I answered. "Another zero is your choice."

He shrugged. He was more than capable, but like a few men over the years who came through our doors, *he* thought he could decide what was required and how it was done.

Mr. Holder sat right behind both of these men. Like Mr. Wilkins and Mr. Tait, he was a black man, but older and wiser—in his early fifties. His peaceful demeanor and round glasses gave him a professorial, dignified look. He was back in school after more than 30 years. Leaving class early in the semester, he said, "I just don't think I can do this, Mrs. Wenzel. It feels like I've forgotten everything I know." Later he wrote about how sad and embarrassed he felt about being incarcerated. He had no idea what a scholarly, exemplary student he would become.

The three of them, Mr. Holder, Mr. Tait and Mr. Wilkins sat together on the side of the room. Mr. Holder was working very hard on each assignment, both outside of class and in it, and from the first week, Mr. Tait and Mr. Wilkins would turn around and ask him for help. I let them, knowing at that point that Mr. Wilkins was tuning me out whenever he could. Four or five weeks later, I began to see a positive change in Mr. Wilkins' behavior. He still said little to me and reported once that he was still mad about the cheating incident, but his work and effort began to improve. At six weeks, when I sat down with them to do a progress evaluation, he let me in on what was going on.

"Holder and I are in the same unit and he's helping me a lot!" he told me. Mr. Wilkins slid through English with a mediocre grade, managing to maintain his frosty attitude toward me until the bitter end. I tried not to let it bother me, but it did. His behavior felt unfair, and though I tried not to take it personally, it was hard.

In 1997, as the next semester began, I opened my attendance notebook to see who had registered and saw both Mr. Wilkins and Mr. Holder in my history class. By then, Mr. Holder stood on solid ground as an amazing student, getting A's on everything and adding immeasurably to class discussions. I was no longer concerned about his confidence level. I was not ecstatic about having Mr. Wilkins again—in history no less, which always presented tough and thorny issues.

Map skills were often nonexistent in my students. I usually started with lessons on basic world geography right away in history class, followed by a map quiz. Mr. Wilkins flunked it flat. I suspected he hadn't put an ounce of effort into it.

"This ain't got nothin' to do with history!" he complained, arms over his chest again and slumped into the chair. He had pushed the quiz paper onto the floor. Sitting right behind him, Mr. Holder picked it up, talked softly to him, hand on his shoulder.

Mr. Holder pulled me aside to ask, "Mrs. Wenzel, can I work with him? I think I can get him to study it." Seeing that we were all in this together, I agreed and thanked him—with relief.

The next day Mr. Wilkins appeared and asked if he could take the test again, saying he had studied it overnight. He wasn't contrite, but at least somewhat civil. To prove a point about what a little effort could do, I gave him one more day. "You could get 100% if you tried," I told him.

The next day, he rushed into class saying, "Give it here! I know it all and I'm gonna get it all right!"

He did. Things weren't perfect from then on, but far better. The day Mr. Holder was named Student of the Month, the men in the program cheered wildly. I caught Mr. Wilkins' eye and he grinned. As we walked back to our classroom, he caught up with me to say, "That was a real nice thing you did for Holder in there!" When I met Mr. Wilkins' family at graduation, he said to them, "Me and Miz Wenzel didn't get along at first, but we ended up okay."

I knew my limits. I don't like to think about where a lot of problem students would have ended up without the help of people like Mr. C, Mr. Holder and Mr. Ryan. I knew there were others, quietly working outside of class, in their units, and in a study hall on weekends. Seeing these older men being so gentle and circumspect made me realize how much role modeling and mentoring went on without me being aware of it. My students talked a lot about their missing fathers growing up, so the gestures of love and support were even more important. So many men were stuck in adolescent behavior, talking out loud in class when other people were talking, getting up and strolling out of the room in the middle of a discussion without explaining, not doing their work and rarely following directions. The day I saw a paper airplane come out of nowhere was not a good one. No one confessed.

I was learning that becoming mature needs to not be so much about changing bad or juvenile behavior, but being witness to and understanding what being a mature man looks like so they can move *into* it. My colleagues and I could teach them as students, but they also needed the example and loving attention from older men like Mr. Holder and Mr. Ryan in order to behave like mature men. Mr. C's daily presence in our room presented them with a grounded, polite and focused person, too.

I learned to provide a safe place and step aside for these amazing "fathers" to help. If I asked them for help, I did it with hesitation—their job was to be in school too, and they almost always had their own stress to contend with. As Mr. C would say they were doing it "quite naturally." I certainly didn't expect to meet and get to know such amazing people, but it was lovely to witness their caring again and again.

A HOLLOW YEARNING

"In all of us there is a hunger, marrow deep, to know our heritage—to know who we are and where we have come from. Without this enriching knowledge, there is a hollow yearning. No matter what our attainment in life, there is still a vacuum, an emptiness, and the most disquieting loneliness."

—Alex Haley

In a classroom filled with people from so many backgrounds and places, ideas and information about cultural differences came up often. Most Spanish-speaking men were eager to share. White men, for the most part, listened politely, but had little to say about their own confusing, hybrid families. Black men, from all kinds of backgrounds, were often angry about their history in this country, though few had been taught—or took the time to learn black history in any comprehensive way on their own. Almost no black students knew anything beyond the current popular musicians and sports heroes. Native students valued their oral history, passed down through the generations.

My students and these discussions compelled me to think about my own cultural heritage and how it had shaped me. My storytelling, very funny grandfather recounted tales about his father's emigration from the Old Country of Ireland to Michigan.

"See, my dad was the second son, so his older brother Thomas inherited the farm in County Cork. When he was only 19, my dad went to Cobh and got on a boat. He went through Ellis Island and got himself here in northern Michigan. He said it looked just like home." Hearing my grandfather talk and remembering Grampa Henry, who used to take off down the road with his old valise to "go

101

home" are vivid memories from my childhood. Ireland worked its way into my head and heart—and stuck. I've loved anything Irish ever since.

When I was halfway through high school, my father was transferred to northeastern Quebec to work an iron ore operation. We lived in a brand-new town on the Gulf of St. Lawrence that served a mine further north. It was in its construction phase, pulling in people from around the world. In its early years, someone counted 21 distinct nationalities in the population. Like many isolated communities, it was an active one with people banding together against the extreme winters and the reality of the long road to anywhere else. I've connected living there to my interest in community education and the opportunities to connect people in the community to students in classrooms.

French Canadians hang on tight to their language, their history, food, stories and songs, their distinctiveness in a largely English country. Several members of my family stayed on in Quebec and have taught me lessons in the value of hanging on to who you are, sparking my interest in other cultures. Learning new stories, music, dances, recipes and traditions—and sharing them—creates community and opens us to other ways of thinking and living.

Mr. C added to my understanding of the importance of a cultural heritage. His grandmother was a powerful community leader and holder of cultural traditions in Jamaica. His Rastafarian background gave him a community within prison and a dynamic identity. He took it further, writing, "I believe it is much easier for a people to be oppressed when they don't have a clear cultural identity. I also believe that once a people have a clear cultural orientation and know who they are, it is very hard for anyone to move them against their collective interests."

Always calm and thoughtful, he became our go-to person with many of the challenges facing the program. He was a voracious reader, so with his scholarship and intelligence, he was able to advise me on course outlines. Because he observed the students so carefully, he could see things I didn't notice.

Mr. C's influence extended beyond the fence. We had the privilege of having a well-known writer and minister of a large church visit an English class late in the fall semester. I gave the group a break between the two hours, and Mr. C cornered our guest to ask questions. The minister saw how Mr. C carried himself with great dignity, asked very pressing questions, and had an easy way with strangers. He was impressed enough to make Mr. C the subject of his Christmas Eve sermon. I was able to get a cassette tape of the sermon, so when I returned to class after the holiday break, I brought it in and set Mr. C up with a recorder and a set of headphones. I can still see his wide eyes of amazement as he listened to testimony that he was perceived to be someone who was living his life in focused, helpful and spiritual ways.

———

From 1964-1968, when I studied in the School of Education at Wayne State University in Detroit, the current educational catch phrase used to describe our inner-city students was "culturally deprived." I remember many discussions about what that meant and came away thinking that if my inner city black students could just get enough time at the art museum and listen to enough Mozart, they had a chance of joining the ranks of "cultured" people. When I was a student teacher in 1967, all of my third graders were black. Being deprived of culture was hardly their biggest problem. They first needed breakfast, warmer clothes and a chance to stay in the same classroom for at least a year. Among the 43 students in the room, one was designated as the "Welcome Person," whose job it was to introduce the new students who joined us every week.

Within the wonderful diversity of my prison classroom, discussions of culture were not always easy, but often rewarding. I stressed the need to learn about the *past*—the compelling history of their people and their family backgrounds, the amazing artistic gifts available to them in art and literature and events in history that so influenced and informed the present. For almost all of the men I taught, pain, struggle, resistance and survival were a huge part of their culture, and I wanted them to explore it. I wanted them to understand the *courage* of their people.

Learning about the past helped my students find heroes and role models. Learning about the artistic culture of their group made them proud. Recognizing the customs, traditions, religious practices and social values of their heritage and their families helped them figure out what to pass down to their children. Learning history helped them define their own value systems.

Mr. C encouraged me to craft an assignment about cultural heritage in my civics class, deciding it fit well into our unit on diversity. We put it together by asking questions about the students' family histories, traditions about how their children were named, family reunions and gatherings, how holidays were celebrated, recipes, music, religion and language. We asked additional questions if and how their larger culture affected what they and their families celebrated. I asked them to identify their cultural heroes and heroines, events in history or anything in the present that they were proud of. The project proved both intriguing and frustrating. As with most efforts around the differences among us, it would challenge and reward us all.

Generations of American students have been taught the winning side of history only. The winners write history textbooks. All students need the whole of the story, to encounter and understand the price so many people paid for progress, profit and prosperity. For my students, most of whom were part of this "other side" of the American story, knowing how they fit in was critical to their identity, confidence and development as students. They needed to know that their people had played vitally important roles, and I wanted them to feel proud. They needed to feel like they were not on the margins, but part of the whole picture. It was a tricky and difficult project to help them see that they could regard their history as a *treasure*. As the years went on, educational materials that reflected the country's diversity became better and better.

My childhood and all of my many privileges continued to feel light years away from so many of their realities. I kept thinking I would start to feel more comfortable in my white skin, but it meant that I had to work harder. Mr. C kept me going as I learned that it took far more than what I wanted to see as good lessons to help many students feel proud of who they were.

LA FAMILIA ES TODO

Spanish-speaking students handled the cultural assignment with gusto—whizzing through the questions quickly and easily, laughing and talking about it in their small groups. They included colorful details about how their moms made tamales, how their families put on a wedding, how much they loved and missed their family gatherings, the food and the music. They dropped recipes on my desk.

It was a rare day when I didn't hear Spanish spoken—with pride. These students represented a wide variety of cultural backgrounds and came mainly from Mexico, but from many other countries as well. I knew many men from Colombia and some from Cuba, Ecuador, Peru, Venezuela, and Puerto Rico, many of whom had grown up in New York City. One day in a civics class discussion, someone brought in a news article about "hyphenated Americans," which immediately generated a lively discussion about what people wanted to be called. Few Mexican-Americans called themselves Chicanos or Latinos, but they liked being referred to as Mexicans and not lumped in with every other Spanish-speaking group. Others preferred to have their country of origin named too. Typically, younger men were not as sure about issues like this. The questions, answers and comments that day reflected the rich diversity of their nationalities, backgrounds and cultures.

Speaking Spanish was the key to their strong sense of identity, no matter which country they came from. The men I knew all wanted to improve their English, but they also insisted on speaking their first language. They often wanted to sit together and would speak Spanish with each other about assignments. They would say, "There's really no way to say that in English," reflecting how closely language and culture are tied together.

Many men had lived in the United States for years without much more than rudimentary English. They were able to greet people and be accommodating and gracious, and they knew the vocabulary of money in order to shop, but not much beyond that. Eventually, with changes in prison demographics, many of these students moved to other institutions, and we no longer needed to offer ESL classes.

I had to teach English as a Second Language for a semester. Every day was a struggle—not for my eager and cooperative students, but for me. It just wasn't anything I naturally did well. I felt humbled and inadequate, but my students didn't seem to mind my fumbling. They worked hard at whatever I gave them to do. The Spanish-speaking men missed their food, talking about missing their mom's tamales and rice and beans. One Friday in the ESL class, I asked for suggestions about recipes to make over the weekend. I tried to get them to speak English, but a lively argument broke out about the right way to fix ceviche, a seafood dish cooked in lime or lemon juice. I insisted that they write the ingredients and cooking method in English and tried to get them to agree on one recipe. No such luck. In Spanish, the room got loud with their insistence that their own recipe was the best. By the end of the day, I had about five recipes with pleas of, "Please Teacher, try this. It is best." I remember being glad to escape. On Monday, they were all waiting to see which recipe I'd tried, and luckily, I had managed to combine a few, telling them I'd try to find time to make the rest of them.

I did not pick up any resistance among other students to hearing so much Spanish, in fact, I knew both staff members and inmates who learned to speak it fluently. When our program was funded well enough to offer Spanish classes, they were very popular. Small groups of men would sometimes organize themselves to learn it outside of class.

My students from south of the border, and I speak broadly here, had positive attitudes about education—and some of them had a near reverence for teachers. They would often articulate how important education was for them. Generally, they were eager, cooperative, fun and hard-working. They rarely caused any classroom problems other than the Spanish "buzz" among them when they were trying to help each other figure things out. Generally, they were very helpful to each other, translating and explaining for each other in class and out. Language and traditions of sticking together and helping one another gave them a strong sense of pride in their identity.

I heard, "My English not too good" all the time, but their willingness to sign up for a class other than ESL and just wade in amazed me. In a history class one day, two Spanish speakers got up to present their conversation between John Adams and Benjamin Franklin. They had worked very hard on the assignment, asking me for a lot of extra help. When they presented it, we all had a hard time understanding them, and something one of them said caused someone to laugh.

Upset, one of the presenters said, "Please don't laugh. My pronunciation real bad, but I try real hard." Properly chagrined, the man apologized. I don't think I ever heard anyone laugh at them again.

Native American students issued invitations to any of the men who wanted to attend a sweat lodge ceremony, and a lot of these students participated on a regular basis.

I felt the reverberations of history pulsating within this group, too. Some of my men had grown up in migrant families, so they understood hard labor for very low wages. They were eager to learn about people like Cesar Chavez and organizations like MALDEF, the Mexican-American Legal Defense and Education Fund, which made strides toward equality in education for Spanish-speaking students during the civil rights movement of the 1960s and 70s.

Mr. Carmel stood out. He worked fiercely hard to learn English, and though very reserved, his positive, thoughtful contributions influenced every group he was in. He said this about history in a course evaluation at the end of a semester:

We as people have to understand that the past is past and history is history. We need to be patient and not take history personally. What we can achieve today will make a difference for future generations. If you want to learn your roots, learn how your ancestors struggled and suffered.

Then teach it to your children. If we cry for the past, we will drown out the present.

Mr. Pecha was middle-aged, not very tall and quite thin. He walked in with an air of determination, sat right down to work and never took a break. Even though he was still struggling to read and write English, he had insisted on moving ahead from ESL classes so that he could enroll in high school and earn his diploma. In a history class, Mr. Pecha chose Thomas Jefferson as someone he admired, using Jefferson's first inaugural speech with its ideas on minorities. Asking for a lot of help, he wrote:

President Jefferson said that he thought that though the will of the majority is to prevail, the minority must also have rights and equal laws to protect them. To violate these laws would be oppression. I respect Jefferson and this quote, because as a minority myself I know to a small extent what it feels like to be oppressed. He had great courage in that time as a white man to voice his opinion on such a heated topic among other whites, knowing that many of them would not like his point of view. He was a great man in my book.

No matter which country they were from, Spanish-speaking men were all about their families, talking and writing about them all the time. Many of them were facing deportation upon release, even if they had grown up and raised families here. Immigration policies put the welfare of their families in jeopardy, so I heard a lot of fear about being separated from their families in another country. In their culture reports, it was family they wrote about, writing about how much they missed family members and the many family gatherings.

It seemed to me like they had more fun than other groups. Mr. C hated winter, often wearing several layers of clothing in the colder months. One morning he came in after a weekend blizzard with a big grin on his face.

"You're looking rather chipper on this cold day," I noted.

"I just walked across from my unit, and I noticed a row of shapely snow *women* instead of snow*men*," he said. "A bunch of Latinos created them yesterday when they were out on the yard." Their sense of fun and their comfort about being from distinct cultures with their language and customs intact seemed to be a good model for other students to learn about their cultural backgrounds. They helped each other learn, and those were examples for the rest of us.

In some years, Spanish-speaking inmates could celebrate Cinco de Mayo, and we would all be invited to join in and hear wonderful, upbeat, energetic music for an hour or so. It was such a welcome treat! When the numbers of our Spanish-speaking population were high, mariachi bands sprang up. Music programs were part of the Recreation Department, and men had access to their instruments, time and places to practice in the evenings and on weekends.

Mr. C often told me how dull and predictable prison was. So, it was fun to surprise my students once in a while. One mariachi band was particularly good, the leader an inmate and someone famous in Mexico. I ran into him in the hall one day and asked if he could bring his band in the last 20 minutes of the week as a surprise. My students were quietly finishing an assignment when they heard music in the hall and looked up with puzzled faces. The band members burst in singing and playing, and it was hard to see who was enjoying it the most—the performers or the audience. I loved it too—what workplace couldn't use that to happily wrap up a week?

THE RED ROAD

Native men who were not in our program graciously accepted invitations to come and talk to us. They shared drum circles, stories of growing up on their reservations and all kinds of wisdom and knowledge about native history and their spiritual values. Their presence honored us. Some had graduated from college or at least attended for a few years; others were largely self-educated. They treated all of us with respect and with a quiet dignity.

One of my students wanted us to know his bunkie, Mr. Terrence, a small man in his fifties who had a soft voice and a gentle manner. He graced our classroom with his wisdom and experiences of growing up on the Pine Ridge Indian Reservation in South Dakota. He told us about the values of the Lakota people and how wide the gap was between people on reservations and the general American culture, saying:

"Our young people have a very hard time when they are growing up. They must keep their feet in two places—one foot in your world and one foot inside the house with the dirt floor on the rez. If they leave the rez, they risk losing who they are and lose being Indian. That is a very bad thing. One of the problems with this is that white people think a dirt floor is a bad thing. They don't understand that hundreds of years of culture are in that family and in that house."

Mr. Terrence went on to talk about the long history of native students regarding white education as a threat to Indian culture.

"We see education as a way to keep our culture going, but for white people, education is a means to economic mobility. We have very different ideas about what it means to be wealthy. For us it is having our culture intact and learning to take care of all the members of our family. For most other people, being wealthy means being able to buy lots of things."

Mr. Hanover, another valued inmate guest, had a white mother and a father who was Oglala Lakota. He often stopped in our office to chat and offered to help in any way he could. He taught us that there is no such thing as an American Indian, that people wanted to be identified by their tribe. The rest of us who were not native people needed that information. I also needed to learn how to reach my native students as I found many of them to be shy and quiet—especially at first. After I'd heard some of their stories, it was easier to understand their reticence. With a firm grasp of the long arc of native history in America, Mr. Hanover stressed that all natives were and are human, therefore not perfect. He talked about a tradition of adapting to change in all tribes, but that a reverence for the earth does not change. He told us about how spirituality keeps tribes united across many differences.

Mr. Atwood was in a small, friendly American history class, but he said almost nothing for weeks into the semester. One day out of the blue he opened up, saying that he had grown up on a western reservation and had spent most of his childhood in a boarding school. He told us about the officials who pulled him away from his mother on his reservation, both of them crying and fighting to stay together. When he was only 7 or 8, he escaped into the desert at night and tried to walk home. He talked about trying to stay warm out in the desert. The next day, people would find him and force him back into a car. He said he knew that boarding school was a way to "take the Indian out of him." Everyone in the room was still and quiet as he talked. One man had tears in his eyes. I couldn't get the vision of a small boy trying to get home out of my head. It made me shudder.

Mr. Keller was another student with a commanding presence. In his thirties, he was quiet but had a dignity that compelled people to listen to him. He listened intently himself, and I think that kind of complete respect made him more compelling. He had long black hair held back by a red bandana and was close to 6 feet tall. He also talked to us about having to go away to a boarding school for high school and how terribly he missed his family. He told us about his first trip to prison and how scared he was when he saw a black man for the first time and how he couldn't understand electricity and running water. "I make more working here in UNICOR in a week than people make in a month back home," he told us. "But, I wouldn't leave my ancestors and family for riches. Having respect is much more important than money. It makes us sad when people abuse the earth for money." He talked about men who were given longer sentences for not looking the judge in the eye, and he explained that when native people didn't look us in the eye, they were being polite and respectful.

We heard stories about their ancestors' resistance to groups of white people taking over their land. As I watched their sober faces and how long it took for most of them to feel comfortable in school, their individual and collective memories of unimaginable loss and pain seemed right under the surface. I was not surprised to see that they had a suspicion of authority figures and hierarchies, nor was I surprised to hear that their ideas about education were not mainstream. I could see that most of my native students needed time to feel trusting and comfortable. When I gathered enough books and other materials for men to use and assigned research projects about native peoples, the only noise I heard was the sound of pages turning.

Native students, except for a few totally recalcitrant men, were liked and respected in class. An older native man taught me a valuable teaching technique with a "talking stick." He made one for us that he decorated with beads in a crafts class; we used it while we sat in a circle on chairs to re-enact negotiations between U.S. government officials and native people. No one could talk unless he held the stick. It worked, and native students eagerly participated.

When assigned the cultural heritage assignment, native students were all over the map. Some learned about being native in prison, attending the first sweat lodges of their lives out in the yard on the compound. Others would write about "the rez," about ceremonies like the sun dance, a ceremony for renewal for the tribe, the people and the earth or vision quests, rites of passage for young boys into adulthood. Older students usually had more to say, but none of them resisted the assignment.

One summer I spent some time on a Lakota reservation. I was there with *Re-Member*, an organization created by old friends to help build awareness, alliances and friendships between the Lakota and white people, mainly young people from church groups. Several of us slept in a tipi. I was awakened by mangy, wild dogs sniffing around us the first morning we were there. I opened the flap quietly and stepped outside. The sun was just rising on what is the most aptly-named land I know: Pine Ridge. Taking up a large chunk of southwestern South Dakota, the land is ribbed with north-to-south rocky ridges dotted in pine trees.

When I walked out and beyond my tipi, I saw land with stark and haunting beauty. Austere outcroppings jutted up, barren in the sun that shone brightly every day. When we toured the whole reservation, including the Badlands dipping down into the northern edges of the reservation, tall prairie grasses swayed in the wind, reminding me of waves on big water. It is a land of buttes, or tables, from which to view vast stretches of land. I felt an expansive freedom, a sense of the long and wide winds helping me breathe. Many of my students came from Pine Ridge, and I wondered how in the world they survived being locked up within four walls and away from such stunning panoramas.

In the beginning years in my classroom, I had native students in every group, most of them having grown up on the reservations of the plains in the Dakotas, from places like Rosebud and Pine Ridge, but we had men from Cherokee tribes in the Southeast and from several tribes in southwestern states. Not all of the native men had native names. Mr. Arnold came from a reservation north of Pine Ridge in South Dakota and was far less reticent. Easy with people and confident about his academic abilities, he loved teaching us about places and people we knew nothing about. One of the best lessons he taught was how a buffalo was properly killed. He drew diagrams on the board and taught us some Lakota words. I wished later that I had video-taped his lessons. He talked and wrote about riding his horse across the plains, his long hair flying in the wind. Lovingly, he talked and wrote about his rez. His confidence kept growing and he earned better and better grades as he shared his cultural experiences with the rest of us.

Mr. Alexander, a veteran from the war in Vietnam, was a small, trim older man with glasses and graying hair, always taking a seat in the far corner of every class. He took at least four of my classes, so I knew him well. From a Menominee reservation in the upper Midwest, he wrote and talked about his home all the time. When I think of him, I automatically picture his beloved world of tall pines, shiny lakes, canoes and rivers. He wrote poetry about "picking blackberries on a black bear's path." He called his tribe the Wild Rice People, and somehow, while enduring a very long prison sentence, his images of home gave him something to focus on outside the fence, and the constant search for more about his Menominee culture shored up his identity inside the fence.

As we listened to men talk about their native heritage and as I read their cultural heritage reports, it was plain that they could not separate their culture from their spiritual practices, the sweat lodge more important to them than anything else. I found it ironic that so many of the native students would learn so much about their cultures from other inmates in jail. After the American Indian Religious Freedom Act (AIRFA) was passed in 1978, the year our program began, sweat lodge ceremonies became an integral part of our school week. Excused from class, our native students participated in the *sweats* out on the yard throughout the year, a few saying it was the first time they had ever been part of it. Only rarely did anyone miss the chance to go. Basically, sweats are ancient rituals designed to cleanse the body, mind and spirit. Participants heat stones in a fire and place them in the center of an enclosed tent or lodge. When the participants have entered and seated themselves around the stones, they seal the tent until it is totally dark. The leader dips pine branches in water and sprinkles it on the rocks to create steam. Often, they are done in rounds with a chance to cool off on the outside, play the drum and offer prayers.

"Sweats are nothing to fool with," explained Mr. Atwood.

I agreed. In 1988, a few years after I began teaching and while attending a North American environmental gathering, I had the chance to participate in a sweat lodge ceremony deep in the cedar rainforests of British Columbia. Eaglestar, an elder from a Cree tribe, led us through its primal power. My biggest challenges were to calm myself enough in the space of five or six hours to really experience something so strange and unfamiliar—and to overcome my claustrophobia inside the small, totally dark and steamy structure. Even experiencing it only once, I have some understanding about how difficult it is to sit around the rocks in a small crowded place, be so hot and shut out thoughts of the outside. Even once, I found it humbling and restorative.

In the first couple of years, I got used to the empty chairs left on the days when sweats were held and worked lesson plans around the reality of missing quite a number of men one day a week. Mr. Thundercloud was aptly named, a bitter young man, angry and sullen. He was not tall or big, but his scowling face and sour attitude affected the whole group. He sat as far away from me as he could. I also learned that he was a voracious reader and a good writer. One day I brought in a book of poetry by young Native Americans. It held a poem called "Old Man, the Sweat Lodge," and Mr. Thundercloud sat right down and copied the whole thing. I asked him if he would like to write about the sweat, but he said it would take too long. I asked if he would be willing to organize his thoughts and speak to the whole class. I was surprised when he readily agreed. All of his angry brooding disappeared. With more energy and directness than I had ever seen from him, he talked for about 20 minutes. He used the word "holy." I told him that he seemed more relaxed on Fridays after sweat on Thursdays.

"Ya, it really helps," he said.

Over the years, many men talked about the sweat, explaining the hard, inner work it requires. Native men welcomed any other men to come, and Hispanics often did. I knew of only two white men who attended, but I'm sure there were more. Native men spoke reverently about the cleansing power of the process, how it centered them and how it was a place where their belief was strong and their heart was sincere. Men talked about enduring the intense heat to suffer and pray for people they loved. I saw that the sweat gave them an opportunity to link themselves with "old ways" and to their people on the outside. I saw the pride in their tribal identity, a way to find out who they are within their relationship to nature, so much a part of their ancient, indigenous culture. Mr. Paul said, "It's a chance to renew myself away from drugs and alcohol. I know a mother who adopted a Lakota son who had struggled with alcohol for years.

"She said, 'He didn't recover until he went to an AA meeting run by *Indian* people.'"

That makes perfect sense to me. Part of the effectiveness of sweats in prison is that it is *theirs,* not another program run by the Bureau of Prisons. They are taking charge of their own rehabilitation within their culture and within their ancient and sacred customs.

Sometimes I felt like I was sitting in a classroom watching a play about American history on a stage. I was reading my students' assignments and listening to them talk about growing up in impoverished inner cities and Indian reservations. Here they all were, assembled in my room and representing the problems we have failed to solve: racism, poverty, unequal opportunity and education.

Mr. Tessler, a young native who did his work thoughtfully but was shy about speaking up in class wrote:

"I feel pretty bad about all the things my people went through and how many of them got killed off for what white people wanted—land. I have a lot of hatred for the white race, but I am going to have to deal with it. I can't go back to the past and change something that already happened. I feel proud to be native though, and when I get home, I'm going to tell the kids and my children about the truth of what the white

men did. I'm not going to lie to them. I'm also going to try to keep our culture going by teaching the kids."

My native students felt a close connection to and responsibility for the people in their tribes. Mr. Arnold had a long sentence and worried about his family. He became a wonderfully capable student with natural leadership skills and was chosen to be part of the graduation ceremony. His poem called *The Red Road* was chosen for the back of the program:

Though he is young
    His ways are ancient.
    Though no elder was there
    To lead the way,
    His truths were from the heart.
    Therefore indisputable,
    As simple and as complicated
    As the moon,
    The earth,
    The sun.
    As fragile as a seedling
    But growing stronger with
    A few well chosen words
    From others who felt right
    Within themselves,
    He found strength,
    He found his way
    Onto the good road.
    Though there are those who
    Will doubt him
    Or his methods,
    None can question
    The belief within himself and

12. The Red Road

Only if he does
Can he stray off the
Red Road.
Others cannot push him
From it, and
As he goes, he beckons and
Tries to make it easy
For others to follow,
Or at least
Make them aware
It can be done.

The Red Road, reprinted with permission from George Archambault, 2017.

THIS STUFF MESSES ME UP!

In a course evaluation at the end of 1994, a student requested a class in African-American literature. I had the summer to work on it, and did so happily, but my insecurities about being white still made me nervous. Surprisingly, there were as many white men who registered as black men. That pleased me. Mr. Curtis was a white man in his fifties who got along with everyone and made us laugh every day. His good humor balanced us on many days. Men who could make us laugh made such a difference in our dreary space.

While I was taking roll and getting the class started on the first day, Mr. Hammon, a young, tall, black man walked into the room, found his seat, fussed around with his stuff and finally settled in— about 10 minutes late. He continued to come late every day, and I marked him down for tardiness. It didn't seem to bother him.

I pulled him aside and asked, "Mr. Hammon, I don't see you taking this class very seriously. You are late every day, and I don't have any assignments either."

"Okay, okay. I know I gotta do what the class is doing, but I just can't get with this African-*American* stuff. I can get with the stuff about Africa, but African American is all about slavery and this stuff messes me up. It messes me up real bad!"

In his early twenties, he came to class feeling upset on many days. He was personable, nice-looking and charismatic. He wanted to do well in school, but submitting to any authority was a problem —and that included me. Every day, he fiddled around with the waistband of his pants so his pants were low enough. "I like 'em low, real low," he'd say.

Asked later in the semester to write what he knew about his cultural heritage, Mr. Hammon wrote:

"When it comes to my cultural heritage I get kinda lost. That's

only because I am an African American living in America. Most people of different nationalities have had a chance to bring their cultures with them when they decided to come here, but black people didn't have that choice. Once a person who had been away from that cultural way of life they once had for so long, it's hard to pass down. As a matter of fact, it becomes extinct."

He seemed to know nothing of his American cultural background—knew no one who had written anything or done anything of importance. He perceived slaves as totally passive victims who simply took all the abuse. He knew Harriet Tubman's name, but saw her courage as unique. He talked a lot, and Mr. C could see that he'd picked up all the stereotypes inflicted upon him, and then like many young people, internalized many of them. He badly needed his own heroes to not only feel proud, but to light his way.

I was encouraged when he did start turning in assignments on time, and it was obvious, in spite of his fussing, that the material had grabbed his interest. I hoped that in time, he would be able to disconnect his own sense of shame about sitting in jail from the shame of slavery, be able to put on new glasses and see his ancestors as people of courage, determination and endurance instead of people who just sat down and took it. I hoped he would keep on reading and learning. I hoped he would learn to feel black and proud.

On the day he graduated, Mr. Hammon approached me with a big smile, wanting to pull me aside.

"I want you to know that I still have all of your handouts and I keep organizing them," he said. "I really learned a lot in that Black lit class!"

That was very nice to hear.

Mr. Hammon had a point about what was lost from Africa. Our Nigerian friend, who had attended Alabama State University, was a valuable guest, talking about his Ibo roots and his tribal village. We loved learning about the African roots of jazz and blues and the probability that the origin of black spirituals came from Africa too.

Like many Americans, my students could identify only a few African countries on a map.

Always, my biggest challenge was to figure out how to discuss any issues around race. On many days, I would have liked to skip right over them. I felt so inadequate in so many ways with my whiteness, my lack of knowledge and exposure growing up, my privileged lifestyle when I left the prison every day.

I got all kinds of pushback. In a new history class, three new black students came in and sat in the back row, obviously good friends as they chatted together. They did not greet me when they came in, and ignored me when I said hello.

"There's no way we're going to learn about us in here!" said Mr. Watts, the oldest of the three, looking like he was in his early thirties.

I smiled as I passed out textbooks and said, "Hey guys, give me a chance!"

"I bet there's nothin' in here that's worth anything in this book," Mr. Watts replied as I handed out a standard textbook.

Still smiling, but a little unnerved that I was already being challenged in the first few minutes, I said, "Well, what makes you think this is all I have to give you?"

The People's History of the United States by Howard Zinn was perfect for my students, the writing so good that men were drawn in immediately. I was learning that their reaction of not learning anything about their history was common, and I understood it. But, when I handed out the chapter in Zinn's book called "Drawing the Color Line" about the origins of slavery, Mr. Watts asked loudly in class, "Mrs. Wenzel, do you think slavery's a good idea? I just can't sit here and listen to this!"

"Of course not," I answered. "We need to tackle this chapter." I was trying hard not to take any of this personally.

When it was time for a break, I pulled Mr. Watts aside in a quiet corner. "Mr. Watts, I can see how upset you are, and I understand just how hard it is to talk about slavery. However, I cannot act like it didn't happen. Can you explain why it's so hard?"

"I can't talk about it because it reminds me of what's going on in here, and I get too upset," he said softly.

I put my hand on his arm and said, "I'm glad you told me. Can you hang in there for a couple of days? Not every day will be this hard."

"Ya, I think so," he said.

Eventually, in a few weeks, Mr. Watts settled down. I had a knot in my stomach on those days, often feeling humbled and defeated, but listening to how they felt helped.

The two other men were not quiet either. They were both young, black men from Detroit. As the 1990s went on and the War on Drugs was in higher and higher gear, more and more people like them were filling my classes. Mr. Baxter said one day in the middle of Mr. Zinn's chapter on slavery, "I just can't sit here and listen to this!"

Time for another break.

"Would you rather go to the library and read it?" I asked.

"I ain't reading any book if it's about slavery," he said.

I was upset and often was not quite sure how to handle men who reacted like them. Mr. C was invaluable. "These guys will be all right. You can't cater to them when the rest of the group is grateful for the information," he said. I let him sit in the library one day, but I insisted that he do the assignments.

I liked copying Zinn's chapters for them to keep. Mr. Stout, a white man from northern Michigan, told me one day when his history class was ending, "Thanks so much for all these hand-outs from Zinn, Mrs. Wenzel. I want to talk about them with my kids when I get out." That was gratifying.

Zinn's chapters on slavery explained how it all happened, beginning with the desperation for labor as early as the 17th Century, the abundant resources available for profit, the growth of the plantation system. But, he also writes about how people resisted, even as slave ships left African shores. I copied all of those chapters for students and we discussed them together. In some classes, things went fine. In others, any assignments having to do with slavery were met with arguments, angst and downright refusal to do them with some students leaving the room. Slave narratives, stories of daring escapes, even poetry written by people during the time of slavery were anxious topics. The idea that "this stuff messes me up" was shared by many of my black students.

The specter of slavery hung heavily over many discussions. When we had to address it, my head hurt. My students were young and black, sitting in a federal pen with hundreds of people just like them. No matter how hard they worked, their top pay would reach only $1.25 an hour. They saw this as the modern version of American chattel slavery. Any attention to the 13th Amendment put us on thin ice.

NEITHER SLAVERY NOR INVOLUNTARY SERVITUDE, *EXCEPT AS A PUNISHMENT FOR A CRIME*, WHEREOF THE PARTY SHALL HAVE BEEN DULY CONVICTED, SHALL EXIST WITHIN THE UNITED STATES, OR ANY PLACE SUBJECT TO THEIR JURISDICTION.

We had some very uncomfortable days. In spite of our best efforts, a few students left as angry and embittered as they were when the subject was opened up. Some young men simply shut down, preferring to sleep or pretend to sleep through painful discussions. That wasn't allowed, of course, and then the struggle heightened. Mr. C's everyday support was critical.

Though I saw issues and events in the modern civil rights movement as the chapters of hope and courage, those discussions could fan the flames, too. Mr. Etter signed up for school with gusto. He was a black man in his fifties, polite and eager to help people in the office and teachers in whatever way he could. He was tall and charming, making discussions fun with his enthusiasm and hearty laugh. He often talked about life in his unit, the jokes they would play on each other and the fun they had playing cards. If I closed my eyes, I could imagine a conversation about college dorm life. Other men were drawn to his exuberance in my 20th Century history class. The fun stopped when any discussion got too close to his nerve endings.

From what seemed out of nowhere one day, he snapped. We were talking about the importance of voting rights in the South when he started yelling. "I can't sit here and listen to this! Mrs. Wenzel, you just don't know what it was like and how many people died. You don't know how hard it was for us. You just don't know!" he said in a loud voice, by then out of his chair and moving around the room.

The last thing I ever wanted to do was to press my body alarm, so I somehow got him out in the hall. "Mr. Etter, please calm down," I admonished in the softest voice I could summon, "please tell me what this is all about."

"My father was killed on one of those marches," he said. "And I watched him die."

I heard too many stories like that. He was right. What did I know of that kind of trauma and its long-lasting effects? I let him sit in the library until lunch. He probably needed to talk about it, but I needed to remind myself I was his teacher. I didn't feel qualified to be his therapist and address all that hurt and anger, and I had the rest of my students to attend to.

With the cultural heritage assignment, most black students balked. They complained and resisted with all of their well-oiled strategies:

"I didn't understand."

"I didn't know that was what you wanted."

"I didn't know you really wanted it handed in today."

"You didn't explain it well enough."

Again, the shame of slavery still had a tight grip on them. Also, the neighborhoods and schools they had come from were not often places to be proud of. Their families were torn apart by poverty, lack of opportunity and mass incarceration. They had not been taught much, if anything, in their people's history to be proud of and honored by. I had to pull a decent assignment out of many of them.

Mr. Peterson was shy and smiled a lot. He was a cooperative, completely conscientious student who got everything in on time and always did his best work. I was surprised that he didn't hand in his cultural heritage assignment. I took him aside to ask why he didn't do it. He looked at the floor and fidgeted with his papers. It was hard to watch him be so uncomfortable, and I asked how I could help.

"I can't talk about my family, Mrs. Wenzel. I just can't," he said. After I talked him through the rest of the questions, he said he could do *those*, but he definitely couldn't talk about his family.

Instead of three pages, which I thought they should be able to do, many of my black students would hand in three short paragraphs. Sometimes the three paragraphs were written *after* several weeks of learning about the history of civil rights in this country, a subject that engaged almost all of them. I wanted them to find people in the recent past they could relate to, find pride in and whose dignity they might embody. I finally figured out that it would take more than a couple of weeks to let the stories of their people's courage, grit and survival sink into their bones. I got discouraged by their resistance and told Mr. C I was thinking of letting it go.

"Just because it's hard does not mean they shouldn't do it," was his response.

Mr. C's guidance was critical to these discussions. The men looked to him as someone who knew who he was, who understood and lived out of his own roots and culture. He would tell them, "Our African culture is like a piece of precious jewelry, a piece filled with diamonds, rubies and pearls. Every time we discover more of Africa's beauty, it's like adding another beautiful stone to the piece, especially when we really understand what it means. Really, we are the gems and we create the beauty when we recover who we are. Learn your African-American culture, too. Learn to love it. You will never be Jamaican or Nigerian."

I also learned to give them a detailed evaluation form at the end of the semester about subjects, units and assignments to evaluate my teaching. Many said they didn't like the cultural assignment at first, but ultimately were grateful I had required it.

One day we read a speech by Barbara Jordan, who served in Congress from Texas. The speech was about activism and being involved, but the black students in that class could not get beyond the fact that she was so educated. "How did she do that being black and everything?" a man wanted to know. I felt deflated when I heard this kind of attitude extended to all black people. What would it take for black men to feel good about themselves?

Occasionally, I had help. Mr. Atkins was older, a small man in his late thirties, with a kind face and impeccable manners. He looked wrapped in softness, his head full of braids, his eyes steady and soft, his voice low and quiet. With this kind of calm, he commanded respect, and other students listened carefully. One day, after I announced an assignment, a few grumbles rippled through the room. We were moving quickly through a lot of material, and I knew I was pushing them. Mr. Atkins raised his hand and said, "I can't believe you guys! Don't you realize how important it is to know this stuff? Without all of those people back then, we'd still be going into separate bathrooms and using separate drinking fountains like that," he said, pointing to a poster with signs saying "White" and "Colored" over two drinking fountains. "You guys need to read and study. You can't expect any teacher to do the work for you. Get the books. Find out for yourself. There's a lot of wonderful stories that you need to know."

One short speech from one of their peers could say and do more than I could in a whole semester of cajoling and assigning. I was so grateful to Mr. Atkins—not only for knowing the material, but for helping other students see their own responsibility in learning it. Other men were angry at their schools for not teaching them positive stories of black history. One young man put it well. "If I'd had stuff about my people when I was in school, I don't think I would have dropped out."

The longer I taught the more I realized the importance of identity in the learning process, and non-white lessons were at the center of this effort. Mr. Bell, a young black man from Chicago, would not look me in the eye for several weeks when he first enrolled in the program. It bothered me.

"Give him time," Mr. C said. "We have no idea what his school or life experiences have been and he may have no reason to trust you."

Mr. Bell opened up when he was given any information about black history, and within a few weeks, he relaxed and spoke up in class. I had him for several classes, and he turned out to be one of my most creative and hard-working students. Recently I ran across a thank-you note from him. "I can now distinguish truth from error. My old education system troubles me because it misinformed and misled me. It bred a sense of *self-hatred* into my undeveloped mind, and I know that my beautiful children are experiencing the same thing."

My students said they did not want to study a white-washed American history, what many of them labeled a "bunch of lies." They wanted the truth, and I wanted to teach it. But, it was another lesson in "if only it were so easy." All students need the whole of the truth, to encounter and understand the price so many people paid for progress, profit and prosperity—and upon whose backs it was built. Knowledge of other people's stories would help bridge the deep divides between us. For my students, most of whom were part of this other side of the American story, knowing how they fit in was critical to their identity, confidence and development as students. Helping them see that they could regard their history as a *treasure* proved tricky and difficult. As the years went on, educational materials that reflected the country's diversity became better and better, so that helped enormously, and it was fun to have my students thumb through the social studies catalogues. I was committed to stories that were as historically accurate as possible. I wanted the strength, courage, resiliency, morality, compassion and humor of African Americans, both in history and in the present, to move my students far away from old stereotypes. I wanted them to see the people in their history as examples of noble values that could counteract and balance their incarceration and the legacy of hatred and self-contempt that they had inherited and picked up in the present. I wanted them to have heroes and heroines who would get in their skin and help them develop their talents. I wanted them to be able to counteract the violence in the streets where they grew up.

I found it painful to understand that my students came in on their first days with only a few names of famous African Americans, usually: Dr. Martin Luther King Jr., Rosa Parks and Harriet Tubman. Some had heard of Frederick Douglass and Langston Hughes, but knew few details of their contributions. One small book of plays for African Americans with short dramatizations about the poet Langston Hughes, Daniel Hale Williams, a pioneer surgeon, Crispus Attucks, a black man and the first person to die in the American Revolution, were easy to read as a group and pulled everyone in the room in. The plays had several themes, which always generated rich discussions. I did not have a class that didn't love these plays, and men would also say how much they appreciated learning about people they'd never heard of before.

"How come we never got any of this in our schools coming up?" asked Mr. Johnston, a young black man who was interested in everything. "This makes me mad."

That feeling of loss and being cheated about your culture was easy to understand, but I also heard people be positive about learning their particular backgrounds.

"It is good to know about people in our history," said Mr. Kern, "and I'm going to make sure my kids know this stuff, too!"

Figuring out a positive identity is not a quick and easy task. Many factors make up the whole of the problem: not enough exposure to black history or culture in school, poor attendance, negative teenage attitudes about school in general, the influence of drugs, no educational role models, and, of course, dropping out—sometimes as early as ninth grade or before. Centuries of racism, both personal and institutional, have left their mark. Poverty and the complexities of surviving hinder the process. I had to learn that imperfect and painful lessons were far better than more white washing or ignoring these subjects. We trudged on.

BEING WHITE

Amy, our Presbyterian minister friend, and by now a frequent visitor, was comfortable with any group of men and warmly welcomed by anyone who had met her. I asked her to come in early for a visit so that she could sit in on a talk by Mr. Terrence from Pine Ridge in a history class. When he finished, Amy said, "Oh, it is *such* an honor to hear your story! I love learning about Native American culture! Thank you so much!"

Without any hesitation, he asked, "What is *your* culture?"

Taken aback, Amy hesitated then painted a quick picture of a typically complicated white family tree. Mr. Terrence then said, "Whatever your culture is, it is wonderful. You don't need to make any fuss about mine. Your job is to learn your own."

We were both struck by his remark. I hear white people talking about their family histories, but I do not often hear them identify a culture. Most family trees are diverse and complex, and many of us do not think of ourselves as white. For most of us, whiteness is normal, simply taken for granted without much thought to how dominating it is. For most white people in the United States, a cultural heritage is a murky, confusing thing.

The one group of white inmates who took pride in their heritage were the Italian Americans. They spent time together, knew each other well, and were well known for their pasta dinners in the unit. Mr. Starr, a very funny Italian student and then program tutor, was known for never forgetting a birthday and his ability to make us laugh all the time. He tutored in ESL classes for a while, and one of the first things his new English learners picked up was, "Fuhgedda-boudit!" I heard Spanish-speaking students saying it all day.

Mr. Fox was the only white man in a civics class, faced with the cultural heritage assignment and completely flummoxed. He was in his thirties, easy-going and got along well with everyone. I sat next to him and asked if he knew anything about his grandparents or great-grandparents. He was immediately interested, saying that some of them were still alive, that he'd heard some stories but realized that he needed to know more before they were gone. He went on to write to his grandparents, delighted about collecting information about where they'd come from and what they'd experienced. Other white men struggled with any kind of ethnic or national identity, but most of them were willing to think about what kinds of customs and values they might pass down to their children.

I saw such important lessons for white students when they were a minority in a group, often for the first time in their lives. Talking about race was often complex and difficult, but the diversity in my classes provided abundant opportunities to stretch their understanding of people who were different. They were uncomfortable and had trouble speaking up. I tried to acknowledge their discomfort, especially if the man was also new to the institution. White students came in, like everyone does, bringing their experiences, the cultures of their home places, the prejudices and tolerance from their parents, schools and communities. Mr. Willis grew up in the Ozarks in Arkansas and told me, "My mother would turn right over in her grave if she saw me in school with so many black guys!"

Men who grew up in northern areas or outside of big cities would talk about never even talking to a person of color until they arrived in prison. Men in that group had to work harder to bridge the chasms of misunderstanding between them. Putting men in small working groups helped form some friendships, the best way to overcome some of their preconceptions. Students who had studied and read outside of class would point out that white people had far more opportunities, therefore more power and money.

Incarceration, however, is not designed to make people feel privileged. None of the men, no matter what their backgrounds were would use the word *privilege* when they were locked up, and there were certainly white men I knew who had backgrounds and childhoods with no breaks at all—let alone anything resembling privilege.

I knew I had to be careful around the issues of being white. It wasn't hard to set off a firestorm.

Mr. Preston, a well-spoken, polite, young white man, enrolled in my history class, one of only two credits he needed to graduate. He came from a middle-class background and good schools. When he found himself in prison, he'd had no time to learn about his fellow students or develop any friendships among students who were not white. He was an excellent student, but he rarely said anything. Though respectful to everyone, he didn't interact with any other students in the group. When he did speak up, he made us all a little jittery by saying things like, "You guys probably don't know anything about Nietzsche, Kant, Locke or Rousseau," a string of philosophers he thought he should mention.

I looked out and saw a lot of eyes rolling. Name droppers or men who flung out big words did not win popularity contests around the compound—especially if they happened to be white in a group of black men. Mr. Preston looked lonely to me, and I had the impression that he simply needed his voice to be heard—even a little. I doubted he had any idea how patronizing he sounded. As soon as I found the right time, I pulled him aside.

"Mr. Preston, I know you didn't mean to talk down to anyone, but sometimes when people use big words, other people feel like you are trying to say you are smarter or more educated than they are," I told him.

"Oh. I sure didn't mean that!" he said. "Thanks for telling me. I will be more careful."

"Thank you," I said. "I know it can be difficult to be the only person who's different in a group."

The prison made rooms available at night for all varieties of groups to meet. One semester we began to discover that posters black men had put up were disappearing. By checking the room schedules in the federal office, we were able to trace it to a group that masqueraded as a religious group but were really a white supremacist organization. Eventually they were exposed and no longer allowed to meet. I had a very young and polite man who was part of that group, but he never gave me any problems in class. It was useful information to know who he was hanging around with, and I used every opportunity to say how well I thought he was conducting himself in class. He rarely spoke and was not a strong student, but I hoped that his experiences in class were counteracting what he was getting from the other group.

When I got a good group, even in one class a day, it made the whole day and week better. I taught a communications class one year in the mid-1990s with a group of older, more mature men of several different backgrounds. They jelled as a group right away and were a great group—open, friendly, hard-working and supportive of one another.

Mr. Lawton was one of only two black men in the class, very friendly and easy with everyone. In the middle of a discussion, he said, "You guys don't always get it. Most white people expect to graduate, but lots of young black kids don't go to good schools and they don't expect to graduate. They drop out because their schools are so bad, and then they figure out how hard it is to get a job and get into drugs."

Mr. Churchill, a white man in his forties who had grown up in a college town, laughed and said, "Well, my town had the best schools and I dropped out too and got into selling drugs!"

"Well okay, but my point is that your experience is relatively rare," Mr. Lawton said. "In my high school, which was mostly black, expectations of students were low, and the experience of school was often really bad."

Mr. Churchill was well-liked all over the compound, walking around with a smile and an easy friendliness. I was learning to stay out of these discussions. They did not need me, and I didn't want to interfere with any open honesty about the highly sensitive subject of race. At the end of the semester when I asked them to comment on the class and how it could be improved, Mr. Churchill wrote:

"I hate to see this class end. Even though I grew up in a town with lots of black people, I haven't ever had an honest heart-to-heart conversation with anyone who wasn't white. I learned a lot from the guys in the

class, and I learned a lot about myself. I've never had a chance to discuss interracial issues, and it was a good thing for me. It's hard to see so many black guys in here, and I can sure see why they make a connection to slavery. I'm figuring out how uncomfortable it must feel. I learned a lot about how many attitudes I have because I am white. These discussions felt so good! We all need much more of this."

When we studied the Underground Railroad, reform movements, or the civil rights movement, I made sure that everyone knew about the courage and sacrifice of the many white people who struggled for justice. Most people need heroes and good role models—white people need them, too.

Discussions were always interesting and could surprise me. Mr. Burke was white man, in his thirties and a consummate student. Absolutely everything was done well, and he came to class with pointed questions and comments almost every day. He was the kind of student who had a ready list of library books he wanted me to find. He could easily slide into facilitating the discussion, and I often let him do that.

"I'm worried about getting a good job when I get out," Mr. Burke said. "It's hard with a record."

"You don't know anything, White Boy," said Mr. Ogden, a young black man sitting in the back row. Mr. Ogden was often angry and prone to outbursts in class.

"See—you did it again! I hate being called 'White Boy' and I asked you not to do it anymore. I don't call you 'boy!'" he said. I held my breath, but nothing happened. It blew over immediately as the other man mumbled an apology.

———

Identifying with any group was hard work when students didn't know very much about their cultures, and multiple identities complicated the process for all my students. If they were poorer, wealthier, gay, disabled, much younger or much older than the rest of the group, came from a part of the country where their dialect and accents were different or if they came from another country, those realities had to be dealt with too. And, there was the invisible T-shirt that said *I'm a felon.* In spite of the pushback, I knew most of them had traveled a long, often painful, road to start figuring out who they were in a larger context. Much of American history is ugly, especially if your people were on the wrong side of the American dream.

There were bumps along the way for all of us, especially in the required history classes. I learned more in these discussions than in any other subject. It was such a joy to be opened up to people and events in our history I knew nothing about. I also learned about the enormous, seemingly intractable problems of poverty, education, drug and alcohol addiction, mental illness and racism that existed on Indian reservations, in inner city ghettos, in barrios, in remote and poor rural areas, all of which contributed to crime rates. None of these is an excuse for crime, but possibly an explanation. In the 1990s, more and more young black men were rounded up in the War on Drugs and imprisoned in county jails, in state prisons and by the federal Bureau of Prisons, and this prison went from a medium security to a low-security facility. I needed to shift my focus and tactics again to meet the needs of far younger students and more men of color. We didn't have the language for what we now call *mass incarceration*, but I knew I was looking at a different reality. I was looking racist policies square in the face every day. Criminal justice was *injustice*.

Education needs to be as much about learning who we are as it is learning about the wider world. The more we know who we are, our backgrounds, our character, our motivation and our desires, the more we can become vulnerable and connected to others.

GOOD MEN,
GOOD CITIZENS

In order to respond to population shifts, Mr. C and I realized that we needed to alter one very important course. Beyond the challenges of race and cultural identity, the word *government* would give me a knot in my stomach when 9:30 would come and men would file in for the dreaded class. The mere word put some students in the red zone, angry before the first day of school started. I could see why. Men were angry about being arrested for nonviolent offenses, angry about the fact that they had been assigned bad or no lawyers to represent them and angry about the long sentences imposed upon them. They were upset that so many black and Spanish-speaking men were filling the prison. They were disturbed about the extreme control they were under and often angry about how they were treated. The *government* was the dark, evil box into which so many students stuffed their grief and losses. My students did not, could not keep it all under wraps. They brought it all right in with them, and their nice white teacher in a government class was an easy target for their rage and frustration.

For several years in Government class, we muddled along with the standard high school textbook and sweated through the standard lessons. Most students were distinctly unimpressed—and said so. There were no safe subjects. Some days felt like everything I said made them mad. They had a sharply-tuned list of descriptions of American government: racist, controlled by money and run by greedy people, crooked from the top down, a bully and cold-hearted. Evil. Sometimes it felt like being around a big, out-of-control fire. Mr. C helped me see that part of the problem was that they did not feel like part of the whole fabric of the country in any way—instead they felt locked away with long sentences and totally forgotten. They were. They were invisible. Warehoused. *Exiled.*

We needed a new plan. They handled any material that exposed them to civil rights with enthusiasm, but we all needed to do some hard work. Students knew very little. I was picking up new information all the time, but good classroom material was hard to find and difficult to buy on our limited budgets. A list for a new class began to grow. Living in close quarters with so many people is hard, and men shared how they coped with staff or other inmates. I could see that living in prison gave them rich experiences in living with people who were different—and in close quarters. Experiencing their courtesy to me, I opened up the idea of civility inside prison walls. I had done some workshops in nonviolence and invited guests in. Talking about nonviolence gave us a logical link to talking about individual ethics and issues around diversity. The new outline for a class called civics happened "quite naturally," as Mr. C liked to say. The change was dramatic. I loved it—from the first day. The men loved it, too.

With a focus on citizenship, the class fit together and flowed well. I put them in charge, listening carefully to what they wanted to learn about. I wanted to help them visualize themselves not in prison khaki and identified by a number, but taking off the imaginary T-shirt saying *I'm a felon* and replacing it with one that proclaimed, *"I'm an honest man and a good citizen."* I knew it had to be their own individual work, not mine, but after listening to them for a number of years, I could see that they wanted to grapple with the big, moral issues of life, and I began to create lessons around integrity. Mr. C guided the process to explain what they needed. He wrote,

"Many of us are not in prison because we have literacy problems, but as a result of the choices we made. Therefore, it is vital that any educational training we receive address the issues that somehow have an impact on our social, moral, political, cultural and ethical awareness. Cognitive and moral reasoning is the foundation of all academic skills, and many of these men lack them. They do not know how to reason well in order to make good decisions."

There was not one civics class in all the years I taught that didn't fully engage in discussions about moral choices, how to live right-fully in an increasingly complex world. They also liked discussing innocence and guilt, and those issues came up all the time when they were discussing the news. As they were grappling with their own innocence and guilt, ideas like these hit them where they lived. The idea of innocence was complicated. My students were *quick* to point out that no one seem to be prosecuted for the corruption and wrongdoing they saw in the government. These were people with a sharp nose for hypocrisy and a keen sense of justice.

We had a visitor one day who proclaimed assuredly, "Well, it's obvious that all inmates claim they're innocent." I heard that more than once. It annoyed me. For a group that was so invisible and disconnected from the rest of us, I found no shortage of opinions about who they were from people on the outside. I assume that there are people who do claim innocence—and some were innocent—but in all the years I was there, I didn't hear anyone *say* that. They did complain about their bad lawyers or their too-long sentences. They were vocal about the validity of criminalizing the use and sale of drugs. One man said he was arrested for a crime he did not commit, but he also said he did a lot he was not punished for. As a whole, I found them remarkably honest, though, of course, not every single one of them. Mr. C said that if I listened carefully, I'd hear them say, "Keep it real now." Mr. C said, "They mean: Be truthful; be honest; be straightforward. They mean: Don't pretend. Be as clear and raw as you can be. They mean tell the bottom-line, unequivocal truth."

Gradually I was learning new ways to help students learn to *think*, to engage in the subject and wrestle with issues at a deeper level that related to the realities of their lives. I wanted them to learn how to be good citizens rather than just passing the class and earning credit. I wanted to arm them with skills in order to make vital contributions to their families and communities when they got out. I wanted them to develop a strong, confident voice and feel like they were as important as anyone else. I wanted them to feel like they were part of the country's future strength and goodness. I wanted to help them see that their lives could have meaning and purpose, even in prison—especially in prison. A tall order, I knew. Occasionally though, I would get something like Mr. Upton's end-of-semester comments about good citizenship: "I've learned that no one person is always right. Every single thing I say is not always a fact. I say my opinions a lot."

Another answered, "I can now take responsibility into my own hands and learn how to make a difference even when I'm standing all alone on something."

In the midst of all of these heavy ideas, they made me laugh all the time. Asked on a quiz to define impeachment, one wrote, "It means you can't lock him up yet."

Mr. Painter, discussing the Montgomery Bus Boycott, wrote: *"The goals of the civil rights movement were started by Rosa Parks when she didn't move for a white man to the back of the bus. She got arrested. Boy, the police who arrested her that day sure did not know what they were getting into."*

Every class loved ethical dilemmas, and I got out of the way when they discussed them. We watched *Gandhi* and studied nonviolence, which churned up discussions for the rest of the semester. We studied the civil rights movement, framing it as beginning when Columbus came and the Native Americans resisted.

I leaned on the ancients. Sophocles' classic play *Antigone* was successful in every civics class. So much about being incarcerated is about feeling powerless. We talked about the difference between power *over* other people, which they experienced with prison guards and rules, and power *within*, when they could figure out what was important and do the right thing. *Antigone* has a straightforward plot: as she has to decide between giving her brother a proper burial or obeying Creon, the king and her uncle, she finds herself standing alone. The themes about which laws to obey—the laws of the state or a higher divine law—were powerful, causing my students to grapple with ideas like arrogance and pride.

Discussions were lively when I asked them to choose which character was the most tragic and which one had the most integrity. Most of them identified with Creon as the most tragic.

"He never listens!" one man shouted.

Creon's grief at the end of the story was tragically familiar to them. The fact that the king must ultimately live with the consequences of his behavior is a state of mind my students understood on an intimate level. The play amplified our lessons on integrity, and I could always count on those days being spirited and wonderful. I claimed the girl part and played Antigone to help them get into it, but then needed only to step back and let the old classics do their work.

I looked for ways the group could teach themselves. The old game of *Scruples* uses moral dilemmas on playing cards. We used the ones applicable to prison and created others. One man at a time led the discussion. One card asked what to do if you send your 10-year-old child to the store and the child comes home with too much change. A typical discussion went like this:

"You gotta be kidding! Keep it!" says someone right away.

After an immediate uproar, I asked the moderator to identify the "bottom-line belief statement" and write it on the board. He writes, "It's okay to keep things that don't belong to you."

Another man would say, "Call it like it is. Just write that it's okay to *steal*."

"It's the store's fault and their mistake, so it's our money," says someone else. More noise.

"You gotta write up there that it's okay to teach your kids to steal!" one said. And sometimes, "It's okay to benefit from someone else's mistakes."

By then, the moderator was pleading for my help, but I stayed quiet.

"So, what if the cashier was your sister and she was having a really bad day. Her boss figures out her mistake and fires her. What then?" asks another.

"If I take the money back, I should get a reward!" states someone else. People argued vehemently on that one. Men would recount how they had returned something and how it was its own reward.

I loved it when they were still chattering down the hall for lunch, and occasionally Mr. C would report that it continued in the chow hall. Sometimes they would come in with their own examples. Mr. Norwood told a story of being overpaid on a job and immediately returning the money. His customers had been so impressed that they found other customers for him. Another told of being honest in his prison commissary job—and getting promoted.

It wasn't all easy. Issues of trust and betrayal lived right at their nerve endings. Prison is not set up to engender trust among its inmates.

Mr. Neal was a young black man from the South with southern manners, greeting me whenever he walked into the room, then striding over to his cherished spot in the corner. His excellent posture and confident walk told me that he knew he was good looking. He liked being a part of discussions and was a positive, cheerful presence in the room.

One day when someone else brought up the issue of trust, he burst out with, "I don't trust nobody!" Then he told us about losing his cousin to gun violence. "I'm working *real* hard on not hating the guy who shot him, and it's hard after that to trust anyone," he said. The room went silent.

My civics students often reported to me that discussions about honesty and integrity were new to them. I saw a connection between immaturity and a lack of integrity. The men who behaved like they were back in ninth grade struggled at first with complicated issues and rarely wrote thoughtfully. I then asked them to tell me how they experienced school as adults compared with being teenagers. They would talk about how disinterested they were in school while trying to survive on the streets. I hoped that the men who did not contribute to discussions or write very much on assignments were at least being encouraged to think more deeply about their lives and their decisions.

I often said, "I teach *honorable* men." I often told them I needed to trust them. Prison policies are set up to put security first, and many staff members are trained to assume that inmates will behave badly. If I said they were honorable, most responded with honorable behavior. I had no tolerance for cheating. A few of them cheated on tests and assignments, but more of them talked about *not* cheating and being honest with me. There were those men who seemed like they would continue criminal behavior, no matter what happened, but I met only a few with that kind of attitude.

———

The mid-1990s brought a new reality to all of us. Governor John Engler and Michigan state legislators were determined to drastically cut the funds to adult education. From then on, all of us, both teachers and students, felt like an ax hung over us all the time, and we worried about keeping the program both alive and viable. Because I wanted to show my students that active, engaged citizens could make a difference, I introduced the idea of writing letters to legislators. I got some pushback from some students. Some said it was a waste of time; others said they could not write a letter that was good enough. I didn't give in. It became a class assignment from then on.

Mr. Day taught me about innocence and persistence. He had been in the federal classroom to boost basic skills and was eager to finally be in a high school class. When he appeared in the front row of my room, it was hard not to watch him. A black man of about 40, he had a wide-eyed wonder about being back in school after 25 years. He said, "I have to pinch myself that school is real. Man, oh *man*! I can't believe I get this chance to graduate!" Every assignment was done perfectly and on time, in a beautiful manuscript worthy of putting up on a bulletin board. He smiled all the time and thanked me every day as he passed my desk on his way to lunch. That year, we were fighting the threat of cuts to a small federal literacy grant, so I told the class they could write a letter to anyone they chose in the federal government. Mr. Day chose Laura Bush, telling me he could just tell what a good person she was. His letter was four pages long and filled with heartfelt pleas for keeping his school. It read:

"Dear Mrs. First Lady Laura Bush, You can't imagine what this

school means to me after so many years. Never in my born days did I think I would get a second chance to get my high school diploma." He finished his letter with a postscript. "You can show this to you-know-who if you want."

I would put money on someone in the White House mail room taking that letter right upstairs.

Another group decided to send a group of letters to then-Vice President Dick Cheney. When I balked a little, they responded with, "You said!" I was as shocked as they were when I returned to school in the fall to find the package of their letters read and signed off by the vice president's office, the Department of Justice, the head of the Bureau of Prisons, the regional director, our warden and finally working its way down to our office. Attached to the pile of letters was a note that said, "Obviously these men care a lot about being in school." My politically active friends were particularly impressed. And, our funding stayed secure that year.

The late 1990s brought us a wonderful gift in Mr. Hurley, an aide in a federal classroom down the hall. He had been a university professor and had taught in the freedom schools in Mississippi during the 1960s. A white man with a passion for racial justice, we could not have asked for a better guide in understanding the people and inspiring events of the modern civil rights movement. He also directed lessons at Spanish-speaking and Native American students. Well-liked and admired around the compound, Mr. Hurley was able to lecture and tell stories, reaching every student in the room. He was warm, fun and funny. Without warning, he would burst into singing and urge everyone in the room to join in. He gave me an opportunity to work with men who were struggling, and I was able to take good notes and write tests. It was a joy-filled time. Watching, I often sat awestruck watching the most gifted teacher I have ever experienced, and I felt like the luckiest teacher anywhere.

———

Mr. Hurley's lessons on fighting for the right to vote fit in beautifully in the presidential election of 2000. *Very* few men had ever voted themselves. As an election inspector for several elections, I had access to all the forms and procedures for voting in Michigan and planned mock presidential elections. I picked up sample ballots, and my students conducted a registration period for the whole compound. They were earnest, excited, and I might add, totally unyielding about the rules. We followed all proper procedures and schedules with a table in the hall where men could register, using their federal ID cards.

One of the co-chairmen said, "Can you believe that guy wanted to vote and he didn't even *register*?"

My students concurred that these were valuable lessons about following the rules in their states when voting at home. I found it hard to tell them that some states barred people from voting if they'd ever been convicted of a felony. They hadn't known that voting rules changed from state to state.

The 2008 election of Barack Obama was particularly exciting. By Election Day, the committee had created a "precinct" and very nice, official-looking voting booths simply appeared. (I did not ask where they came from). When the day arrived, I saw my committee members outside waiting in the cold with big smiles, ready and waiting to get in. The day went well, with lots of excitement.

Voter turnout was huge, and I was in another room as they were shutting everything down. When the committee came back with ballot boxes stuffed to overflowing, they might have been as excited as Obama's real-life committee members.

Before we started counting ballots, the chairmen, taking the whole assignment very seriously, had a confession to make. "Miz Wenzel, we have to tell you something. Old Jones tried to get over here all day, and finally his boss let him go. He had to stand outside for a long time waiting for the next move and somebody to open the door. When he got in here, we told him the polls had closed and he was too late. Miz Wenzel, he was so upset. He said he had never voted before in his whole life, and he was so excited to think he could vote for a black man. I'm sorry Miz Wenzel, but we broke the rules. I know we shouldn't have done it, but he was registered and we let him vote. Not only that, but we just didn't have the heart to tell him that *these* votes don't count."

The two people who worked hardest on the project were young white men, one of them determined to go out and be an election inspector himself. I assured them they had done the right thing. I could not have asked for a more poignant lesson in what it means to not be able to take the right to vote for granted.

Voting lessons had their underbelly, however. We had a hard time figuring out which states would let them vote when they got out. Some states allowed people to register and vote as soon as they were *off paper*— "off parole and out of the system." Other states deny the right to vote forever for people with a record. There is no consistency and still much confusion about the issue. They followed the issue of many ex-felons being denied their vote in the 2000 election, and it made them angry. I had a few misgivings about this lesson, knowing that many men would go out and discover that there were huge roadblocks to voting—even when they were off paper. But, I also wanted to teach them the lessons of political activism and how important it is to make their voices heard. Most men were shocked by the stories of oppression and brutality endured by women in their very long struggle for suffrage. I hoped all of these stories gave them resolve and courage.

They were learning how the government worked and learning that they did have a part to play. One of the other words they used to describe how they saw their government was *confused*. Mr. Gonzalez wrote this, *"A healthy democracy should have a proper relationship among freedom, rights and our responsibilities to each other in order to reduce the chaos and disorder in a society. We have not figured that out yet."*

While learning about our confounding system, they would puzzle over the way things were done—or not done. When they found the textbook photograph of senators reclining on cots during the infamous filibuster during the civil rights era, one student said, shaking his head, "I can hardly believe this."

One Sunday night after a weekend out of town, I showed a friend my lesson plan book for the coming day. The old Girl Scout motto and the first rule in college education classes was: Be Prepared! I was not. The pages were empty.

"Don't worry," my friend said. "Remember, you *always* know more than they do!"

I did not always know more than they did. They were not empty vessels in which to pour my knowledge. Our most successful days came when I stepped aside to let them design some lessons in the course, facilitate discussions and be in the front of the room to report or explain or interpret. They needed ownership of their learning—and I needed to get out of the way. I was turning a corner.

I taught summer school for five years in the early 2000s. One summer three students approached me about a civics II class. They wanted more about civil rights. It was exciting to plan it. I'd had all the men before, and I knew they'd do well in groups. I copied original documents and had them figure out the distinctions among the three branches of government and how they worked together—or did not. For instance, how did the Chinese Exclusion Act of 1882 come about and how was it fixed later? Every group was on fire. The room buzzed. In the final presentations to the whole class, they sounded like lawyers. I made another turn around the corner as I was figuring out: I needed to trust them with the harder language of original material, with the research they needed to do, with working productively in groups. The more they talked and argued, the more they thought and wrote, the more their confidence grew. When they gave voice to what they believed in, the more they knew what mattered to them. I was walking on air as I stood by and watched that summer. I loved teaching civics, shuddering when I remembered how disastrous the old government classes were. Someone on the outside once asked me, "What are they getting out of when they sign up for school?" I wish he'd been able to see all the eager faces and their palpable excitement on so many days.

Our lessons about being good citizens came all the time and were too many to count. Their friendly warmth to me and to each other as we all moved around the place made me realize how important friendliness is anywhere. I watched them disagree with each other and not make it acrimonious. I observed their honesty and how they wouldn't let people "push them off their square." For them to become good citizens, I had to create enough space for them to try it out, to act like good citizens. We agreed that the task of becoming a good person and a good citizen is a hard one—and lifelong, but their lessons in being kind to each other, being honest, standing up for what they believed in and their examples of building a prison community seemed like a good place to start. They welcomed these discussions with eagerness and wanted to figure out the best parts of who they were. They wanted to determine the directions of their lives themselves and not always respond to the pressures around them, hard as that could be. Some learned to feel more comfortable standing alone against the group when it was important. They learned the hard truths about themselves and their bad decisions—and to move beyond them, beginning to see themselves as good and honorable men. These were profound lessons for me too. The more I taught, the more I learned that goodness is inherent in almost all of us, even when people are damaged as children and often make bad decisions. I learned that these men were teaching me to be a better person every day, and they were doing it lovingly. I learned that working together can be very hard, but it is necessary to create a healthy community. I learned to be a better listener from my students as together we learned that it takes a lifetime to learn to do the right thing.

SOWING SEEDS

Bad classes and bad semesters came along, sometimes teaching in this classroom could feel like a bad joke. I had these frequent thoughts: *What am I accomplishing here? Will this day ever end?* I had a lot of bad days, long hours with too many interruptions, too little energy on anyone's part, too much grief sucking the oxygen out of the room. I had lots of students who were not just difficult, but created all kinds of upset and havoc. I could call a few of them *nightmares*. I had Mr. Flanders and would feel a shudder every day when he walked in. He seemed to get along with other men, but I could tell he was itching to make trouble. A black man in his thirties, he was determined to argue with everything I said, sneering when he asked a question. Finally, one day, things changed.

"What in the world are you talking about, Mrs. Wenzel?" he blurted out. "I don't understand a word you are saying."

Trying to keep the sarcasm from my voice, I answered, "I am not surprised Mr. Flanders. You've been talking since you came in here this morning."

"Ya, well you told us we were supposed to talk in civics class, so I'm just doing what you told me to," he said.

I was afraid to lose my cool, so I ignored the last remark, but when he kept talking near lunchtime, I said, "Mr. Flanders, you are not free to leave for lunch until I talk to you!"

Then I did lose it. "I have totally had it with your rude behavior, and I'm tired of your interruptions and rudeness. You have one more chance to act like an adult with good behavior, or I will have you removed from this class. And, this is the end of any discussions," I said, shaking with frustration and anger. He flounced out of the room and slammed the door behind him. It helped to know that other teachers were having similar problems with him. It was a relief for all of us that he stayed quiet, though sullen through my class. His mid-term points did not look good because he refused to contribute to the group.

"These are your choices, Sir," I said. "You know perfectly well what polite, mature behavior looks like and what this class is about. Just look at any other student in the room."

Occasionally, immature and extremely dysfunctional behavior would take over the atmosphere and demand everything in my bag of tricks. Over and over Mr. C would tell me when I felt discouraged about my students' progress or by a lesson gone badly that I was simply sowing seeds. He would say that they would sprout and thrive when and if the time was right.

"Give them time to grow up. You are not in charge," he would say.

My students were anything but blank canvases on which I could brush layers of paint. I read about Michelangelo once and how he carefully chose his pieces of marble. He thought his sculpture was already *within* the stone, and his job was to chip away the outside so the figure could emerge. That proved true and useful for my students. What they needed to succeed was already within them. My job was to help chisel away their lack of confidence, their bravado, their preconceived notions and negative experiences in school. Also, I needed to raise my standards and challenge them as much as possible.

I had moments of truth when I had get out of my comfort zone and chip away at my white, middle-class ideas of the world in order to take in new painful realities, to tough it out like any teacher and to learn from my mistakes. Learning to be comfortable with conflict was not an overnight lesson, and there were days when I did not learn it at all. I had to make room in my head and heart for the painful truths of America's historical and present racial and economic realities. I had to hear students' opinions that were different from mine; I had to hear and try to understand views of the world that came out of such painful experiences in their pasts. There were many days when all of this drained my energy.

Mr. C often reminded me that my students were in cognitive

dissonance with new information that challenged their previous worldview and made them uncomfortable. I had to learn to present hot-button issues that I knew were hard for them to accept, but do it in a way that did not step on their tightly held, comfortable truths. For instance, when a news article came up about teaching evolution in schools, Mr. Avila flounced out of the room, saying, "Mrs. Wenzel, you're really upsetting *everything* I know today!"

I had to learn to let them vent and, if possible, seize a chance to talk to them alone. I found a quiet moment with Mr. Avila and told him that I understood his confusion. I told him he didn't have to agree with me, but that my job was to introduce evidence accepted in the wider culture. I didn't like seeing him so uncomfortable, but often new knowledge is like that for all of us.

It was a huge job for many of these men to overcome childhood hurt and damage, bad schools or no schools at all, in order to grow up, survive prison and then go home and make it in the world. They had committed crimes and now had the chance to redefine themselves in new ways, not ignoring the past, but pulling it into the present in healthy ways. Most of it remained hidden from me in seeds that I hoped had been sown. Mr. C, with his quiet eyes, would tell me that he could see *transformation*, especially if we had a student for a long time. I could see awareness begin to grow about how to make better ethical and social choices if I listened to discussions and carefully read their papers.

Mr. Rice was a young, black man who needed to earn many credits when he enrolled in the program. He lobbied hard at the beginning of every week for movies on Friday. "That's what they do in regular high schools," he'd say. "And if you'd try really hard you could get some really educational ones about ..." and then he would list relevant subjects. He tried to sleep in class and had a knack for doing a minimal amount of work to get by. He played the games of What Page Are We On? or I Don't Have the Right Book. At the very end of the semester, he missed the day that we counted points and figured out grades. He did not have enough points, and he discovered it when he asked people in the office. He came into our room talking to other men about how unfair I was.

"I need to see you in the hall, Mrs. Wenzel," he said.

"You will have to wait until they call lunch," I said. I saw a few students glance at each other. Most men hated this kind of anger. He kept talking, so I told him he would have to wait in the library. Mr. Rice was pacing the hall and came right at me as other men were leaving. "How come I don't get any credit from you?" he demanded in a loud voice. Other men turned around to see, and one man stayed behind. I know he was trying to protect me.

"You had every chance to turn in missing assignments, and you did not earn the 60 points even for a D-," I said, adding, "You need to cool off, and then come and talk to me."

He was uncharacteristically quiet for the last day and asked to see me in the hall.

"I'm so sorry I took things out on you about flunking, but I've had a little time to think about it. I can see now that I didn't do enough work, and flunking it was a good thing to happen to me. You are going to see a really good student next semester."

We did. He turned into a responsible student, not setting the world on fire, but certainly working much harder and putting the games away. I could see how a long list of classes in order to graduate might feel overwhelming at first. They needed to learn to take things step by step.

Accepting responsibility took longer for other men. Mr. Guyer was in my room for many semesters. I found it hard not to be annoyed by what looked like lazy behavior. A tall, young black man, he walked around with a wide, disarming smile, used, he thought, to great effectiveness. He came in with what seemed like a plan to do as little as possible. Claiming a back-row seat and trying to be invisible so that I wouldn't call on him, a writing assignment early on demonstrated his solid academic ability. Soon, every expectation I had for him became a problem. Assignments were handed in late or not at all with a whole litany of excuses. After learning how well he could write, he then turned in work that was barely worth reading. He started to sleep in class. Frustrated, I called him out in the hall to ask what he was doing there.

"C'mon, Miz Winslow, you're just not gettin' how tired I am from workin' my job," he said, flashing his beautiful smile.

I asked him what he was doing in school if he couldn't handle both a job and a few classes.

"I want to *graduate!*" he answered.

We were not on the same page. He barely passed.

The second time, he had another grade right on the edge, but he had figured out that English was easy for him, and he didn't have to work very hard. He didn't seem to mind the D on his report card. I told him he was making all the decisions, and I paid little attention to him. The next semester he signed up for an art class and told me proudly in the hall one day how well he was doing, what great grades he was getting. He needed only civics to graduate and forewarned me in the hall that he hated the government. I said I'd heard that before and that he might want to figure out what *work* looked like. I'm sure there was a tiny hint of sarcasm in my voice.

He contributed nothing to the group but resistance, and assignments did not come in on time or at all. I warned him in writing, but I said nothing. At the end of the semester, he didn't have enough points to pass, but he made no attempt to count them. I ignored that too and left for the Christmas break knowing he would be very upset when the reality of "No Credit" hit him. He was waiting for me in the hall when I got back, still wearing his smile, but I could tell he was upset. He slouched down the hall, his pants dragging along the floor.

"I can't believe you wouldn't give me credit just because of a few little papers," he said.

"I know. I can't believe it either. I'm having trouble understanding why you would throw away a whole semester for just a few hours of work," I said.

"You know what Miz Winslow, that lady in the office says that I have to repeat the class to graduate, so you're going to get me all over again," he threatened, "you could give me another chance right now if you really wanted to." I said the discussion was over and kept walking. Fortunately for all of us, he took a semester off.

The next fall Mr. Guyer reappeared, still smiling, but did not go to the back of the room. "You're gonna see a new man because I really want to graduate this year, and I don't want to be that old person anymore. You just wait!" he told me on the first day.

I admit to feeling skeptical and told him he was capable of an A, since this was the second time around with the same material. Papers came in early and were done with effort and care. Mr. Guyer was always on time for class and volunteered to help where he could. When he went to the hole for a week for some minor problem, he wrote me a frantic note saying how worried he was about what he was missing. "I'll do whatever you say to make up the work," he said the day he came back. I finally had to tell him to relax a little.

Other teachers were noticing the turnaround too as Mr. Guyer walked more quickly down the hall and stood up straighter. He pulled his pants up and tucked his shirts in. The day he was measured for a cap and gown (Mr. C's favorite task), we could have peeled him off the ceiling he was so excited. It was more than realizing that school was serious and not a place to play games. He really was a new person. He was spending less time in the hole and growing up all over the place. Seeing him on graduation day in his cap and gown was a thrill—his tassel swinging, his shoulders back and his smile wider than ever. He caught my eye as the line passed, and I choked up. It would have been easy to give up on him. My sense is that he knew he needed a semester off to think about how much his behavior was hurting him. I would love to know what he was thinking in those long, transforming months.

Everyone has a right to fall apart at some point. Everyone has a right to learn and grow at their own speed. I got annoyed with the games and excuses, but I was learning with a point system to let students figure out how they would succeed and at what rate by themselves. To be successful in school requires some humility, facing themselves in the mirror to see that the present plan just isn't working. I had no idea how many other obstacles at home or elsewhere in the prison these men were encountering. If a man kept coming back to school, I was learning that at some level, he wanted to be there and to succeed. I had to get out of the way.

Students needed to learn to take responsibility for their own learning, and I had to learn not to take any away from them. I was getting there, developing my own identity as a good, fair and effective teacher. It required humility, self-awareness, time to discern my priorities and where my energy needed to go. It required making mistakes—and learning from them.

"Make failure our friend," Mr. Gill said.

"The more I learn, the less negative stuff I do," Mr. Lane said.

Mr. Carmel, our resident philosopher, wrote one day, "Success is like a seed. If you don't plant it in the right soil, it won't grow a good tree." The good soil seems to be readiness. Getting there had to be painful though, and when they could admit they needed to be new people, it took courage. They were teaching me that people grow and thrive in a garden-like atmosphere that is nurtured and praised for good work—not in a climate of punishment. If given a chance to be responsible for the required work and accountable for adult behavior, the great majority of my students became responsible and accountable. Finally, by the mid 1990s, I had a system that worked for this particular group of students: points for assignments (and one less for every late day), a contract to sign and a clarity about what was my job and what was not. It all worked. Overall, things went well in my room.

EXUBERANCE

I listened to stories of high school teachers having to follow strict curriculum guidelines with specific textbooks, and it made me realize just how lucky I was. How ironic that my isolated classroom, where the phone rang all day and I had to stay hyper-vigilant about prison rules awarded me the freedom to teach whatever I wanted. My program directors were always supportive about new courses I wanted to teach. My students and I were learning together—and all learning what we *loved*. By the end of the 1990s, I was "feelin' a vibe," Mr. C would say, and feeling much more confident about meeting my students' needs. Finally having enough of the right materials made a huge difference. Our needs were coming together.

I loved learning about people and material I had known so little about. Poems from Maya Angelou, Rita Dove, Nikki Giovanni, Claude McKay, Paul Laurence Dunbar and Langston Hughes, among many others, were working their way into my heart. I was learning more and more about the towering heroes in the civil rights movement: Fanny Lou Hamer, who started her own political party and stood up to the white powers that resisted her efforts; Ella Baker, an unsung heroine who kept things organized on a wide scale and believed in grassroots organizing; Diane Nash, whose courage and creativity helped her organize the lunch counter sit-ins and stand up to unfair laws and policies. My world had opened up—and it had changed my perspective on the country I was living in. I wanted to be moral and courageous about the "other side" of our history and culture, and these heroes provided me with role models.

Mr. Weaver worked in the kitchen, so he came in after lunch in his white coveralls instead of the khakis that everyone else wore. He was a tall and stocky black man, wore glasses and loved being back in school after 30 years. A stocking cap kept his bald head warm. He sailed in every day with a hearty greeting and a big smile before he settled down in the back row where he said he could "concentrate better."

One day, as he was putting new vocabulary words in sentences, he was struggling with a new word: "exuberant."

My rule was: No "black dog" sentences. If you have the word "black," then explain that your dog is as black as coal and can curl into a corner at night where no one can see him. Don't write, "I had a black dog."

Fussing with his dictionary, he said, "Miz Wenzel, I just can't figure this one out."

"Well, you know cheerleaders, right?" I said, sitting next to him.

"You bet!" he said, grinning.

"If cheerleaders are exuberant, who else do you know like that?"

"Sooo-py Williams!" he said without a moment's hesitation.

G. Mennon Williams, better known as Soapy with his connections to the Mennon family, was Michigan's polka-dotted tie-wearing, grinning governor from the 1950s. He was indeed exuberant. Perfect. Takes one to know one.

"So, put him in a sentence and tell how he was exuberant."

Mr. Weaver's school skills were, as he put it, "a bit rusty." But, he was long on patience while he started his sentence. I helped him spell "Soapy."

After a few words, he stopped abruptly. "Miz Wenzel, we got a real problem here." I thought maybe he needed another word spelled.

Putting his pencil down, he turned to look at me, eyes wide. "Miz Wenzel, Soapy Williams ain't exuberant. He dead!"

What we were all feeling, my men and I, was a growing sense of exuberance about learning. Our horizons were being stretched; I was listening better and feeling more confident, and we were encountering countless American treasures—in literature and in history. It was heady and exhilarating.

Prison provides enough breathing room for learning. As adult learners, who were curious and eager, my students were able to focus without the day-to-day worries and distractions of employment and families to support. They were there to learn and in a space that allowed it. In such an uncomfortable, austere, cramped, noisy and distracting environment, inmates crave a place to work that is orderly and peaceful. The private "bubble" of space they created around them, a prison coping mechanism that they eventually learned in order to concentrate, never failed to impress me. Some needed time to adjust to being in school and some needed to reduce their school schedules. But for most, being back in school while in prison was a huge positive. I tried to discover what ignited their passions and allow them access to as many materials as I could gather up, and they would report that studying took them away to places outside prison walls.

For a lot of men, access to books and libraries was new. They had no access to the internet, though an occasional googled piece of information from Wikipedia or some other on-line source would come in from a friend or family member at home. I did not miss this lack of access to the web, because we had to rely on *books*—and my students loved them. Some of my favorite days would be when I unlocked a large cabinet with huge drawers with all the books I'd collected, spread them out on a table and let the men choose what they wanted to read and study about that day. Eventually they would need to do some kind of assignment about what they were reading, but they were soon lost in subjects they knew little or nothing about. I could see that many of them felt like true students, taking learning into their own hands, getting excited about it and letting what they were reading take them into new worlds.

Mr. Waring looked like a scholar. He was a black man about 40, slim and tall with professorial-looking glasses and an intense focus on learning. Other students called him "Professor." He wrote, "My escape comes in many forms, but none is more important than books. With these wonderful tools, I can go anywhere in the world. I've been to places that if I'd taken a plane or a train would have cost me thousands of dollars, but books take me free. I can even go back in time!"

Once during a summer session, I had a small English class, and Mr. C suggested that they learn to write a research paper. With some discussion, they gave me general topics they wanted to study. I took boxes of library books in and arranged "research tables" for them by putting four desks together for each person so they could spread materials out. They spent some time with a pile of books and then chose a topic. They got totally lost in their research, hardly lifting their heads for hours on end. They could go outside during moves, so I pushed them to at least get some fresh air. I was moved by their concentration and delight in learning what mattered to them. When they presented their projects, they radiated a pride about having some expertise about a person, an event or a place. They were exposed to material that was also taught in college—and I liked letting them know that. So many of them *belonged* in college.

Watching them make personal connections to the material was so satisfying. Mr. Ferguson, a middle-aged white biker guy, covered in tattoos and with a long ponytail, simply could not get enough to read. He read *Walden* and told me on the way out of class one day, "You know what I'd like, Mrs. Wenzel? I'd like to sit down and talk to Henry David Thoreau tonight. I feel like we share the same values and I really know this guy!"

Mr. Finney was a young black man who came into class with a huge smile on his face every day. When asked what time was the best in their lives, he said that he thought it was when he was young. Then he said, "No! That's what got me here. I think my best time is now because I'm learning so much I didn't know." The more they engaged with the material, the better their assignments were—and the more pride they took in their work.

Mr. Wade knocked his knuckles on my desk as he left every day, telling me to drive carefully, watch for deer and take care of myself. As he put his assignment about his grandmother on my desk one day he said, "You're going to need some milk and cookies when you read this one!" It was a delightful paper about love and devotion, and it stood on its own—even without milk and cookies. These energizing, inspiring little interchanges happened in my early years, but they became more frequent as the years went on. By the 2000s, I was not surprised by positive reactions to school, but they still got me up in the morning.

Mr. C's keen observations became part of my teaching language. "They need quiet eyes," he would remark, explaining how starting from a place so lacking in confidence and knowledge gave them the humility they needed to be open-minded and focused. We hear a lot about Life-long Learning in Community and Adult Education. When allowed so much creativity and flexibility, I could not only teach some of the lessons and subjects I loved, hoping my enthusiasm would rub off a little, but I could let them lead me toward the subjects that really grabbed and held them. Prison provides time, and I wanted to teach them how to find good material and how to approach learning it.

THIS LITTLE LIGHT OF MINE

All along the way, my students were teaching me that education is about changing and enlarging identities, about becoming someone new. They were people trudging on a long road to dignity and becoming the men they were born to be, in spite of being locked up in a dehumanizing place, in spite of the pain and suffering in the past. Like most of us, they want to learn to wear many hats comfortably, to make all the moving parts of their identities fit together. Nothing said they were new people more than being able to wear a cap and gown and participate in a commencement ceremony. Being able to take their diplomas and shake the superintendent's hand was a pinnacle experience.

There is absolutely *nothing* like a prison graduation. Accomplishing this kind of goal makes me think about the sources of joy in our lives. Some are expected events: a wedding, a baby born, those first steps, the ecstatic smiles when a child finally takes the training wheels off a bike. But, I wonder about joy that comes from the *inside* and how that's different. How does our level of joy affect us when we finally master our own fears and get it done, discover we really can accomplish something that has been high on our list for a long time? How do we possibly measure the blood, sweat and tears that accompany the long journey to wholeness that graduating represents? A high school diploma is a vital benchmark of success in American culture, and when men could hold the certificate in their hand and pose for the camera with parents, children and friends there to watch, it seemed to me like a glorious sunrise.

If a man had to leave before graduation day, we put him in a cap and gown and had a small ceremony in a classroom with all the students attending. For many years, we were able to conduct the ceremony out on the yard so that other inmates could be there to watch their friends graduate. Under a bright blue sky, their red caps and gowns looked beautiful. As administrations changed, worries about security with family members ended outdoor ceremonies, so our graduation was moved to the rather awkward and cold visiting room. When weather permitted it, at least everyone could go out onto a patio for a reception with their families.

We made name tags for the guests that said, "My graduate is_____." Having family members there was so important—and so difficult to arrange for some people. Mr. Foley was a white man in his forties, very popular among his fellow students for being an all-around nice guy. He told and wrote a little about his troubled childhood. The paperwork for families to attend had to be in weeks before the ceremony, and he had submitted his with no response from anyone. Dressed in his cap and gown, he kept looking out the small window to see if his family would show up. "I know they're not coming, but I can't help myself if there's even a small chance." I knew no details about his family, but he made my heart ache that day.

Usually the teachers were sitting where we could watch both the graduating class and the families in attendance. The children were wide-eyed, the mothers and fathers proud and choked up. Spontaneous cheers and applause would sometimes come from families, like one mom who stood up to say, "That's mine too!" when her son received his diploma. I loved meeting the families and being able to tell them how well their son had done. Graduation represented a new identity for family members too. I did not enjoy watching the men who had no one from home in attendance as they stood together on the side looking sad and forgotten.

Mr. Starr's parents were both there when he graduated. He pulled me aside to say, "Do me a favor and please don't tell my mother where we are. She thinks this is *Harvard*!"

Each man wrote out a "graduate response," illustrating what being able to graduate meant to them, and then we published them in a booklet that had a drawing on the front done by a graduate. The booklets brimmed with pride, amazement, appreciation and gratitude. Seeing their fathers graduate was a powerful experience for the children, and I loved watching the kids with their proud fathers and seeing them get their pictures taken together. The ceremony lasted about an hour and the reception about the same. There was a degree of let-down to see the men have to say good-bye to the families, take off their caps and gowns and line up to go back to their units for the 4:00 stand-up count. It bothered me when graduation was over, but Mr. C assured me that there would be parties and celebrations for many of the men back in their units. It was a festive day for the whole compound.

Mr. C used to talk to me about when he and Mr. Newman were bunkies. "He simply refuses to understand that he has graduated. He still sees himself as a student and even tried to re-register. He cannot accept the fact that he can no longer be in school, and if he could have done anything to hinder the office getting his transcript, he would have. I wonder if he will ever stop coming around and wanting to be in class."

One year, my students asked if our friend Amy could come to graduation, and it seemed obvious that she should be our graduation speaker. We could still hold the ceremony outside at that point, as the sun shone brightly and a row of dignitaries sat behind her. When she finished her address, she stepped out from the podium onto the middle of the tennis court with hundreds of inmates in the stands watching, ready to cheer their friends in caps and gowns.

"*Everyone* stand up!" she said, scooping her hands in all directions, including in the direction of the (very reluctant) dignitaries. She proceeded to lead us all in song, "This little light of mine, I'm gonna let it shine. This little light of mine, I'm gonna let it shine." It seems to me that's what it's all about.

Graduation is commencement, a beginning. Who knows *what these men may be?*

III. BECOMING A VILLAGE

> *"Without a sense of caring, there can be no sense of community."*

—Anthony J. D'Angelo

> *"Sometimes reaching out and taking someone's hand is the beginning of a journey. At other times, it is allowing another to take yours."*

—Vera Nazarian

> *"Do not neglect to show hospitality to strangers, for by doing that some have entertained angels without knowing that."*

—Hebrews 13:2

WHEN JOHN ENGLER became Michigan's governor in 1991, he

was determined to drastically reduce adult education. We had experienced small cuts for a few years, and then in the fall of 1996, an ax had fallen. Adult education funds in Michigan had been at $312 million, but were now cut by two-thirds. We had 54 sections of classes in 1995, but plummeted to 16 sections in the fall semester of 1996. Students, teachers and office staff felt miserable. Many teachers were laid off, and the ones who weren't were severely cut. I lost half of my classes. Rumors about funding cuts brought students to our office door who were worrying about graduating. All of us were increasingly worried about the survival of the program.

But, in spite of the ever-present budget problems, my students and I were having more fun and more success. I'd read their end-of-semester comments and was learning to implement their suggestions. By then I knew them—and what they needed—far better. I was learning that most of them loved working and learning *together*. They might have fussed and resisted moving chairs around to make "table groups," as they called them, but once the groups settled in to address the task at hand, I could hear an excited, eager buzz. Mr. Carson liked writing poetry and would come in and do workshops with English students. He called the compound "our village." The image of a small, coherent community intrigued me. I hoped leaders would emerge and they would learn to work together for the common good.

As much as adult education students needed individual help, this particular group of students also needed to work and learn together. Many of them were working in a group for the first time. A culture of celebration continued to develop, and I was discovering just how much they loved and needed *rituals*. I often told them that many workplaces had people in teams, and the ability to get along with other people would be one of their most important skills in finding a job. As they lived through their days in crowded conditions, a few of the men I knew were lonely, living completely on the margins away from anyone. But, I saw a growing sense of community. I was learning to have groups of tables all set up when they came in the door. The room buzzed with their discussions—and spirited arguments. Then with a man from each group to report on conclusions, they created a camaraderie among the whole group. By singing together, with Round Table Discussions—and by writing and producing plays, my students were having fun, feeling a *whole* by including everyone and creating *hospitable space.*

OUTSIDERS ON THE INSIDE

One of the most salient features of prison was that appearances and first impressions could be completely deceptive. When I met Mr. Shakir for the first time, it was impossible not to imagine a very together person. He didn't just have an aura of dignity about him, he looked like he could have been a fashion model for prison garb. He walked slowly and deliberately with perfect posture that seemed to reflect a confident sense of self. Entering my classroom for the first time and ahead of other students, Mr. Shakir met my eyes steadily through round glasses and softly said, "Good morning." His perfectly arranged dreadlocks moved in front of his dark, smooth face and a neatly trimmed beard. He headed straight to a tiny corner of my oddly-shaped room. He was thin, not very tall and impeccably dressed in khaki pants, ironed with a crease, a shirt that fit perfectly and was neatly tucked in. His high-top black boots had obviously been carefully polished to a noticeable shine. His cream-colored, crocheted Muslim kufi sat neatly on his head.

Pulling a desk into the corner that was built to hold the moveable wall when it opened, he proceeded to get organized into a space in the corner that was just large enough for one desk. I'd never seen anyone want to sit there and was a bit alarmed by his obvious resolve. I went back to talk to him.

"You don't want to *hide* back here, do you?" I asked, trying to tease.

He assured me that this was where he wanted to be. I thought I could ease him into the group if I gave him some time. I watched him from the corner of my eye. That first day, he spent at least 10 minutes getting organized, lining up books on the floor in a geometric pattern and crisply positioning papers and notebooks next to a straight line of newly sharpened pencils.

"Good morning," he would say in a soft voice each day with a small smile. I had several conversations about his corner, but he simply shook his head.

As the weeks went on, he turned in perfect papers exactly on time, but he said absolutely nothing to any other students nor did he ever speak up in class. I looked for any connections I could make with him, noticing and making a note of his birthday. When the day came, I pulled a chair next to him and whispered a greeting.

He looked up at me quickly, obviously startled, and held my gaze for a few moments with a smile, whispering, "Thank you. That means a lot."

But, he stayed right there, silent and solitary in his corner. No matter what I did, no matter how friendly and welcoming other students were, he would not budge and refused to join any groups throughout the entire semester. I learned that it takes only one person who isolates himself to affect the whole, and in our small room his alienation was hard for other students to ignore. They would turn around and gesture to invite him in. Eventually he refused to talk about it with me, simply looking down and shaking his head. As the weeks went by, other students started to protest having to put their chairs in a circle, and I finally gave up on any group activities. I had Mr. Shakir for another class the next semester, and again, he came in early to claim his corner, and again stayed completely away from the group. He completed all of his credits to graduate but was transferred before the ceremony. I wondered if we could have possibly convinced him to participate, wear a cap and gown and stand in a group with his class. Mr. Shakir's outward, dignified and deliberately perfect appearance gave me no clues about why he needed to be isolated and unable to relate to any other student, and I didn't ever know what caused his isolation. His behavior was a reminder of the need for groups to have an integrity, a wholeness with no one in the room left in a lonely corner.

———

Mr. Grulke enrolled in my Global Studies class. He had dropped out of high school early and had been imprisoned since his teenage years. After he arrived in this institution and passed the ABE test, he wanted to take some high school classes, but people in our office reported that he looked very nervous. My Global Studies class seemed like a good place for him. On the first day of the semester while I was taking roll, other men said that Mr. Grulke was standing in the corner of the hall outside of my room. I tried to be friendly and welcoming as I got him into the room, but he headed to the far corner, turning his desk slightly away from me and the other men in the room. He was not very tall, had long straggly blond hair and wore the same dirty clothes for weeks on end. Many of his teeth were missing. He continued to move his desk to the farthest corner of the room, but he loved the maps and the chance to look in some books and encyclopedias. I could tell by his reading and writing skills that he was bright and curious. His conversations with me were minimal, grunting a yes or no, but I could see him waiting in the hall when the class before his was finishing. As soon as those students left, he marched right in.

As the weeks went on and he became more comfortable with me, he wanted to be my *only* student, needing and wanting more and more attention. He began coming into the room and pushing his desk all the way across the room next to mine with a resounding clunk. He learned continents and countries, examined books and encyclopedias as if they held vast treasures. Though he did a lot of work, he absolutely refused to participate in group discussions or share what he'd written. Other men tried gently to reach out to him, calling him "Cowboy," and the name stuck. That at least drew out a small smile. In our Friday groups, the students sat in a circle and would say, "C'mon Cowboy—let's hear what you have to say." I finally got him to at least point out the country on the world map that he was reporting on, but he complained that other men didn't like him and he would not, under any circumstances, read anything aloud.

He had grown up in Idaho and began to talk about it with me. Within a few weeks he brought in some dog-eared photographs of some horses he had cared for. I asked him if he would like to pass them around, and he reacted by saying, "Hell no! These are *mine!*"

As he became more comfortable, Mr. Grulke began to demand all of my attention during the breaks. He got mad one day when I was too busy and stormed off to the office, looking for anyone there who would listen. Over time he told them about being beaten as a child and being hungry a lot as he grew up.

He signed up for my civics class for the winter semester, but I decided I could be stubborn too. I did not want to let him off the hook. He did his desk trick on the first day, slamming his against mine, but by then, I wanted and needed a little more space and asked him to move his desk a few feet away from mine. He fussed, asking what was so wrong with being next to me. I didn't answer, not knowing how to say that I wanted him to grow up a little. I thought he could handle the Friday Round Table discussions about current events academically, but I also knew I was in for a fight. When I said participating in the group was not optional, he went storming down to the office saying he was dropping out. I decided I needed to talk to him away from anyone else.

I found an empty, quiet room and pulled my chair close to his. I leaned forward. "I'm not doing you any favors by letting you be on the outside of the group. How is it fair to the rest of the men that they must do this in order to get credit and you do not?" I asked.

He was quiet for a moment while he thought about it. "Fine," he said. "I'll just drop out."

I waited a moment and then said, "I know you, Sir. You love school. Give me one good reason why you should drop out of the program."

He said, "Because I'm gay, and those guys hate me."

I caught my breath, surprised. "I told him what a nice group of men he was in and that I also knew how much he enjoyed being in school. I asked him if he would feel better dropping or would he feel better if he at least tried to read his assignment to the class. I suggested that before he dropped, he could try at least *once* to be a part of the group.

"I ain't movin' my chair. No *way!*" he responded, but that seemed like a hopeful sign. I could let him sit by my desk without needing to be all the way inside the circle.

He looked at the calendar every day to see when the group would get in a circle. When the day came, he told me he didn't think he could do it. I smiled and ignored him. Another student helped me set up a circle of desks, and we configured a big open spot in front of Mr. Grulke's desk, still putting him outside the circle but in a place where everyone could easily see him. Other students were nonchalant, acting like this was nothing new. The facilitator that day asked casually, "So Cowboy—wanna be first?" The class ignored Mr. Grulke's trembling hands, but he did it! He got all the way through it, and other men joined in to discuss what he'd written like he'd been participating all along.

I sat back in awe as I watched, knowing the courage it took for Mr. Grulke to finally, after months in school, be part of a class. I was also awed by the ease and grace other men displayed as they smiled and laughed with their "outsider," even though they might have been nervous on Mr. Grulke's behalf. I was certainly nervous as I watched Mr. Grulke's shaking hands. It was a powerful lesson in what learning in concert can do, in what students can learn from each other, and in the loving concern for someone who lived outside and lonely on the edge of everything. After the first week, Mr. Grulke was totally into it, wanting to be first every week. I wondered who gained the most in this experience—Mr. Grulke or the rest of the men who so lovingly included him. I wondered how Mr. Shakir and Mr. Grulke functioned in their units, and I wondered how in the world they would function in a workplace.

Mr. Grulke took one more class, but would not even discuss the idea of graduating and said, "Why would I need that? If I ever get out of here, I'm gonna commit another crime so I can come right back. There ain't nothin' or nobody out there for me." Close to graduation, he dropped out of the program. Mr. C told me that Mr. Grulke looked alone most of the time around the compound. I hope that school gave him some measure of joy and satisfaction—and a sense of belonging, however small. Mr. Grulke taught me that it often takes time for men to integrate into a group, and more importantly, he taught me that I certainly couldn't do it without the help of other men.

I was not surprised that my students felt isolated from the rest of the world. They were completely cut off, except for watching television in the units and talking to people at home, and many men didn't even have that much. I remember Mr. Kovacs telling me in a soft voice, "I haven't talked to anyone on the outside in over 15 years." They would often say, "Nobody out there cares about us."

ROUND TABLES

I believed in evaluations—for everyone, including me. *After* grades were calculated, I liked to have each class evaluate how things went, what they liked and did not like, what they would do differently if they were in charge. What would they tell other students about how to succeed? Did they have any good ideas for the next group coming in? One man suggested in civics class that each person read a news article every week and then the group could sit in a circle and discuss current events. From that discussion, the beloved Round Table was born. It built community, and it was so much more than sitting back and listening to the teacher. I was concerned about the really quiet men, who were either too shy to talk or lacked the confidence, sometimes both. I decided to try this circle discussion idea using the news, and knew that if my students could connect what was happening in the news to what they were learning about how the government works, the lessons would make far more sense.

I had to limit the subject matter for Round Tables. We talked about all kinds of media sources, and because many of them watched television news in their units, they received enough information about crime. I wanted to focus on local, state and federal government news, so I said no crime, sports or entertainment. The vast majority of my students were not in the habit of reading daily newspapers, so they usually balked at first. They could also use reports from NPR, and one week I assigned only the radio. The Round Table format was simple. The men had to have current articles, state the source and the date, summarize the articles in their own words and then add their own comments. It was such a simple thing, but so successful!

I sat in the circle and listened in on the first Round Table, but immediately I could see my mistake. They did want me in the room, but it was *their* time together and I told them they were in charge. I did need to keep my attention on the discussions in case someone was misinformed or misinterpreted a topic. Once in a while I asked to join them about a topic of particular interest to me, and they were always welcoming. If they didn't get all the way around the circle to include everyone and I forgot to give them time the next day, I faced a noisy revolt.

A different person facilitated the discussions every week. Most leaders were very good about hearing people out, about keeping things orderly and making sure each person was heard and not interrupted. They were discussing the dreaded *government*, so occasionally someone would burst out with, "You don't know what you're talking about—those politicians are all crooks—all they want is money!" or "There's no way those guys in Washington are thinking about us!" Generally, most students were happy to put the government down, but they would not abide put-downs of their fellow students.

As I observed how valuable current events were to understanding the workings of government, I suggested that they look for articles about the president if we were studying the executive branch and articles about Congress if we were discovering how legislation happened. I was always impressed by how totally professional they were.

Once in a while, a man would say that his article wasn't really about the government or anything front and center of the weekly news, but he thought it merited discussion. I remember one report vividly. One week, a man's report was on spousal abuse.

Mr. Walsh, who had the report, declared, "Sometimes it's necessary to show her who's boss!"

An immediate uproar filled the room. Mr. Benton, an older, well-respected black man said, "Let's settle down here. We need to talk about violence and how little it solves."

"I gotta have my respect!" answered Mr. Walsh.

Mr. Millman, another wise and quiet student, said, "Respect comes from the inside. We don't get it by harming other people—especially defenseless women. There are better ways to solve problems than by hitting people."

Mr. Dickerson added, "Ya. My dad hit my mom all the time, and it sure didn't help anything."

Mr. Orr said, "Can we talk about anything else? I don't like talkin' about stuff like this."

Mr. Walsh got quiet. I hoped he was listening and taking in the wisdom of the other students.

I sometimes had a hard time being quiet, but it was far better to let more mature men speak up—or have a quiet man be angry enough to make his voice heard. Another time, someone had a report on child abuse.

I wanted the men to learn how to handle these sensitive topics, and almost all of them did. Other subjects involving racial tensions or police brutality were charged and sensitive, but I did not have to intervene to keep order more than once or twice in the many years of the Round Table.

Many new students were very nervous about speaking out in front of the class, and some had poor reading skills. Inmate tutors were available to help if they wanted to practice, but they were still nervous and scared the first few times. Being in a circle was essential as it equalized the group and created a safe place. The circles ensured that every man's contributions and participation were equally important.

It was fascinating to observe how leaders developed. Noisy, boisterous men did not always fare so well at first, and sometimes the quiet men found an inner strength to patiently keep the group moving ahead. The men who focused on other people were the most successful. I hoped those lessons would be remembered out in the world and provide tools for working together in their neighborhoods and communities when they went home.

One day I heard two students talking. Neither of them had started the semester with any competence or confidence. I heard one of them say, "I just read about that bill in the newspaper, and it will go nowhere, because there's not 60 votes. The other party will filibuster." Their level of understanding surprised me and made me want to celebrate!

Round Table became precious time. Mr. Alexander appeared on a day he should have been in the sweat lodge. I went over to ask him about sweat, and he said, "Mrs. Wenzel, you know I could never miss the Round Table." Over and over their evaluations would say that they were interested in the articles and topics that *other* students chose to read and present.

Mr. Piper, a Native American from Michigan, wrote in his end-of-year evaluation:

"I took the civics class from 9:30-11:30 unless they were serving fried chicken and then we get out earlier. Mrs. Wenzel was sometimes frustrated by that. These were not, and I underline not my favorite classes when I tried high school as a kid. I really like the Round Table in this class because it's a wonderful way to learn and it's fun. Sometimes guys get downright colorful and their opinions aren't for the faint of heart to hear. The teamwork is something a lot of us have trouble getting used to, but I can see the benefits of it."

"I like the Round Tables because it keeps us in tune with what's going on in the world. Because everybody is a part of it, we learn about other things than just our own article. Another thing I like is that you have a chance to express your feelings honestly and just listening to different opinions about what we can do to make things better makes a lot of sense," noted Mr. Glenn.

"The Round Table gave you freedom to talk about something, but it was your responsibility to back up what you were talking about. It meant a lot to be me and say how I really feel about the government, even if sometimes guys would tell me I was wrong," Mr. Wade noted.

I was getting to know my students in new ways as I sat and listened to these discussions: what they cared about, what they were interested in, what made them angry and how much they needed to connect to the outside world. Most men liked and appreciated knowing what was happening and talking about it, but they still felt disempowered. I often heard, "There's nothing we can do about anything."

But, there we all were, feeling like our program would disappear as budget cuts became more frequent and more severe. It didn't seem like we had any friends or advocates in Lansing, our state capital, and it also didn't seem like anyone knew about what we were doing. Our staff began to write to legislators and attend rallies. At one rally on the capitol's front lawn, one of our former students was there, happy to be rallying for adult education and greeting his former teachers warmly. I had hopes that many others would be at rallies and write letters after they were released. I hoped that the Round Tables prepared them for discussions in their neighborhoods and communities, their own villages.

I hoped their enthusiasm in the Round Tables would stay with them. I hoped they would keep up with the news. Mr. Nolan, who did well in civics class, did write the program and say, "Tell Mrs. Wenzel that I listen to NPR every day!" In the meantime, in prison, in the company of fellow classmates, they were finding and strengthening their voices.

COMPANY'S COMING

I called on other inmates to come in as guest speakers. It was easy to contact them through prison mail and then simply put a man on "call-out," the computerized daily list of where men needed to be if different from their regular assignment of school or work. Men who were businessmen, bankers, professional and amateur teachers, or men who had a special love of certain historical figures or events were happy to visit and enjoyed putting a lecture together and sharing it. Mr. August, an inmate, taught basic skills classes down the hall and would come in any time to talk about credit, banking and businesses in preparation for men who were going home. I hope I thanked Mr. August and others enough.

Two major universities within 15 miles provided an abundance of resources. People were so nice when I asked them to visit, and I could count on one hand the number of people in 25 years who turned me down. In my early years, the required visitor's memo was as simple as the person's name, and we could get it around to the captain's office and various department heads and signed within a week. As the years went on, the process became more restrictive. The form needed to be signed by the visitor, and then background checks were needed. Things sometimes hit a snag with the wrong date, the memo getting lost on someone's desk, or guests not understanding the urgency and importance of getting it in on time. Occasionally I had guests turned back by a fog restriction or a general lock-down, when all inmates were sent back to their dorms.

When a guest arrived, it was always worth the effort. The men loved company—and they needed the attention and interaction with people from the outside. I learned to write out what guests could expect, and what not to bring. People were immediately sent back to their cars with items like cell phones or pagers. It was so much easier if I came in with them, but if I could not, many people reported feeling intimidated by the paperwork, the metal detector and surrendering their driver's licenses. When an escort would arrive, some reported feeling strangely apprehensive when the second grille would slide shut behind them.

I prepared my students too, telling them that they needed to soften the experience of our guests who were coming into the institution for the first time. I explained the importance of making people feel welcome in the best way possible. I always had a student introduce the speaker—and then asked the students to introduce themselves. It was not unusual for each student to spontaneously stand up one by one when they said their names and where they were from—nor was it unusual for the guest to get a rousing round of applause after being introduced.

In the days before the guest was coming, I did hand-shaking lessons with every student in the room, encouraging them to grip my hand with firmness. They resisted, not wanting to hurt me, but I kept at it. Because a few people were very shy and wouldn't look at people, we practiced making good eye contact. Without being reminded, they took extra care about how they looked on those days too, and it isn't easy to make khaki look much different from the day before. Without being reminded, they hung up coats for guests, found more comfortable chairs, brought in water, helped with equipment and cleaned the board. I knew from both written and verbal comments how much they loved meeting new people.

I invited all kinds of people: musicians with horns, fiddles, harpsichords and violas; politicians, professors, lawyers, writers, artists, a storyteller, people with interesting experiences to share. For a couple of years, we had a drummer come in with enough drums for the graduating class. We were able to convince a graduating group into thinking they had to take yet one more standardized test while we helped the drummer put the chairs in a circle with a drum on each chair. It was quite wonderful to watch them file back in the room for their hour-long drumming "test!"

I asked my former English professor who taught film if he could visit, and he eagerly agreed. Mr. Gill introduced him with, "We are most honored lady (with a nod and a smile to me) and gentlemen, and we are most proud to have a real professor here with us this morning. He teaches at a real university and is filled with high esteem."

The professor was overcome and quickly insisted, "Please—just call me Pete!" He was relaxed and fun as he talked to us about genres and directors. The next week he wrote personal letters to every student in my class. He came back, and my students then decided he would be "Professor Pete." I loved to just sit and watch these kinds of interactions, not knowing who was getting the most out of them—the guests or my students.

One of the most successful programs involved college students. Our good friend Amy, who was becoming well known to most students in the program, was a campus pastor, and she brought groups of college students to mix with mine. Together they discussed big ideas involving the philosophy and the spirituality of education. Her students loved it too, one commenting about how grateful my students were to be in school and how much she took this for granted.

Many days things did not go as planned. I could get fairly stressed out about people having trouble at the front desk or the mechanics not working very well. The worst situation involved my dad, who was coming in to talk about being a Red Cross volunteer in Puerto Rico after Hurricane Hugo. He was a warm and friendly person, but after living between the United States and Canada for 45 years, he had lost his patience with border hassles and officious behavior. I really wanted him to visit, but could not be with him at the front desk. When he hadn't shown up after an hour, I was pacing the floor. When I called the front desk, the person said, "Mr. Patterson is in the warden's office." I pictured him incarcerated. As it turned out, his driver's license did not have a picture on it, so the warden took over and they were chatting in his office while someone took his picture. Then, his artificial hips set off the metal detector. He finally appeared, and my students gave him a standing ovation when he walked in the door. Mr. DeSantos from Puerto Rico insisted on introducing my dad. They loved Dad's slides and asked many questions. All in all, a success, even with the shortened time.

All the guests were wonderful, but a few other memories will warm me forever. Percy Danforth played the bones, a percussive folk instrument played with animal bones or pieces of wood. He was known in folk circles as a charming national treasure and was in his late eighties at the time he visited us. I put the men in a circle on chairs as I was instructed to do, and Percy passed out a pair of bones for each man. One man leaned back and slid his legs forward, to Percy's great dismay.

"You need to sit up, young man," said our new teacher. "You have to play the bones by the seat of your pants!"

Percy played for graduation the next year when it was held out in the yard. We had some accompanying music, and he stood in the middle of the big group to play his bones. The men went wild when he finished, giving him a standing ovation with many cheers and whistles. It was a hot and clear day with the sun blazing down, turning his bald head red as a strawberry. I got worried as the ceremony went on and there was no easy way to get him out of the sun.

The minute it was over, I said, "C'mon Percy, you're getting badly sunburned and I want to get you inside!"

"Oh no you don't, young lady," he replied. "I've been looking for a group to play with that doesn't *tour*, so I need to go talk to my new young friends over there," he said, heading for the graduates with their red caps and gowns. He was 90 years old.

We were honored by so many people: an extraordinary citizen and activist came over and over to work with my students about nonviolence; a man from Mission Control during Apollo 13 came in to talk about the qualities of a good leader and what made a well-functioning team; writers came to read their own work and then listened intently as my students read theirs and artists came with slides—and attended our art shows. People brought their passions and preparation: lawyers came to explain complicated Supreme Court cases; political activists came to tell their stories; an extraordinary birder came to teach my students to look up and watch the migrating flocks that flew high above the prison compound; professionals in the employment field came to instruct and encourage. A group of black women from a book club came and talked about books, education and families, and their presence was especially appreciated by a class of black men. All of my siblings put forth a lot of effort to visit.

"The guests were always willing to help us and treated us as real people and not inmates," Mr. Hyde said.

"The guests were not only brilliant but down-to-earth too," Mr. Guyer wrote on a course evaluation.

"I think we need more strong women to talk to us so that we can see that all men need strong, assertive women. I was impressed by all the guests and the sheer magnitude of their caring," Mr. Vogler wrote.

In such a restrictive environment, I will be forever grateful for my friends who came again and again to be part of an audience, to people who took time out of their busy lives to visit, widening all of our horizons and enlarging our village in such graceful ways. Many guests wrote back to individual students and to groups saying how glad they were to meet my men. On many days, we needed all the stimulation and good will that we could soak up.

WHO'S MY BROTHER?

Prison is a place of paradox. Incarcerated people become both their worst selves—and very often the best people they can be. In such an alien environment, estranged from the world, people reach out and form friendships that sometimes last long after they are released. Prisons also hold distrust, fear, violence and racism.

"If you weren't a racist when you got here, you will be one when you leave this place," said a younger man in a class discussion.

"The longer you are here, the more compassionate you will become, believe me," noted an older wise man, to another group.

Both statements were true. Federal prisons hold men from all over the country and across the world. Depending on where they come from, some men might experience diversity for the first time in their lives when they arrive in prison, and if they brought racist attitudes in with them, living in such close quarters complicated the process of getting used to people who were different. It was also true that prison could be a crucible of transformation as the men's perceptions of people widened and they formed friendships with each other. Occasionally, arguments got heated and once in a while two students argued loudly, but that happened rarely. I watched how politely they treated each other—and how caring they were every day. I recognized a code of civility among them.

Men self-segregated into comfortable groups, like most of us do in unfamiliar surroundings. People from an inmate's old neighborhood or country made a difference when men first arrived in the institution, even if they hadn't known each other on the outside. Men called them *homies* or *home boys*. Native men from the same reservation would stick together; Spanish-speaking men from the same countries would too. Groups who congregated in the chow hall liked to sit near each other in class and hang out in the halls during breaks. It wasn't unusual in a class to see "neighborhoods" form in my room, a group of men speaking Spanish in the back corner, a couple of white students sitting side by side in the front row and a group of black students grouping up. I sometimes found it hard to break them up, knowing that they needed to feel comfortable at first. I was looking for ways for all of them to work together, for them to feel the whole as well as the parts, but many groups resisted. Men from white rural areas would say that they had never talked to anyone who wasn't white.

Mr. West had grown up in the Ozarks. His long brown hair was pulled back in a ponytail. He sat in the front row in an English class right next to the closet so that he could have easy access to the books of poetry on the inside shelves. He was a consummate student, loving the newness of poetry in his life and wanting to do something with poetry every day. He sat right next to Mr. Vaughn, another white man, and they were a tight pair from the first day, both working hard but ignoring everyone else in the room. One day in an effort to mix them up, I arranged tables of desks with names where people needed to sit. They fussed, so I repeated a line from my grandmother, "It will get better before you get married." They worked together in their groups for one of the two hours of class for several days, and then I asked them to write a few comments about the experience. Mr. West wrote, *"My mother hated black people, and she would be surprised by how much fun I had. I have a long way to go to change my attitudes, but this was good."*

Because they could have so easily ignored each other, I was always moved by black and white students helping each other and becoming friends, overcoming their initial stereotypes and misgivings. Mr. Hadley was a 19-year-old from Iowa farm country, tall and thin with a shock of thick red hair and a spray of thick freckles across his face. He looked like a gangly middle schooler and told me he was a recovering addict. He always looked like he'd slept in his clothes. When his transcript arrived, his file bulged with special education evaluations and reports of truancy and failure. He had a very hard time being back in school, wandering in the halls when he was supposed to be in class and looking totally lost. He seemed unable to focus or get any work done. He sat right in front and liked to tell me how much he missed being with his younger brothers and sisters. If he hadn't been so tall, he could have easily passed for an 11- or 12-year-old.

Mr. Kitter, a black man about the same age, sat right next to Mr. Hadley but hung out with all of his black friends. He had his own problems, no solid skills and damaged confidence, but he worked hard and was always polite.

Mr. Hadley came in one day with his long hair all messed up. He didn't greet me when he came in. He had a blank look on his face and promptly put his head on the desk. I asked him if he was sick, and he seemed to not have even enough energy to answer. I finally heard him mumble, "I didn't get no sleep last night." When Control announced lunch, Mr. Hadley stayed in his seat and put his head down. Mr. Kitter turned back, went over to him and gently rubbed his shoulder and back.

"C'mon Buddy," Mr. Kitter said, rocking him a bit. "You can make it. You can't stay here for lunch, so I'll walk with you to the chow hall." They ambled off together. In subsequent weeks, they began to chat and laugh together while Mr. Hadley began to engage in school. Mr. Kitter began helping Mr. Hadley with his work, and they often pulled their desks close together.

This kind of caring helped quell the competition that often seemed rampant in my room. I would hand tests back, and my students would seem as interested in someone else's grade as they were their own—and in broadcasting their own *higher* grade. I said I didn't want to hear competition in my room. This was like talking to the wind. Many men were into sports and had grown up in a competitive culture, and they saw nothing wrong with competition They argued with me saying competition was always good. But, I wanted them to at least be exposed to the idea of cooperation, to the idea that everyone gains more when students help each other. Competition about test results lessened as the semester went on. I put them in charge of review days when they had to work together.

Another pair sticks with me. Mr. Weiss was a young white man who swaggered in as a new student, ignoring my greeting. Small and short, he had completely shaved his head. "What are we doin' in here?" he asked with a sneer. "I need to tell you that I hated history in high school."

When I handed out the first assignment, he said, "This looks really boring." Within a couple of days, I wanted to hide in the closet when he came in the room. Very smart, he jumped at every chance to let the group—and me—know exactly how well he could do, and it took a while for his sneering sarcasm to lessen.

His first week did not go well. After written and verbal warnings, I locked him out when he tried to return to the room 15 minutes late from a break. Then, in a discussion, he made a terrible racist comment, not at anyone in particular but using offensive labels, prompting a talk with me in the hall. I had to be careful how I handled his behavior. Instead of scolding him, I acted like his remark was a big slip-up, and I acted like he was a very nice guy—his behavior making that a stretch. I told him I didn't think he meant to offend anyone, but we, especially black students, would not accept that kind of language. He shrugged and went back to class. After a few weeks, he quieted down and did his work. I could tell that history had hooked him when he started asking for extra material.

Mr. Bashir sat next to him. They were about the same medium height, but the similarities stopped there. Mr. Bashir was black and a devout Muslim. He had a long beard and a shy, peaceful personality. Mr. Bashir struggled with confidence, especially with tests, telling me quietly that he had never done well and was worried about passing. I hated handing back D's on his tests. He hardly talked at all, and after two tests, he was beginning to hang his head.

I was looking for ways to help when I noticed Mr. Weiss and Mr. Bashir talking in the hall.

"Do you guys know each other?" I asked. They responded that they lived in the same unit.

I went out on a limb and pulled Mr. Weiss aside. "You are so nice," I attempted. "Is there any chance you could help Mr. Bashir study for tests? He knows the material when we review, but he panics when the test is in front of him. I bet he would be really happy to have some help."

"Sure," he said grinning. "I can do that! We'll start tonight."

I discovered later that Mr. Weiss had four brothers and *all* of them were, or had been, incarcerated. I wondered what kind of parents he had, what his childhood had been like. I wondered if anyone had ever suggested that he do something nice for someone else.

I was nervous watching them take the next test, but Mr. Bashir handed his in with a smile. "I know I did a lot better!" he told me. They walked out of class chatting and laughing.

I was delighted to hand back a B-, but the best part was Mr. Wiess' interest. For once he was interested in someone else doing well.

"Whaddya get, Bashir?" he immediately wanted to know.

"I got a B-, thanks to you!" Mr. Bashir said.

"See, I knew you could do it!" said Mr. Weiss with a wide grin. Mr. Weiss' bad attitudes disappeared, and the two new friends enjoyed the rest of the semester together. I wondered which of them had been most helped.

Watching these kinds of interactions kept me encouraged, but issues of race were impossible to ignore and often painful. On the one hand, all the many cultural groups made teaching a joy. On the other hand, the painful prison realties of overcrowding and an increasing number of people of color being incarcerated were in our faces every day. Any mention of racism could be a flashpoint and easily slide into loud and angry arguments. Walls were thin, and we did not need teachers and students in the next room complaining, nor did we need an officer having to step into the room. I wanted to let my students have a voice, but I had to be careful when their voices got too loud or they got out of control. I introduced them to the powerful, authentic voices in slave narratives, in black, native and Hispanic poetry, short stories, and novels, but I had to be careful about who was in the class and what we could talk about.

With hindsight, the classroom scenes and the larger forces at work have become clearer. Now I can see that there was no way to avoid the conflicts, misunderstandings and the wide differences in backgrounds. There was no way that people in all the groups, whites included, were not going to be occasionally upset. Race was the most emotionally loaded topic we had to deal with—and the proverbial elephant in the room.

Hundreds of my students enrolled, came to class, got their work done, participated in class and graduated without causing any problems for anyone, and then there were some who often made me wish I was anywhere else. Mr. Ferry could create an argument about an apple sitting on my desk. His intelligence was as sharp as the tools that carved tattoos all over his tiny, bony body. His blond hair was cut so short he appeared almost bald, and he had a small pointed beard. He was the only white man in my civics class one semester, and words like *government, poverty, racism*—and occasionally *assignment*—could ignite his anger like a match to a pile of dry twigs. He and I were on a collision course from the first day. His idea of work and my idea of work were miles apart. He was smart, capable and eager, but *he* wanted to decide what he should do and what didn't need to be done. He wanted all A's, but his work was done in a hurry without much thought, and losing points for late papers made him mad enough to leave the room. I wanted him to work harder, to see his keen mind match the current assignment.

Students like this sapped much of my energy and made it difficult to attend to other students—and to the daily lesson plans. But, I found him compelling. He looked vulnerable and isolated, talking to no other students in class, and seemed angry so much of the time. One memorable morning in civics class, we were working on the vocabulary about diversity and things turned ugly. When I talked about racism as a system of white control over people of color, Mr. Ferry jumped up with his fist clenched, yelling that he wouldn't "listen to this kind of crap" and headed down to the office to drop the class. When he didn't show up for the next two days, and I couldn't locate him, we all had a much-needed break. Finally, when he came back and sulked in the back of the room, I was able to pull him aside to see if I could cool him down a bit. It took some careful discussion and good listening in the office before he calmed down. He told us about an abusive father and the poverty he'd experienced. He let his anger out about the bad schools he'd attended and the chances *he* did not get. With his intelligence and creative energy, Mr. Ferry was hurting too. I had hit a raw nerve, and I saw damaging effects of disinvestment in poor white children too. He came back to class, but something had changed in him and he stopped talking in class completely. I didn't handle him as well as I could have. I wish I had put my hands on his frail, skinny arms to make a stronger connection. I wish I'd hugged his tense little body. I rarely felt like I had enough time and emotional energy to do what so many men needed.

These discussions were hard and they drained everyone, but Mr. C kept reminding us of America's problems talking about racism—and classism—in all of their forms. The problem with ignoring race issues in a prison classroom, especially in social studies courses like history and government, was that these difficult problems were all right there—in our faces and in their lives every day. Issues of inequality and the pain about not getting an adequate education, living as children in dangerous and destitute conditions came up and there was nowhere to hide, even if I'd wanted to.

I knew Mr. Muskin, a young, light-skinned black man, as a troubled person before I ever had him as a student. He was not very tall, dressed neatly and would put his face close to whomever he was speaking to. I would overhear him in the halls and in chaplains' offices, arguing with anyone who would stand there. He stopped by one day *before* he enrolled to inquire what kind of materials I had and asked if I was teaching only white history. As he argued with me about leaving black history out and distorting it, he seemed unhappy to discover that I was trying hard to teach the whole of the story.

When the class started, he interrupted me and other students with angry questions and a lot of talk about "the black man." Any discussion of race or diversity had him out of his seat and yelling, making other students reluctant to say anything. One of my frustrations were the pamphlets that circulated around the compound, filled with conspiracy theories and all kinds of misinformation about politics and history. One of them said that the United States government started the AIDS crisis to kill off black people. Another pamphlet claimed that people in the White House were responsible for 9/11. I did not know where the pamphlets came from, but I got very tired of them and hearing my students referring to them as gospel truth, "But, it says right here!"

Mr. Muskin brought them in all the time—and wanted to share them with the class. He was angry when I refused, and he and I spent a lot of time in the hall. That was risky too. He was one of the men who just wanted attention—positive or negative—either one would do.

I sensed his vulnerability and some deep hurt, but I had no idea where it was coming from. One day during a break, he let his guard down and told me about an abusive, white stepfather, and how hard it was growing up. It occurred to me that my classroom seemed like a safe place where he could act out and express his anger. Over the weeks I was able to convince him that he was not my only student and that his too-frequent outbursts were interfering with other people's learning. I think I convinced him that he had a lot to offer the rest of the group, but he needed to do it appropriately and get his work done. He finally settled down. I had him only one semester as he was on his way home. When he came in to say good-bye, on an impulse, I pulled him aside and hugged him hard. I told him I really cared about him and that I knew he would do well. He seemed stunned.

It was hard to not ever know what happened to people like Mr. Muskin.

Mr. Riley was the man who thought I had treated him with respect when I held the door open for him. The next semester he appeared in my class and mentioned the interaction. "I still remember when you treated me good," he said. *Off to a good start,* I thought. I was very wrong about that. Mr. Riley was so absorbed in racism that he would add the word to a vocabulary matching list on a test when it wasn't even there. He was not a strong student, and his victim stance was frustrating. He blamed "the system," the government, the BOP and his poor education for his incarceration. I knew a lot of those points had merit, but when he was in and out of the hole on a regular basis and blamed his unit officers every time, my patience grew thinner. Being out of class for several days or a week posed problems, because getting books and assignments to the hole was always difficult, and his long list of excuses for why his work wasn't done was annoying. He didn't like losing points and tried to use the hole as an excuse.

One day after more of his excuses, I pulled him aside and said, "You know—you are playing right into the hands of the people you think are too hard on you. The fact that you refuse to take any responsibility for where you are, for all the time you spend in the hole or for the work that you need to do in this program feeds right into the idea that you are not capable. That allows them to take even more opportunities away from you." He left, angry and upset.

Later, just before he graduated, he asked to speak to me. "I've really thought about what you said about responsibility Mrs. Wenzel, and I keep trying," he admitted.

His remark startled me. I was not used to him taking any responsibility, and I had to recognize that I had no idea about what his life had been like—or what anger and hurt were fueling his behavior. I hoped that being in school had helped him.

Generally, in student evaluations at the end of the semester, if students talked about difficult discussions, the white men said things like "we got too deep into racial issues," and the students of different backgrounds would say that it helped to "vent our fears and talk to each other."

After one particularly painful, upsetting morning when issues of race came up, Mr. DaSantos, a mature and charming man from Puerto Rico, held back when the room emptied for lunch, put his hands flat on my desk, looked straight at me and said, "All this anger is about their *pain,* Mrs. Wenzel." I agreed. Their pain about their backgrounds and their pain about being among so many other people of color who were stuck in prison for years and years was palpable.

The 25 years I spent teaching in prison coincided exactly with the dramatic rise in mass incarceration of black men. New mandatory minimum sentencing laws were put in place shortly after I got there. Men were being sentenced sometimes for decades for drug offenses. I can still see my first groups in the first year, which were made up of white or Hispanic men and an occasional black man. From then on, we had a steady increase of black men until some of my last classes would have only black men. Neither Mr. C, my students nor my staff had a name for what we now call *mass incarceration* and the overwhelming and disproportionate number of people of color in prisons. I didn't know at that time about the specifics of the War on Drugs, and I didn't want to anger them by talking about the demographics in our program. I suspect it was too painful a subject for any of my students to address. Black men often mentioned poor schools, their housing projects or their dangerous neighborhoods. I remember hearing a man from Detroit say that he hadn't ever known *anyone* who had a good job.

I handled many days badly. I could have done so much better. I could have used some training, but hadn't been offered a course in college about how to handle racism in a prison classroom. I had many days when I felt nothing but my own prejudices and biases come through and many days when I felt like a failure. But my men and my mentors, there every day, made it work. The pain, the conversations, the arguments, the upset, the hard listening that we all learned to do pulled us along the path.

———

I often wondered if the men extended courtesy to each other as a coping behavior necessary in such crowded conditions—sometimes with very nice men and sometimes with men who were obnoxious and difficult. I could see that their efforts at civility and kindness in my classroom helped to bridge their differences. I decided to put together a unit on civility for my civics classrooms, and I knew it would have more success if I had some help from the men.

Mr. McCall's smile seemed to precede his arrival in my room. He was short and completely bald, friendly and warm to everyone. I had him for several classes, and after he graduated, he made a habit of dropping in to say hello on a regular basis. As a student, he was constant, daily sunshine. A young black man, not over 30, he had the wisdom and composure of a much older man, coupled with a happy playfulness. I asked him one day if he ever had a bad day.

"Sure, Miz Wenzel," he replied. "Everybody does. But I just don't think that gives me the right to take it out on anybody else. It's hard enough to be locked up in here."

It was fun for all of us to have graduates back to facilitate discussions, and Mr. McCall was an obvious choice to talk about civility. He seemed to treat everyone on the compound with respect and compassion. He was delighted with the invitation. The first time he came, he had an outline ready and proceeded to say how grateful he was to be there. He noted that he knew several of the students from his unit. Inmates changed units fairly often, work shifts ran on opposite schedules, so it wasn't a given that they knew everyone in their units. If anyone knew a lot of people, I would guess it would have been Mr. McCall. He then went on to talk about how he tried to deal with men who were brand new to the institution, saying:

"I tell guys, especially the younger ones who come in here, that it's okay to let your guard down. They see a whole lot of dumb stuff on TV and they're scared to death when they get here. I try to take 'em aside as soon as I can and let 'em know things are gonna be cool. I try to give 'em soap and shower shoes right away till they get set up. You know where I learned that? I learned that from the Mexicans. You just watch them. They take care of their own. For me it doesn't matter though. It's hard to come in here and I just try to help whoever. You gotta tell 'em that you got their back."

Mr. Hale, who was in his forties, agreed and added, "You're just always cool, little brother. I never see you when you're not smilin'."

Mr. McCall responded by saying, "I use you as a role model man! I see you getting hot about something and then checking yourself, so I know I can check myself too."

He went on to mention trust, which struck a chord.

"All of us have had trust broken," someone said, and there was a murmur of assent through the room. "But we gotta get by it or it will eat you up man!"

"You gotta find trust in your heart!" said another man from the back row.

Mr. Hale spoke again, "Trust has a whole lot to do with forgiveness." More murmured agreement.

"As black men, we gotta stop killin' each other," said Mr. McCall. With so many of them coming from impoverished inner-city neighborhoods, this subject came up often.

Mr. Ogden, another man in the back who said little, spoke up. He was new to me and seemed quite shy, but whatever he said was worth listening to. "I think it all goes back to slavery and how we couldn't trust each other back then. The system set it up that way so they could keep us down. We gotta break the same chains that are holdin' us down now. We're narrow and divided in our thinking and how we treat each other."

"It's not about what state you're from or what city in here. Sure, it's nice to hang with guys you know or know your hood, but this home boy stuff is the silliest thing in the world. No home boy, no other inmate, nobody's gonna make me behave in any way that's not right. I decide!" another said.

"You're right," someone else chimed in. "It's never about where you're from!"

"We don't like people we don't understand. TV divides us and we're jealous of all that stuff we think we gotta have. Jealousy and envy are killin' the black man," Mr. Ogden offered. "We're real fast sometimes to blame others—mostly white men, but we're doin' a lot of this to ourselves and we gotta stop."

"It *all* starts with self, and we gotta work together," our facilitator said. "You just can't be around someone around here for a long time, sharin' the same cell and stuff without building up a bond. We gotta care about each other.

"You there," he said pointing and laughing at someone he knew well, "I'm gonna take care of you 'cause I love you, and I'm not afraid to stand right here and say that in front of all of you. Now's the time to step up and be men—for real!"

Mr. Riley had his hand up. I held my breath. He was such a loose cannon. This day was different.

"It's about seein' the *God* inside all of us!" he said in a preacher's voice. "It's not about where we're from or whether we're Christians or Muslims. It's about seein' the *God* in each other! We gotta *unite* and be there for each other. Otherwise, we're gonna keep *dyin'*!"

That got some applause and answers of "Tell 'em like it is, brother!" and "Yessirr!"

Mr. McCall said, "Religion is just one word for me: discipline. I have a little book I read all the time and it never fails to set me straight. The other day I read that when we criticize someone else, we need to look at our own behavior because it's probably something we do and don't like about ourselves."

Some of my best days were when I slipped to the side and simply listened. They sure didn't need me that day. Even the difficult people shared profound insights. They were smiling and laughing as they gathered up their things to leave for lunch. Mr. McCall stood by the door as they either shook his hand or hugged him when they filed out.

"That was REAL nice, Mrs. Wenzel!" many of them commented.

———

Now, several years away from them, when I think about that day and many others like it, I realize that civility was too small a word for what these men acted out on a daily basis. Civility connotes the common courtesies of *pleases* and *thank-you's*, the *Good mornings* and the *Have a nice days*. Civility means holding the door open and helping out, none of which are small things in a place like prison. But I can see now that men like Mr. McCall and many others like him, created a way of meeting strangers and taking care of the people who lived with them that went far beyond the surface definitions of civility, into a territory that held great fear and many hardships. They were *mindful* of each other, raising the concept of kindness to new heights. They had to learn how to get along with all kinds of people, and few of them had any prior experience with people outside of their own groups. They learned to treat each other like family, and they also learned to have all kinds of fun with each other. They demonstrated how a good and healthy community functions. The crowding and overcrowding, the need to have a handle on their anger and frustration so they did not end up in the hole made their coping skills simply remarkable. Not only did they get along for the most part, they shaped a new meaning to the word *brother*.

SWEET SINGING IN THE CHOIR

When my students sang, either with me or by themselves, it brought us all together. During the civil rights movement, Pete Seeger declared, "Singing moves people off the fence." If you are a part of a chorus, you are part of a whole. No one wants to be an unintended solo like singing something in the wrong place—doing it once usually cures people. Doing prison time well means having plenty of distractions and singing, like many artistic pursuits, can be completely absorbing. Singing simply feels good and provides an emotional catharsis, something else needed to cope with the emotional struggles of being locked up. In my personal experience, singing is a stress reducer, a feel-good, good-for-the-soul thing to do.

My history classes were natural places for singing, bringing events to life. Whenever I first mentioned it in a class, the new students had a she's-got-to-be-kidding look. They rolled their eyes, glanced sideways and generally looked too busy for such nonsense. I told them that singing has always been a part of the American story. I would point to a poster of an African woman dancing that says, "*If you can talk, you can sing. If you can walk, you can dance.*" If needed, I would tease and say, "No singing, no credit." I would say that it was fine to sing *badly*, that there were no singing police in the hall. I put the music on and passed out the lyrics. Pretty soon, a few brave souls would join in and then more and more. I loved it when they would forget how they might look and just sing out! Even if they had nice voices, they seemed so uncomfortable at first that I wondered how many music classes some of them had ever had.

When I would talk about work songs and how much easier the day went on a sailing ship when the shanty man sang the verses and everyone else sang the chorus, it made learning about crossing the ocean more real. I could always count on a few good sports to mime hauling in an anchor or hoisting the topsails to the rhythm *Heave away, haul away* or *Blow the Man Down*. We sang lots of sea shanties like *Rio Grande, South Australia* and *Drunken Sailor*, (the latter being their favorite). In a few classes over the years, our own shanty man would emerge, and then they would *ask* to sing.

Railroad work songs were also instructive. We sang *John Henry* and acted out a little story about him, "driving that steel drill down" and "dyin' with a hammer in my hand!" Another favorite was *Low Bridge, Everybody Down* about the Erie Canal. Once they learned it, they would say, "Again!" I began to understand that singing was more than fun. It took them to the emotional level of a historical experience. When we sang songs like *Bound for the Promised Land* about moving west or *Bread and Roses*, the anthem of the women garment workers in Massachusetts, they could feel and understand the lessons in a new way.

All of my students loved black spirituals or "sorrow songs." I once heard an American college choir sing a few of them in Notre Dame in Paris with the crowd around me visibly moved. I remember learning a few spirituals in grade school and high school, so I was at first shocked, then saddened to realize how few African-American students knew *any* of the famous treasures. I had many CD's of spirituals, and students would ask for them when they worked quietly at their desks. One very young man asked me if he could come in during breaks just to listen to the CD's, saying, "I just can't get enough of these songs." I wasn't surprised. We sang along to these too—sometimes badly, but with great spirit. *Sometimes I Feel Like a Motherless Child* was a favorite.

We learned songs that began: *Oh freedom, oh freedom, We shall not, we shall not be moved* and *Woke up this mornin' with my mind stayed on freedom*! The men loved these songs.

One day when Mr. Hurley, who taught our history classes, was talking about being in the South during Freedom Summer, he said, "Let's all stand up and get in a circle. Before anyone could object, we were all crossing arms, holding hands and singing all the verses to *We Shall Overcome*, led by his rich baritone voice. Another time, studying the labor movement, he stopped abruptly and told us to clear our desks. Then he sang all the verses to *Joe Hill*.

Prisons are full of people with many talents, music among them. One man I didn't know came into the Complex with amazing keyboard experience and organized a small group to sing in their spare time. Mr. C told me the keyboardist had no formal musical training. I wondered where he would be if he'd been trained and could have used his prodigious talent to make a living.

In 2006, I was able to organize a high school choir. I first tried to find a graduate student in music from a nearby university, but I couldn't interest anyone. One woman I talked to was horrified that the class would meet at 7:30 in the morning, a "very bad time for voices!" Prison affords no such luxuries. When the word was out, two inmates eagerly stepped up, one to direct, the other to accompany. The class filled quickly with both students as well as anyone else around the compound who was interested. There were men willing to lose a couple hours of pay in order to sing. They met officially twice a week, but quickly added other sessions in the evenings and on weekends.

Young men with absolutely no experience joined the choir. Mr. Tyler, a new student, was asked how school was going for him after a few weeks.

"Man, do I love that choir!" he said.

Mr. Briggs, a man who was not enrolled in the program and was serving a long sentence, said, "Thanks so much for organizing the choir, Mrs. Wenzel. I used to sing a lot when I was growing up, and this is the only time I forget I'm locked up."

Mr. Dale behaved like an unruly ninth grader in my history class. He went straight to the back row on the first day, talked out of turn, laughed with anyone who would listen and fussed about the rules all the time. When I talked to him privately, he said, "You're always picking on me." Or, he would say with some annoyance, "Other people talk, too, you know." Things got somewhat better only when I used threats removing him from class. He made my head hurt, and I was sick of the effort it was taking to keep him in line. Then one day—ah ha! I discovered that he had a rich, baritone voice and loved to sing! I asked to see him in the hall.

"You have a great voice and the choir *needs* you!" I implored, thinking maybe that the choir did not, but it was worth a try.

He agreed to join the choir, and I would watch him out of the corner of my eye in the baritone section and marvel at his much more grown-up behavior. He knew he had to do what he was told because it would be too embarrassing not to, and he didn't want to risk the scorn and dirty looks of the older men in the group. Singing in the choir may not have had anything to do with his improving behavior, but it all happened at the same time.

The choir was made up of many cultural groups, who mixed and sang together beautifully from the beginning. Men with more experience who were able to read music carried the ones who approached the page like it was filled with hieroglyphics. I was nervous that they might be singing too many Christian songs, but when no one complained and they were all so proud of being able to sing *Ave Verum* in Latin, I relaxed, because, well, they sounded like *angels*. Catholic masses and Protestant services were held almost every week, and the choir was asked to sing for both of them. Some of the younger men complained to me that they were too nervous to perform, but I told them their nervousness would pass and that performing might even be fun. So, the extra church experiences were valuable.

Joshua Fit the Battle of Jericho and *Brothers Forever* became their signature songs, and the first big concert was eagerly and nervously anticipated. The local Rotary Club generously donated a badly-needed new keyboard, and about 10 Rotarians came to the concert, thoroughly charmed by the sound of such lovely voices and the wide smiles in the choir.

The choir sang for a couple of years and was able to sing for religious services, school concerts we organized, GED graduations and other ceremonies in the institution. At its high mark, the choir had about 35 men. At the warden's request, they put together a Christmas program. They darkened the room, except for twinkling lights on some plants and on one spindly Christmas tree. In a processional, they sang a song in German, crisscrossing as they processed and stood in their places. At the end of the concert, the choir invited us all to sing along. We stood together, inmates, staff and guests to sing *Silent Night,* all equal and all moved by the power of singing together.

I learned that singing and listening to singing in prison does feed the soul. Mr. Briggs and Mr. Tyler were not the only men who expressed gratitude and excitement about the choir, but men also said they enjoyed hearing all the singing when they were in the hall. "Their singing softens the place," said a man in the hall. I watched them develop as a group and learn to work—and stay together. It amplified my belief that everyone needs beauty in their lives, these men maybe most of all.

"WHAT IS ALL THIS JUICE AND ALL THIS JOY?"

—*Spring*, Gerard Manley Hopkins

From the first day that I passed out a play for everyone to participate in, I knew I had a valuable teaching technique. There was not a class that didn't love to read them aloud together. We read all kinds in several different classes: African-American history plays about Frederick Douglass, Langston Hughes, Mary McLeod Bethune, *12 Angry Men*, Greek plays and after some pushback, some Shakespeare too.

Because it made the setting more real, arranging desks proved to be a key element to success. But, it was not easy to get students to move, to put it mildly. They staked out territory in our room like the Sooners in Oklahoma claiming territory in a land rush. Getting them to move once class began rarely worked, so I learned to move the chairs myself before class started. Then, something wonderful happened when they simulated a jury in a group shaped like a square—or when they sat stiffly in rows in the graveyard of Grover's Corners in *Our Town*. Something magical happened when a kind of stage was created, and they felt that they were all part of a whole. We were all transported to a place inside the story, and no one was left out.

Reading someone else's play was fun, but doing their own had even more wonderful rewards. During the 1990's in my early high school academic years, I had about a dozen men in a history class, all eager, committed students. They were all on time or early every day, and none of them ever abused breaks. They got their work done on time, and class discussions were lively and interesting. Several were outstanding students, doing extra work out of class and were involved in activities around the compound, playing on sports teams and getting involved in religious groups. I thought that this history class needed more challenges, but I was feeling overwhelmed with preparation for classes I hadn't taught before and an eight-hour teaching day. This group was capable of organizing a project that would take some of the responsibility off me. On a whim one day, I said, "How would you like to write a play about some period of history and present it to other classes?" Within minutes they were buzzing in small groups. By the end of the two-hour class, a leader had emerged and they already had an idea of what to do. Because my history classes were scheduled from 7:30 to 9:30 a.m., we put the play on early in the morning. Though no food was available, I called it *Breakfast Theater*.

We were studying 20th Century history, so they focused on World War I and the Great Depression. One man played the lead as a grandfather looking back and reflecting on his life. I hadn't yet figured out how important it was for students to work together, but I learned quickly from that group that *they* had to own the project, crafting a plot and figuring it all out. By the time they performed, they had included music from the 1930s and '40s, projected large images in a darkened room and included some humor. I found an old plaid shirt, suspenders and a hat for Grampa, and somehow, he found a pipe. The final product was a huge success.

The next effort in another class focused on the problem of writing the Constitution with slavery still included. For this effort, flexibility became the operative word. The white man appointed to be the slave owner was someone known to be a totally nice guy around the compound. Students in the class objected saying, "He's just too nice for this part!" So, word got out and a black man who had some theater experience appeared and said he could be "mean enough." Oh well. The point my students wanted to make about slave owners was made.

More and more black men were being incarcerated and enrolling in our program, so I began to see the plays as not only a way for my students to learn to work together, but also to learn about the cultural heritage of their own group or about another group, both valuable. The year that Stephen Spielberg released *Amistad*, another history class wrote and produced *No Ticket for this Train*, a play chronicling *hundreds* of years of African-American history. Why do just *one* story? A few men created a huge steam engine out of cardboard for the backdrop, arguing about who would get to paint it black.

"*Nobody* touches *my* train!" announced Mr. Tait, who was incidentally about 6-foot-4 and over 300 pounds.

Opening day came. When the lights dimmed, Mr. Simms and two back-up singers took their places to sing Curtis Mayfield's *People Get Ready:*

People get ready
There's a train a comin'
You don't need no baggage
You just get on board
All you need is faith
To hear the diesels hummin'
You don't need no ticket
You just thank the Lord!

The characters got on and off the train as the story unfolded. The most enthusiastic group was the one that researched the Harlem Renaissance. Students reported that they had known nothing about it before they did the research. Other groups looked at Reconstruction and Jim Crow laws.

Mr. Simms, with his resounding baritone, played the conductor. We thought he needed a special costume, so I borrowed a navy sports jacket, white shirt and tie from one of my sons and bought a conductor's hat. I got in trouble about the costume—not a good idea to put inmates in any other clothing than prison khaki, especially with so many guests coming in and out. Nothing happened to Mr. Simms, but I heard about it from the federal staff and was told to never do it again.

Typically, we would perform for other students during school hours, and then I would invite as many outside guests as I could to an evening performance. The students were nervous about that, but adrenalin is always useful. The only painful part was the time to mingle with guests and enjoy their hard-earned appreciation was cut short by the need to get them back to their units for the evening count.

One of the most difficult and complicated projects was *Things Fall Apart*, an adaptation from Chinua Achebe's world-famous novel. Mr. Abah, a man from Nigeria who had toured several continents with his dance troupe, wrote and directed it. He decided to add some dancing at the end. *Things Fall Apart* is an astonishing story, which traces the life of a tribal leader and then the confrontation between tribal customs and Christianity at the time of British colonialism in Nigeria. The title reflected how things would go for our project every day. We didn't have a big enough class to fill all the roles, so we recruited people who were not students to dance and be part of the cast. At the time, we had lots of men from places like Togo and Liberia in Africa, who were delighted to drum and learn some of Mr. Abah's dances. A white man with a long white beard tried out for the part of the Christian missionary and got it. Perfect.

Rehearsals were, in a word, rugged. At least half the time people had work conflicts and didn't show up. The script kept changing. Almost all of the participants preferred drumming to the tedious task of learning lines.

Mr. Abah fussed and fussed, saying, "I have *never* had these kinds of problems!"

Since most of them were not my students, I had little power to make them be responsible, except to dismiss them from the project. We had fewer people than we needed, so that wasn't an option. Mr. Abah insisted that I have a part, so I was the storyteller who introduced the play. Someone had to set a good example, so I tried to do my part as best I could.

A group of inmate carpenters I'd never seen before came in and quickly assembled a small wooden "hut." I was learning never to ask questions about the origin of such things, but when a large covered screen magically appeared, I asked why. The cast was a bit dismissive, mumbling something about needing a place to change costumes. I was getting suspiciously nervous as both the warden and the superintendent of schools were coming. I didn't get why they needed to change and nobody wanted to talk about the costumes until one man took off his shirt a few days before the play was to open.

"Oh no you don't," I said. "We are not going to have a lot of skin showing here!"

They assured me all was well, and the dressing area stayed in place. I began to feel like things were spinning out of my control.

There are a few people behind bars who tend to be just a *bit* slippery.

Mr. Abah was already upset that he did not have the final say on things and felt that his reputation was at stake. I tried (quite nicely, I thought) to explain that I would not put the program in any jeopardy, and that he needed to understand who was coming from the outside.

"Hurrrumph!" was his response.

Play Day came. Everyone in the cast showed up, much to my relief—we were never sure they would, and the dancers were in the dressing room with about half an hour to spare. Then, there was some kind of kerfuffle about how the chairs would be arranged. I hit the wall with their infighting and got out of there. Our program director arrived and saw me casually leaning against the wall with a cup of tea. Hearing loud voices in the room and looking very worried, she asked, "What are you doing out here? The visitors are already in the lobby!"

"I can't handle that much testosterone," I answered. At that point, I just wanted the day to be over.

The guests began to arrive, take their programs from the ushers and take their seats.

I will admit to a stomach full of butterflies with a very long list of things that could go wrong. The lights dimmed. I opened the play with my storytelling, and away they went—flawlessly! There is *nothing* like an audience to make things right. Chinua Achebe's story is a heart-stopper, and Mr. Abah's abridged version spun the tale about the life of Okonkwo, the tribal leader needing to prove his manliness. They got it all right—the clash between Christian missionaries and the native Ibo community rang true as a bell. The audience was spellbound with the timing, the drama, the awful climax at the end with the hatchet coming down and the lights going out. People leapt to their feet, their sweet applause filling the air.

Then, it was time for the dancing. The drummers began to drum and out they came—

four of them—no shirts, white streaks painted on their chests, arms and legs and...grass skirts! I gasped—held my breath, amazed at what were obviously prison-issue sheets, somehow dyed green and cut in long thin strips! The dancing was wonderful—Mr. Abah had taught them well, and it was a perfect ending to the play. The crowd loved it. It was also lunchtime, thank goodness, so the men were dismissed and all the official people left too. I didn't have to answer any questions about sheets or bare bodies or green dye. I didn't ask any either.

I told people that year if they wondered where their federal tax dollars went: "Sheets."

By then I was seeing how valuable these plays were. Not only were students learning to plan and rehearse together, solving their inevitable conflicts along the way, but they were learning to rely on one another. If the student in charge of the lights didn't have his timing exactly right or the music didn't come at the right time, things *all fell apart.* I was enjoying their success as much as they were, and we were all having so much fun!

In a class called cultural connections, my students wrote and produced an Indonesian shadow puppet play called *wayang*, complete with beautiful, intricate puppets made by the art class and authentic Indonesian music, brought in and shared by my friend who played the gamelan. My students were particularly intrigued with how *wayang*, these outdoor, public performances, were sometimes used as devices to criticize and complain about the government in Indonesia. With that information, I got more vigilant, not wanting anything like grass skirts on my hands. Again, a stage magically appeared that men placed in the smaller corner of my oddly-shaped classroom. The stage was a large wooden frame, covered with more sheets and lit unobtrusively from the bottom.

Mr. Schmidt asked to be in charge of the "house," our own classroom-theater. He was from a farm community in the Dakotas and said that his mom loved having company—and he did too. The chairs were arranged in perfect rows, and then he cleaned every surface in the room within an inch of its life. He asked if we could possibly have flowers, so I brought in a huge bouquet of orange tulips. As he smiled his bright smile and graciously ushered people to their seats, the guests felt especially welcome.

We darkened the room, turned on the gamelan music and the puppets appeared to show off their beautiful shapes and march across the stage behind the sheet. It was totally enchanting. During the intermission, the director decided to have a short *sick call*. He played the physician's assistant on duty. Other cast members lined up to tell him their ailments. "No, no, no!" he said. "It's Wednesday! No sick call on Wednesday. You're all *well* on Wednesday!" Just a little jab at Health Services. Not too bad. It could have been far worse.

One play had an important function. Within our school district, our program was suddenly under siege—faced with a massive budget cut. Our students asked if they could put on a play for the school board that would show what their high school program meant to them. Mr. Marley volunteered to chair a committee to write the dialogue. He was a middle-aged black man, normally quiet and focused on his assignments. He was always cheerful and eager to do good work. Often, he did extra work outside of class, and as he started writing the play, he was so excited about it that he wrote most of it himself. He told me he'd never been to a real play, and he could not have been more excited about the project. After a lot of discussion, the class settled on a title for their play: *Light from the Cage*.

The cast decided to construct a segregation unit of side-by-side cells, the *hole* or D-Block, assuring me they could get enough card-board. (I imagined by then that there was a cardboard factory hidden somewhere on the compound). The plot centered on conver-sations among the men in each cell as they talked back and forth: They thought they would never have the opportunity to go back to high school and how much school meant to them; they told one character who hadn't yet enrolled what it was like and how hard he would have to work, but how satisfied they felt with jobs well done and good grades. They talked about how much fun they were having and how proud they and their families would be when they gradu-ated. There were a few lines about how much easier it would be to get a job with a diploma in hand when they were released. Mr. Marley had a natural flair for dramatic lines, and the story moved smoothly along.

Within days large pieces of cardboard appeared, and the cast created seven prison cells. During rehearsals, the cast quickly figured out that the windows could be cut so that each character in the play could sit on a chair, have their script in their hands—out of sight—and voilà! They wouldn't have to memorize anything! I didn't say anything. They were in charge, and, as it turned out, their inge-nious lap plan saved the whole project.

The Bureau of Prisons was doing a major shift in populations right then, transferring men to another facility almost every day. Our pleas to keep the cast there until our play was finished fell on deaf ears. So, we kept losing characters like water through a sieve as invi-tations went out to guests and the school board. Every day became a mad scramble to replace the people who were being shipped out. Mr. C scouted the Complex and came up with some men who were good sports and willing to fill in the vacancies. Being able to read their scripts on their laps made it all work in such a last-minute situation.

Then, a week before the play was to open, we were dismayed to realize that Mr. Marley was on the transfer list too. When he came to tell me, he could hardly express his frustration and disappointment. I tried to call the right people, and he pleaded for help with anyone who would listen to at least keeping him there until the play was over. When that didn't work and the day came for him to leave, he showed up to say good-bye to everyone and express his regrets at not being able to see the final product. He called me out in the hall to thank me and could barely keep the tears back. He had been so excited about his playwriting and so invested in the process as it unfolded. Missing the final production was a cruel disappointment.

On the day of the performance, we filled the room with guests. The adrenalin kicked in, and the story unfolded perfectly. No one could tell the actors were reading from their laps and their voices rang out with conviction. One student, who played the part of an officer, was especially convincing as he roughed people up and patted them down. When the last lines ended, the audience immediately leapt to its feet. One school board member rushed over to hug me and say, "I've *never* seen students who cared this much—this was just wonderful!" Soon after the performance, the threat of a budget cut had disappeared. Everyone in the program was relieved, but the students who had put the play together were *jubilant!* A loud cheer rang out when I told them while their fists pumped in the air.

A few more productions followed, smaller in scale but still fun. We had poetry readings, dramatized short stories and events in history. We did readers' theaters. We did a presentation on kinds of dance, and Mr. Wheeler, an extremely good sport, volunteered to demonstrate some ballet. He did some arabesques and then some rather dizzy pirouettes—all with a straight face. The audience roared.

Some of the students' comments about participating in plays were:

"I was able to face my fears about getting up in front of people."

"I loved working with the group. I never knew that we could come together as we did."

"It is not easy to accept others' ideas, criticism and comments, but we learned that we are all different and together we can be a unit."

"Working in a group brings out the best in all of us!"

"I didn't know I could make people laugh."

"I want to be a star player in the next play."

Mr. C and I noticed that their efforts to put the room in perfect order was a huge part of their welcome. The company from the outside gave the men the chance to present themselves in a much more positive light and counteract the awful prison stereotypes. Though nervous at first, they were always glad that guests had been invited once it was all over. I made special certificates for each student for the after-glow or day-after celebrations. Mr. C video-taped the performances, so we all loved watching it, laughing and rehashing all the fun. What I appreciated most was how they pulled every man into the project and gave each other all kinds of accolades—providing their own hospitable space.

One play stands out as a hands-down favorite for me. The performance happened just before the Christmas break, a perfect time. The few weeks between Thanksgiving and Christmas were such a struggle. The men missed their families, so it was hard for them to fight their inevitable depression and lack of energy. I had a hard time getting work out of them. But, one year, they pulled a Christmas gift out of a hat. We had lots of talent and energy in the program right then, and a group of students from two classes approached me to see if they could write a play putting Santa on trial for not doing his job adequately. I readily agreed, telling them they had to do all the work.

Many groups were sensitive to not leaving anyone on the sidelines, so the script writers gave everyone in the two groups a part. *Everyone* was in it: Scrooge, Tiny Tim, the Grinch, and both Clauses from the North Pole. Extra parts went to a bunch of elves clumped together at one side of the stage and members of the jury who sat in two neat rows off to the other side. We had Mr. Wheeler, our very own resident Santa, who was short and round with a white beard and twinkly blue eyes. He wore a very nice Santa suit that a warden's wife had made him for the annual children's Christmas party in the visiting room. He took his appointed role *very* seriously—and his sweet personality made him popular all over the compound.

The students pulled out all the stops. Somehow, the men made Santa a sleigh on a BOP cart that rolled through the halls with Santa on a chair bellowing, "Ho, Ho, Ho!" and calling to his reindeer. The halls were full of men, eager to get in the chapel to get a good seat. I looked at the crowd and thought they looked like kids at a circus, laughing and talking, an air of expectancy filling the room. The jury marched in soberly and sat in their box. Santa rolled into the room, waving and smiling to the wild applause that drowned out *Here Comes Santa Claus*. My colleague, who had offered to help, stood with me at the door of the chapel and we smiled at each other, thinking things were off to a great start. We had yet to deal with Mrs. Claus, who was waiting in our office closet for last-minute help with his costume.

Mr. Tucker had insisted on playing Mrs. Claus. He was a black man, well over 6-foot tall, and had barely said a *word* in my class. We helped him get dressed in the office closet; an apron barely reaching around his middle. At the last minute, he decided he wanted to wear a hat, so he plopped a mop on his head, fingering its white hair to blend in with his dreadlocks. Though we had monitored rehearsals, somehow neither one of us had heard him practice his lines. As we helped him with his mop, I kept thinking, Who is this guy? We ushered him down the hall, and as he approached the door, ready to make his grand entrance, we noticed a wicked gleam in his eye. My colleague gave me an *uh-oh* look. Sure enough, down the center aisle he staggered—seeming very drunk.

"He ain't never give me any bling!" he blithered.

The laughter was deafening. I gave quiet thanks that we hadn't issued invitations to the general public or any prison or school officials. Santa was found innocent, of course, rolled back down the hall in his sleigh and the season was saved by spritely Christmas spirits.

Now, I love thinking about that day. I can still see men who were bent over in their chairs they were laughing so hard. I can hear the laughter and cheers, the loud claim of, "The defendant has been found ... *innocent* of all charges!" I can hear the applause and see the cast members marching single file out for lunch while their audience stood and cheered wildly. Now I see, in that grim and lonely place, in a grim and lonely time of year, that they were determined to have as much fun as they could—cast members and audience alike. In a dry and boring place, they had juiced things up. Now I see that they were not only creating hospitable space, but creating at least a couple of hours of fun and happiness—for themselves and for each other.

It was as if they felt *a responsibility to joy*.

IF A MAN BE GRACIOUS

"If a man be gracious and courteous to strangers,
it shows he is a citizen of the world,
and that his heart is no island cut off from other islands,
but a continent that joins them."

—Sir Francis Bacon

Like any prison with its cramped living arrangements and more than a few volatile inmates, this one had its underbelly of ugliness: fights, gang activity, stabbings and betrayals. Only once, with a young, angry student, did one man threaten another in my room. He held up his fists, angry with another man for taking his book. Mr. C intervened immediately, speaking in an even voice to say, "Calm down, gentlemen. This is the kind of behavior that gets you kicked out of class—and puts Milan High School in danger." Things went back to normal immediately. As teachers, we were almost totally sheltered from all that went on outside our area. We heard vague rumors of trouble, but usually only when someone was in the hole. Even then, the men tended to be reluctant to tell us any details about why the man had been locked up.

What I saw was their graciousness. I saw them form friendships, become like family to each other, create tight-knit groups that became safe places for them to discover each other and the best in themselves. I witnessed their grief about leaving their good friends behind and feeling lost when a good friend went home. In these groups, they created kindness, understanding and consideration. By trying to include every man and encouraging each person to add into the group, they learned to know themselves, learned to free their own fearful hearts. Learning to welcome strangers, they became robust citizens of their own world—and created their own continent of caring.

For some of them, it was their first encounter with people who were different.

"For me, being in the group reminds me of being on a cross-country bus trip I once took," Mr. Piper said. "People stopped at various stations, but basically we stayed together for the whole trip. By the end we were all taking care of each other. Now when we see each other from class, we have a bond and a caring we didn't have before."

A man who grew up in the gangs of an inner city, wrote, "I have learned that no matter what race or color, everyone has struggles and has been discriminated against in some way—from blacks to Mexicans, gays or women. It's only after we learn how it feels to be wronged that we learn how to treat each other right."

In their circles, no one was left out and men felt equal to everyone else. They were not only learning to form bonds in their circles, but they were also learning how to turn suspicious people into friends.

Mr. Shafer noted:

"It's hard living with different kinds of people and get along. That's why you have black people who stay in their own neighborhoods and white people stay in theirs. Society is so messed up. But, we can come here and get along. The thing is that everybody looks at one another the same. We're all prisoners and have families we're trying to get home to. You have white people in the law library who are good with the law and they work with everybody, no matter what color they are. They are happy to help with no fee. Everybody wants to see one another get home. It's a good sight to see everyone living in harmony. The big question is when people get home, are they going to treat everybody the same way and help each other out?"

My classroom became a safe haven for me too. I watched and I marveled. I shed tears with them and about them. I wrote things down and I was moved beyond words. I laughed a lot. I was looking at and felt part of a small, caring village in which people knew and cared about each other, knew how to have fun and build community.

One winter, all inmates were issued new knit hats. Picture fifteen hundred men wearing a nice, bright neon orange. Mr. Morgan, a young tall black man, had shaved his head. He tended to be more than a little flaky about getting to class on time and losing assignments. One chilly day, he left class and then a few minutes later, came back.

"Miz Wenzel, I can't find my hat and it's *cold* out there!" he said. I helped him look, but we didn't find it.

He insisted we look a little harder the next day, but it wasn't there. He left, shaking his head. The third day, he burst into my next class, interrupting it.

"Miz Wenzel, they won't give me another one and I gotta find my hat—my head is too cold!" he insisted, putting his fingers on his bare head.

Okay. I have lines and he had crossed one. I didn't look kindly on anyone interrupting a class that was already in session. I asked to speak to him in the hall, impatient and annoyed. I closed the door behind us, put my hands on my hips, looked way up at him.

"Mr. Morgan, I've had it with you. Just how is this *my* problem? Do I look like your *mother?*" I asked, my voice rising.

Towering over me, he leaned back, hand to chin, thoughtful for a moment. "Ya know? Ya *do*! She real light-skinned!"

I laughed hard. He had me. They had me.

We're all family.

IV. HOLY GROUND

---

66 *"It's not so much the journey that's important; as is the way that we treat those we encounter and those around us, along the way."*

—Jeremy Aldana

66 *"Wholeness does not mean perfection; it means embracing brokenness as an integral part of life."*

—Parker J. Palmer

I DIDN'T GO to prison to find the presence of God. I went because I badly needed a job and because I was intrigued with the idea of teaching in a place—and with people—I knew nothing about. At the time, I was an active member of a large, mainline Protestant church—happy there, but knowing the container for the sacred was certainly bigger than that beautiful old building. In the years before and as I took this job, I'd had some dark and unsettling times: a long

227

and painful divorce, a big move to another town, loss and pain for my children and some financial challenges. But, I had the loving-kindness of new friends and old, the generosity and support of my extended family, my children finding new courage and doing well.

Through it all and as I settled into a new town and this job, I felt that love had hovered around me and held me up. I also learned a lot about my own reserves and coping skills. My life was deeper than it had been. I was feeling the presence of forces larger than I was. It was a continuous discovery. In very concrete ways: God was love.

I knew that people who were locked up and isolated had to be hurting. So much was taken away from their lives: the love and solace of families, the freedom to move around, the ordinary comforts of daily living. I did not expect to find, in this harsh and barren place, my students' laughter and joy, their kindness and generosity. I did not expect my students to be so grateful about another chance to graduate. So many men seemed to have a fist full of resolve in their search for direction and purpose. They wanted what most people want: good jobs and to support their families in whatever other ways they could; they wanted to be good citizens by mentoring young people; they wanted to be of use. I had a poster in our classroom that read: *Use all of your gifts. The earth and its people need them.* I could see that my students were working on being their best, most authentic selves. They were discovering their gifts. They were giving themselves another chance in a world that had failed so many of them. Being their authentically best selves seemed to be about God too.

I knew many men who conducted themselves like monks, staying calm, quiet and contemplative. Except for the fact that prisons' main functions are punishment and security, prisons have a remarkable similarity to the monasteries and convents I've visited. Monks live in simple, cell-like rooms too, and prisons, except for the fact that no one can leave them, are cloisters. Both monasteries and prisons are austere places where people can retreat and reflect, though that's far harder within prisons with noise and too many people in a small space. Both groups are housed in places with restrictions like predetermined daily schedules. Monasteries have daily rituals, and I found that my students loved (and often insisted on) rituals like our Round Tables every week. Monks dress in simple clothing. I saw monks in prison-issue khaki, and there were many days when they transformed this clanging, disagreeable, dissonant place into a kind of church.

In the ways they responded to literature, to poetry, to the lessons of history, and in their efforts to write and to journal, I could see them trying hard to be the people they were born to be. I saw what Quakers call "that of God" in them. I did not expect to experience the presence of God in this most unlikely place. God is sometimes revealed in brokenness as the light of love comes out of the darkness, so present in prison. I saw, felt and understood God as a verb, not as a noun, in the loving, life-giving connections among us. God is love, and the men I knew further defined love as compassion and caring, generosity and gratitude, joy and pain. We were all on a quest for wholeness.

MANY RELIGIONS,
MUCH UNDERSTANDING

The years were stretching on and we turned the corner into the 21st Century, and it seemed like I had been going to prison forever. At this point, I still faced many challenges, but I was also moving in a comfortable rhythm with my students. I was experiencing the same challenging complications as a white woman, a person raised in privilege, *and* I was becoming much older than they were—enough to make a difference in what we paid attention to in popular culture. I have never been tuned into popular culture, have never known much about things like television characters, pop music or sports. As I got older, those gaps became wider. At the same time, I was learning to be more real, to relate what was happening in my life as a way to expose my students to wider perspectives. For instance, I could offer my ideas about raising children, managing money, aligning time with values and living simply. I started this job with students who were my age, then with younger students when our security level changed, I could have been most people's mother. In my last five years, I could have been their grandmother. That was okay. Grandmothers and their experience have their important place too.

We had moved into a new room right next to the chapel, so we were closer to the religious services that went on every week. Adding to the monastic atmosphere, we were surrounded by religious rituals all the time—in fact, we worked in a swirl of organized religion. Sharing with chapel services meant sharing rooms, programs, time and men. I did not always have a tip-top attitude about the patience, flexibility and cooperation required. I would have a lesson or a test all organized, and the call-out sheet would have too many men scheduled to be in other places. If there was an Islamic holiday, a medicine man coming to visit, or a marriage seminar the men had signed up for, I had to move to

Plan B—or C. Sometimes religious guests would arrive without any notice. Most of the services were held on Fridays, a day when energy was at a low ebb anyway. Lesson plans always needed stretch and flexibility, and I couldn't count on my students being aware of something coming up. Few of my students handled calendars well.

When I didn't let myself get too locked into firm plans, I would recognize the rich diversity of our learning environment. We would see a rabbi in the chaplaincy area conducting a Seder meal, watch federal staff carry the tarps to the yard for a native sweat lodge ceremony, and see Muslim prayer mats lined up on the floor in the chapel. We would learn about the month of Ramadan from crescent moon to crescent moon, and be able to tune into what the fasting meant to Muslim students. The moveable walls, which were not good sound barriers, meant we might hear music from a gospel choir or preaching voices next door. We had to learn to keep our noise down too. Interfaith and ecumenical understanding meant: *understand all the time.*

The benefits of this rich religious diversity were many. I knew Protestant chaplains, Catholic priests and Muslim imams over the years, and we invited them in. If a Native American visitor was in the Complex, a student would ask if the visitor could come and talk about what he was doing there. The chaplains had offices and shared a lovely room with large windows and several televisions where men could watch religious and cultural videos. We used the videos too, especially from a large collection of Native American documentaries, some of which I could not have obtained anywhere else. One semester, an English class did a collaborative research project on world religions and students could simply walk across the hall to a chaplain's office for an interview or ask men they knew at work or in their unit for information.

The main bulletin board in the area had a long list of the various religious services available. Some groups were small. Rastafarians would read Psalms in a small group on Sunday mornings, for instance. In spite of logistics, the men usually had resources, support, clergy, chaplains and space in which to meet in small groups, permission to wear headwear and access to sacred objects.

There were many Christian programs in our prison. A large contingent of religious volunteers came in to have individual visits, Bible studies, help with church services and special holidays. For many years we had a full-time Catholic priest on staff and always a full-time Protestant chaplain and a Muslim imam.

———

We all have specific memories about where we were and what we were doing on the morning of September 11th in 2001. I often remember that day. What happened subsequently affected everyone in our program.

My civics class was struggling to understand the difference between political and economic systems, so on Sept. 11, 2001, our wonderful inmate tutor Mr. Hurley suggested we play *Star Power*, a game that simulates capitalism. Needing more people, we invited another class to join us. We set it all up in three groups that were given tokens to trade with each other. After each round, our tutors counted the profits of each group and posted them on the board. The idea was to manipulate them so that one group would do far better, one group was in the middle and the third group would be left either in the hole or with barely any gains at the end of the game. Having them stay in their original circles when the trading was over, we discussed how it had gone and how they were feeling.

"How come you didn't reach out and help us?" asked an insightful student in the poorest group.

"All I could think of was to keep making more money!" answered his friend in the richest circle.

When the students returned from a break, one of my students had a small radio he was struggling to hear through his earphones. Radios were not allowed in the Complex, but this was an older man who wouldn't dream of breaking the rules or causing trouble. The student, sitting in his wheelchair, had pushed himself into a quiet corner and motioned me over. With a steady and quiet voice, he said, "Mrs. Wenzel, the United States has just been attacked. Huge buildings are falling down in New York. I think you need to stop the game and talk about this." In that ironic setting with many people who had so little, we learned about this attack on capitalism.

We relied on news from the radio and luckily, we had a little time before lunch. I remember feeling stunned, like so many of us did. A young white man, who had been in the program a while, asked, "What if they come and attack us?"

"Yeah, right, like anyone knows we're here—or cares," a young black man said.

Mr. Hurley took over the discussion, much to my relief. I could see how vulnerable and helpless the men felt. They talked and decided that even if the attack had not been motivated by Islam, they would be the first people blamed. Almost immediately, one man suggested and others agreed that "we put our arms around the shoulders of our Muslim brothers in the chow hall." Mr. C and Mr. Hurley reported seeing people trying hard to put Muslim men at ease by eating with them and making a point to talk to them for the next few days. Those open, loving gestures have stayed with me, and I keep what happened within our institution on 9/11 close to my heart as an example of interfaith understanding at its best.

I knew so little about anyone who wasn't white and Christian when I took that teaching job. I had never talked to anyone who was Muslim nor did I know anything about Islam. Prison taught me to examine my Christian privilege. As I recall our discussion of President Barack Obama's second inauguration, my students noticed the distinctly Christian flavor of the ceremony. It seems we as Americans try to be inclusive and celebrate cultural diversity—certainly that was evident in the participation of several Hispanics who read poetry and gave the benediction, but our civil religion is still distinctly Christian. We don't think of a Muslim or a Hindu God when we say, "In God We Trust." President Obama would have fueled an already long list of rumors about him being a Muslim if he had even vaguely strayed from the Christian context. In America's efforts to celebrate religious diversity, we have a very long way to go. In our program, we had chances to learn about and celebrate all kinds of religions and religious practices.

Prison has been a birthplace of many Black Muslims in this country, patterned largely after Elijah Mohammed and Malcolm X. I don't remember a semester without having several Muslim students in my classes, nor do I remember any Muslim men who did not take their religion, its practices and services, very seriously. The Nation of Islam was active every week throughout my time there. Jum'ah services were held every Friday and the Moorish Science group also met on a regular weekly basis. I had Muslim men from Syria, Palestine, Iraq, Iran, Turkey and Indonesia, among others. Our First Amendment unit in civics class provided a context for men to explain their religious services and experiences, and discussions were held with a remarkable degree of interest and respect for differences—especially about Islam.

September 11th created sweeping changes for all of us in the Education/Religious Services Complex. For a couple of years after 2001, no group, not even Christian ones, could hold a religious service without having a federal staff person present. Then cameras and microphones were installed in all the rooms, adding a whole new dimension of security. We learned to adapt, but it sometimes felt like Big Brother was in the room. In spite of that and hectic, disruptive Friday afternoons, I value how many opportunities I had, personally and as a teacher, to get to know so many people from such disparate backgrounds—and see them honor and respect each other. The activities in the Complex and the students themselves would be the envy of many social studies teachers.

ALL AROUND THE EARTH

It took me a while to understand just how intimately my history students and I were connected to the stories and the pain that native people have endured for so long. Because many of the men I knew were Oglala Lakota, the story of the massacre at Wounded Knee held particular pain and poignancy. In December of 1890, Chief Bigfoot and his band were killed on the Pine Ridge Indian Reservation by U.S. Cavalry troops. Hundreds of people died, the majority of them women and children, and were buried in a mass grave. In my early years, before I was able to get more inclusive and sensitive materials, the native men found only one reference in our history textbooks to Wounded Knee, labeling it a "battle" and not a massacre. Most textbooks had no mention of it. Wounded Knee's despairing story came up with a reserved sense of continuing heartbreak from the Oglala Lakota men from Pine Ridge. Over and over I would feel saddened and humbled as I listened. It is difficult to separate native spirituality from native culture. My native students would tell us they are the same, and as we learned about Wounded Knee and how it is commemorated now, their spirituality became clearer.

Mr. Terrence, an inmate guest in our program, had been so helpful with his explanations of native culture, and he was always pleased to be invited to speak. He had an ancestor who had been a baby in 1890 and had survived the massacre at Wounded Knee, kept warm from the biting wind by her mother's body until the remaining soldiers rescued her. When these heartrending stories came up, there was a respectful quiet among the other men in the room, a *solidarity of pain*.

I did not begin to understand my students' depth of suffering until I went to Pine Ridge with a program my friends had created and stood at the top of Wounded Knee's lonely hill myself, trying to take in the enormity of the now old, long, fenced-in massed grave.

Feeling its sorrow and remembering my students' connection, it felt right to stay. An elderly Lakota woman lived in a small house at the base of the hill, and she asked the leader of our program if volunteers could clean up and weed the graves outside of the fence. I volunteered and felt like I was doing a small task to honor the dead and the immensity of this tragedy.

Discussions of events like Wounded Knee were so hard, particularly for the men who had lived with the story in their own tribes. Every major world religion values compassion. My students demonstrated their compassion by creating a hush in the room, listening carefully and asking questions. We learned this: if these awful stories are not told, taught and discussed in compassionate dialogue, two kinds of stories travel through time together. The native story is passed along through the generations as a way to honor the dead; the story from the soldiers' side rides silently through the years in the shadows—neither thoroughly discussed nor compassionately understood. Consequently, potent fear and shame accompany the white, government side of the story without any reconciliation between native people and most of the rest of us.

In the Native American section of the prison's chapel library, a film called *Wiping the Tears of Seven Generations*, captured my students' attention. It is the story of the Bigfoot Memorial Ride that takes place every year in December when native people ride hundreds of miles on horseback in bitter winter weather to honor the dead and heal the wounds of Wounded Knee. For each day of the week, they honor a different group of people: the elderly, women, children, those in prison and those caught in the traps of material possessions. I gave my students an assignment to write what they would honor and why. I never had a student who did not take it seriously nor fail to do it thoughtfully. I loved watching how this tradition became meaningful for men who were not native.

Mr. Donnelly was a white man in his twenties, very bright but careful about not sounding arrogant. Like many men I knew, he practiced meditation and read widely about many spiritual traditions outside of class. Mr. Donnelly's paper about what he would honor for every day of the week reflected his meditative habits. He would honor love and the gift of life; courage and strength; the earth and its bounty; truth despite consequence and being honest with the world; the beauty of sound and speech; insight and the ability to see beyond what our eyes can see and on the last day, he would honor moving beyond the physical and into a higher plane of existence. I read his paper over and over.

———

Mr. Fulton, another inmate guest, stopped in one day to talk to us. He was in his late thirties, and had a white father and a mother who had grown up Lakota on Pine Ridge. One day he said, "When people have a hole in our spirit, we try to fill it. White people fill it by shopping and things, and Indian people fill it with alcohol and drugs." Like Mr. Terrence, Mr. Fulton was wise and informative. Both men were soft-spoken and thoughtful. They not only knew about native spirituality, but practiced it as closely as they could. They attended sweats regularly and worked with chaplains to bring leaders from the outside in for ceremonies and celebrations.

Every year the Native American inmates were also allowed to have a dinner and invite other inmates and staff. The chow hall is not a place for an optimum dining experience—it would not receive a high mark for ambience. But when we walked in, the Native American inmates and guests greeted us with the warmest welcome possible.

We needed to be *very* hungry. A typical menu listed buffalo steaks, rice and beans, mushrooms and salsa, fried bread with cinnamon sugar and blueberry dessert. The men serving the food tried to fill our plates with as much as possible and then came around to offer seconds. I loved the chance to sit down and eat with them.

When the meal was over, we gathered in a circle. One year, a visiting Shoshone chief unpacked the peace pipe and bowl ceremoniously, and as it traveled around the circle, people scooped the smoke into their faces. Called *smudging*, it took a while to complete. I always struggled to slow myself down on a Friday night in order to feel part of it.

Within the circle one year, a young man spoke softly and slowly saying, "My prayers are for me not to judge a man except by what is in here," tapping his chest.

Anyone could speak, and when everyone who wanted to offer something was heard, the songs sung, and the drum finished, the giveaway would begin. A table in the center would be filled with handmade native crafts, and the teachers and staff were invited to simply take anything we wanted. They were *created* to give away, but we protested, as our consumerism got in the way. Gradually and still a little uncomfortable with the process, we chose pieces of jewelry, beaded items and things made of leather. I felt a sense of wholeness as the native men shared such sacred customs with us.

I often think about what my classes would have been like without our native students. In their reserved, respectful ways, they set an important tone and modeled ways to behave. Generally, they listened before they spoke and had a respect for other students and for differences in cultures and attitudes. They were eager to learn about their own cultural ways from other natives.

"Prison has been a place to learn about my native culture. I conduct myself in a good way. We welcome everyone. We respect everyone," Mr. Alexander said.

The other men in my class were also respectful and asked many questions. Some of them accepted the open invitations to attend a sweat. Many Hispanic men with their indigenous roots were actively involved in native activities of all kinds.

"I don't understand why they aren't angry all the time after what happened to them," a white man noted.

I wondered too and saw a lot of anger and depression over the years. But being able to be native, band together, play their drums, sing, go to sweat, welcome representatives from the outside, and host an annual dinner all helped to reduce their anger. I saw them recover a sense of their dignity and self-worth with people who understood and wouldn't judge them.

One day, Mr. Fulton was sitting comfortably with all of us in a circle. "Indians don't have a word for religion. You can't chop up life. The Indian way is a way of life. We honor the earth, because she is our Mother and the source of everything. The only way we get more than we need is to give it away. The depth of your soul is the depth of your suffering. It's not what you have that makes you happy, it's what's in your heart."

Being white and Christian in this country can blind one to difference, minority struggles and the legitimacy of being "other," culturally, politically, economically and spiritually. We live so separately in this country. A dominant group tends to feel "normal," therefore regarding other realities as outside of what is right, acceptable and truly American. I can fall into that trap. I think some of it comes from the fear of losing power and what we regard as precious and vital. Some of it comes from simply not knowing people who are not like us. I hear lofty words and angry political posturing regarding First Amendment rights for Christians, but very little about protections for other religions and the freedom to practice them.

The United States has a long history of trying to make native people more *white* with efforts like trying to turn native people into farmers and putting native children into boarding schools to "take the Indian out of them." My native students needed to be who they were in all of their goodness and wholeness. We could all learn about respect, generosity, humility and gentleness from native people. I was humbled over and over, moved beyond measure, and learned more than I taught. An elderly man from a reservation on the plains explained his prayers to me one day, "I pray at night for the Great Spirit to take my prayers all around the earth while I sleep. When I wake up, I know that in some way, my prayers will be answered."

A REAL INNER LIFE

Evelyn Underhill, writer and pacifist, noted, "After all it is those who have a real inner life who are best able to deal with the irritating details of outer life." Rainer Maria Rilke wrote, "The only journey is the one within." Many men complained about the difficulties of overcrowding in prison, but learning to value silence and learning to be contemplative helped.

Mr. Fullerton, a middle-aged white man, called himself a "hard-rock biker dude." He was about 40, with a long, thin face, a lot of tattoos and a long ponytail. He paid attention to other students when they spoke up in class, and often followed up with questions for them. He was good-natured with a wide smile and an easygoing way about him, and it wasn't surprising that other men paid attention to him too—and smiled back. He was a joy in any class, eager for new books and new ideas.

"Silence is essential to the exploration of one's self. I don't think everyone realizes it, but silence is an absolute necessity to maintain our sanity," he said.

Mr. C said it well too. *"I crave silence, I revere and cherish it, and the good things that I've discovered inside this 'zoo' where I live, is that I am able to find silence even when there is an abundance of noise and distraction. I find silence in my own realm of existence, no matter where I am. This silence is golden and I need as much of it as I can possibly find.*

"Through silence, I've learned to see what isn't obvious, notice what tends to stay hidden and listen to what is not said. It connects me to my inner source of energy. It helps me to reflect upon the things I learn every day. It moves me closer to my center and I find the balance that I need every day. Silence uplifts my soul and makes me more whole. Silence is my monastery, my temple."

Mr. Lando wrote: *"Silence is like a medication to me and a way to find peace in myself. I need to reflect at the end of the day on what I'd done wrong and what I'd done right. Sometimes when I make mistakes, I get mad at myself later and think that I wouldn't have done them if I had sat in silence and thought it through."*

Both the meditative silence and writing in a journal helped them hear an inner voice.

Learning to write anything was difficult for many of my students. I saw this as a consequence of dropping out of school. I knew they had opinions and values, but I had the sense that many of them had not tried nor had they any inclination or encouragement to put words on paper. The power of writing, especially in a place like this, was profound.

"Paper listens," I said.

The deeply personal dimensions of writing can soothe, reduce anger and anxiety and help to figure things out. It makes time disappear. It warms my heart to hear about writing programs in prisons across the country.

After a lot of trial and error, I figured out that learning to journal was a helpful way for the men to figure out who they were, what they stood for and was a way to develop an inner voice. Students arrived in class over a 15-minute period, especially in the early mornings, so I played some soft music, put a quote on the board almost every day, and the instructions were to come in quietly and write about what the quote meant to them. They told me they liked the quiet to start the day. I watched and listened carefully. Some of the younger men balked at first, claiming they had no idea what to write. Men wrote as the class gathered, and then they could share what they wrote. It was important not to force anyone and to respect their privacy. There were always men eager to talk about what they'd written, so gradually other men learned how to do it. It was satisfying to watch them become more and more comfortable with writing. One of their favorite topics was about distinguishing wants and needs, and one of the best quotes about this came from the English writer, poet and philosopher G.K. Chesterton who said, "There are two ways to get enough. One is to accumulate more and more. The other is to desire less."

An older black man wrote: *"I have talked and thought about the difference between my wants and my needs in prison. I now realize that I don't need all the things I thought I did out in the world. I now want the simpler things like having picnics, having coffee with my wife in the morning and doing fun things with my kids. Prison has made me fine tune my life and not want any more frivolous living."*

Other responses sounded like this:

"When I was out there, I thought a great car, some good clothes, some chains around my neck, a pretty woman and some great tennis shoes were what was important, but now my babies are growing up without me and I cannot help my mom."

Another black man in his forties wrote: *"My own life has gone down a dark road, not knowing which way to go. It caused me to take to the streets for acceptance and I never want to go back there again. I've learned that the only thing that matters is my family."*

When they filled out evaluations at the end of the semester, many of them wrote that they liked to journal and would continue to do it.

In civics classes, I assigned Victor Frankl's *Man's Search for Meaning*, the story of his experience in a Nazi concentration camp. I had learned how important it was to stay out of the way by inviting a former student to facilitate the discussion. I told them I knew nothing about being incarcerated. We bought more copies of Frankl's books almost every year as they would simply disappear. Mr. Hanover was known as a great athlete and bodybuilder. He didn't say much in class until the day we discussed Frankl's book.

"I've never read a book like this, and I just can't get over the stuff this guy says about your attitude. It makes so much sense to me," he said. "Can I *please* keep it?"

Locking hundreds of people up in a small space creates problems of anxiety, frustration, loneliness, depression, mistrust, aggression and violence. Inmates learn to adjust by all kinds of methods, discovering coping skills they did not know they had. They learn that in order to survive, they must know and trust each other. They read, go to school, play sports and have fun. When a teacher is available, they practice yoga. They tap into their old or new religious rituals and traditions.

Mr. Donnelly, who had learned to meditate, wrote:

"For many years, especially when I was involved in criminal behavior, I really mistrusted other people. As a result, I treated other people poorly and aggressively. I didn't ever approach anyone with a kind and open heart. Therefore, I never received kindness in return. I was cynical, always questioning the motives of others. I felt that people would take advantage of kindness and generosity and see it as a weakness. Once I learned to meditate and open my heart to others, I began to see the error of my ways. If you are pure of heart and trust the actions of God, then you can trust others. You can know that human nature is to be kind and give love freely."

I was hearing echoes of the same kind of cynicism that Mr. Donnelly had grown away from in people outside the fence: mistrust about who was behind bars, a few people willing to say, "They are all sociopaths." I heard a willingness to treat incarcerated people poorly and agreeing with the use of harsh punishments, like the widespread use of solitary confinement. I heard politicians' aggressive rhetoric.

But, the longer I was there, the more I believed Mr. Donnelly's thinking: Our basic human nature is to be kind and give love freely. Not that I didn't run into manipulation and bad behavior. I did. All the time. But, I also saw it in the context of prison life, where manipulation was often a survival skill and bad behavior in crowded, spare, uncomfortable conditions was inevitable. I also saw, as they wrote in their journals, meditated, worked and learned together, that they helped to correct bad behavior in other men—and in themselves. I saw them move beyond tolerance of differences among themselves to understanding, appreciation and celebrating differences. In an environment designed to be humiliating, they learned to swallow their fears and their pride enough to be corrected, to be able to learn and grow. They were finding their inner voices— and discovering the depth of their own goodness.

MICHAEL JORDAN GOING
FOR THE BASELINE!

The arts—music, dance, drama, poetry—stretch our imaginations and perceptions, allowing us to become self-aware and jar us into alternative ways of thinking and feeling. Works of art like paintings, stories, novels and photographs could all help a student see himself in a new way, or they could reveal the complexity of an experience he'd never had. By expressing different perspectives in vivid ways, creative works moved them emotionally, acting as a portal to finding common ground and common humanity with others. In a place like prison, art helped all of us feel less alone and opened us up.

Mr. C wrote:

"There is inner beauty in all of us. The artistry of Langston Hughes or Claude McKay has the ability to touch us. Pieces of literature help us find the inspiration and encourage us to form bonds with others. We identify with characters in the stories who can make us more compassionate. Classes about art and literature can be seen as a form of cleansing and redemption. Our human yearning for symmetry, order, and beauty becomes almost a craving in a place that is so harsh, cold and dry."

Our program has always had an art class. For men who were back in school after many years, scared and needing to work on most skills, being in the art class was a way to ease back in, to enjoy the company of other students and to be creative. Being creative takes courage too, however. To make anything new requires stepping out of one's comfort zone, being willing to gather up one's own emotional energy, bear a more intense kind of vitality and sometimes hold it up for scrutiny. Our students had more creative talent than we could keep up with. They were visual artists, drawing, painting and crafting works of beauty, grace and meaning. Men sang and played instruments, sometimes without any formal training. And, they were wordsmiths, loving poetry most of all.

Poems worked whenever, however and wherever I used them. In a place where it was difficult to display feelings, poetry hit them where they lived. I tried to keep four or five poems in a folder, and then as they waited for the day to end with coats and hats on, ready to spring, I would say, "Can you listen carefully to this one?" A hush would fall as I read. Almost always men would ask for a copy of the poem. A few favorites came up in every group. Paul Laurence Dunbar's "We Wear the Mask" would have won an all-time favorite poem contest. These men knew all about wearing a mask and hiding what and how they felt about being black or native or Spanish-speaking Americans. The poem drew a straight line to their hearts.

In the 1990s, Michigan had a fairly active and visible militia movement, organized to resist what they perceived as aggression against citizens from the federal government. Our program was shut down for an entire week when one of the suspects of the Oklahoma City bombing was housed temporarily in our detention unit. I had a few militia sympathizers, always white men from rural areas. They tried to make their views widely known in class discussions, Mr. Lennox among them. Having him in English classes balanced the discomfort in history or civics when he wanted to rant about the abuses and danger of the government for as long as possible. When he enrolled, he had few writing skills after dropping out before high school. But, once he got going in school, he would be the first one in the room and could not get enough work. In spite of a burning hatred of all-things-government, I found him polite and friendly. In a smaller English class, his writing assignment was to describe the person he admired most. "Paint the picture so that we get to really know them," I instructed.

Most men chose people in their own families, most often mothers and grandmothers, spinning out tender words about growing up and feeling loved or about losing these people, sometimes both. I made a big deal of their willingness to keep rewriting, asking at the end of the project if anyone was interested in reading the polished products aloud to the rest of us. Proud of their results, they eagerly put their chairs in a circle, even asking people in the office to join us. Mr. Lennox went last. He hadn't found any friends in the group, and his flirtation with militia ideas was no secret. The rest of the students looked a little nervous and leaned forward to hear. But to their shock, the person he had decided he admired most was ... Emily Dickinson!

He was besotted with "Miss Emily," as he called her. Earlier in the semester, I had gathered poetry anthologies from the library, and he focused on Emily Dickinson right away. As he read through them, he would call me over to say, "Just look at this!" He learned about her reclusive life, and somehow that resonated with him. He was fascinated by her poetry and wrote about what Miss Emily had to say about death. He had worked hard on his paper, and the room was still and quiet as he read it—and for a moment after he finished.

"Hey! That was real good man!" someone said, and then there was applause. He grinned. He copied many of her poems to keep in his cube. I never would have conjured up this particular pair of people, but Mr. Lennox fell in love with Miss Emily, and we all got to watch.

I had to be careful with the technical aspects of poetry, such as rhyming patterns or deciphering fourteen lines in a sonnet, because their eyes glassed over and those lessons needed to wait until an advanced class. I did want them to think.

I asked if anyone knew what figurative language was, and one man's hand shot up.

"It's those puzzles in poems you gotta figure out!" he said.

They wrestled within the layers of a poem, learning the magic of metaphor and letting their senses get tickled.

I asked a fairly recalcitrant new group one morning just before lunch (I admit to killing time), "Can anyone give me a good definition of poetry?" I got a few standard answers: "Lines that rhyme" and "All that stuff that's hard to understand." The room went dead. I stole glances at the clock, longing for lunch. Scoop sat in the back of the room. We barely knew him as he had been out on writ (a court date about his case) and seemed shy and uncomfortable about joining the group late. We all startled when a sudden verbal explosion came from the back of the room. Scoop had jumped up.

"*Where you dudes been, anyway? You gotta feel poetry. Poetry's like this: It's taking your shorty to the park on a nice day; it's hangin' with your woman; it's Michael Jordan going for the baseline!*" as he dribbled an imaginary ball around the room and then shot for the clock when lunch was called. Saved by the bell and the ball!

Beautifully, they strung words together and made their own poems—to their children, parents and grandparents. They poured their hearts out about being locked up and what they longed for. They created images about the people and things they missed. On and off, we had Mr. Carson, an inmate and published poet, who loved to come in and do workshops for us. He wrote in a booklet of collected student poems, "There was much more to the experience than the simple writing of poems. There was the joining of men at the common task of empathy, a willingness to share themselves with a courage and honesty seldom found in a correctional setting." A few of their words are here:

"*When life unveils its holy face...*"

"*My fingers hold it as if it were the
     twist of a bristlecone.*"

"*Mango ripe, mango sweet
     I want a penny to buy...*"

"*Take good care of memories...*"

"*Beauty then approached me*

and said, 'Fear not, because I
have opened the eyes of everyone
who has met me.'"

"Have you ever captured an animal?
Held it captive and all alone?"

"Do not forget me when I'm gone..."

Mr. Benjamin, a middle-aged black man, hung in there as he worked through the courses to get the required credits. He had dropped out in ninth grade, was with us for years, but he didn't ever exude much confidence about himself as a student. One day he wrote a poem and was so pleased with himself that he passed it around for his classmates to read; they finally insisted that he stand at the podium and read it to the whole group. He got up, stood tall and grinned, reading it not once but twice.

"Man, I just never thought I could be a *poet!*" he said, shaking his head but still smiling as he left the room.

I've heard poets say that the best stuff comes from where the pain is. The poet Michael S. Harper says you can draw on suffering as if it were a well. Writing poems is a way through grief, as Jane Kenyon said, "The pleasure of the poem works against the sadness." No wonder prison is such a good place for poetry, a powerful tool for self-discovery and a road map into their inner grace.

APPLES AND A BLACK-EYED PEA

The institution had explicit and implicit rules about the lines between inmates and all other staff, which kept all of us ever-watchful. Beyond the Native American giveaway during the annual dinner, staff was not supposed to accept gifts from inmates and, of course, not give them either. Greeting cards were in their own category, and I got get well cards and sometimes Mother's Day cards. The problem was that my students were very generous people, needing positive ways to express themselves. Many bright, shiny red apples appeared on my desk after lunch over the years, pilfered, of course, from the chow hall. One day, a big juicy pear sat tilted quite nicely on my desk after lunch. It made me laugh.

Our Native American students were vocal about their value of giving. Mr. Alexander wrote:

"For life to be a full, rich experience, I must give as well as take, serve as well as lead. Without the student, there is no teacher. Without the listener, there is no message. In my native culture, when we take from nature, we give something in return. Life is a continuous exchange of give and take to complete the moving circle. We measure wealth by what we give away rather than by what we possess. When you hear 'Indian giver,' this is what it means."

Mr. Hamden was the president of the Jaycees in a year when an inmate club was organized. He was tall, blond and had a clean-cut appearance, was extremely polite and *very* well-organized. He discovered a program that would collect coupons of many kinds and then contribute their value to the Easter Seal Society. Mr. Hamden was on a mission, collecting, cutting out, organizing and mailing as many coupons as he could possibly gather up. Staff members readily participated, and other inmates from around the compound helped.

I would love to know the end value of his efforts, but I remember that he raised thousands of dollars in redeemable coupons.

Our upholstery program, taught by the same person for more than two decades, gave many men wonderful skills to take out into the job market. In addition to upholstering furniture, they made hundreds of "Happy Hats" for sick children in nearby hospitals, accompanied by huge cards signed by the men with cartoons for children included. When the upholstery teacher finally retired at age 80, we had a huge party for her, and men lined up to help. One of her classes had upholstered a chair in green corduroy that sat in the office. When men were sent to the office to work out a behavior or other school-related problem, they sat in the Green Chair, often uncomfortably.

At her party, several students escorted her into the room, placed her in the same chair and presented her with a dozen roses. The student given that honor, one of our most upbeat students who seemed to never stop smiling, went down on one knee and proposed. Turning around to the big crowd of men, he announced, "She's *mine*—got that?"

The program had funny stories and skits from her classes, and then they presented her with all kinds of handmade gifts made in her classroom. We ended with a song, rewriting the lyrics to *My Old Kentucky Home*, accompanied by a small inmate pick-up band, mostly bongo drums. She loved it—and so did they.

After having a man for several semesters, I thought I knew him well. I certainly knew them as students, but rarely did I get to know the whole person. Mr. Dunn was middle-aged, gruff and grumpy most of the time. I rarely saw him smile, and if he did, it didn't last very long. He wasn't a very confident student, so he said very little. He did do all of his work. Students could get very territorial about where they sat—and want the same seat in another semester. I can still see him sitting in the second row, second seat. He didn't contribute to class discussions, and I thought I wasn't reaching him at all.

One day in a Round Table, issues of sexual orientation came up with some unsavory language and an argument, heating up as it went along. I tried hard to stay out of such conflicts, wanting the men to learn to solve them. All of a sudden, Mr. Dunn's deep voice rang out. "I can't believe my ears!" he said. "What in the world is the difference between how you're talking and the prejudice we feel as black people? Gay people are no different than any of us, and I'm not going to sit here and listen to this!" You could have heard a pin drop—and the subject was dropped too. I was as surprised as everyone else, but grateful for his courage. Several months later, as he was getting ready to go home, he appeared at my door one day. Many students came to say good-bye, and I assumed that was why he stood there.

"Come out in the hall, Mrs. Wenzel," he said. "I have something to give you. I know I can't give a present to you, so this can be part of the program. I know you don't have it because I've checked out the poetry books for a while now. I know you'll like it."

Nikki Giovanni's *Quilting the Black-Eyed Pea* was in his hands. A wide smile spread across his face. I was learning that God is generosity.

ALL MY HEART AND SOUL

I have a folder filled with thank-you notes that came to me over the years. Our students expressed their gratitude in every way they could. In addition to apples for the teacher and in greeting cards, they expressed their gratitude for school and their teachers' efforts at the end of the semester when they were filling out evaluations, in notes and letters, in Teacher Appreciation Day assemblies and in graduation booklets and speeches. They wrote us notes of gratitude as they were leaving to go home. They thanked anyone who gave them anything. Someone we did not even know donated a much-needed set of encyclopedias. Mr. Day ended his thank-you note by writing, "Mrs. Lent, we need more people like you in this cold, cold world."

My precious collection includes more hand-made cards than the Hallmark variety they could buy. They drew and painted roses and tulips; they made them black and red to reflect the school colors; they made them with quotes on the front.

Our outside guests provided a spark to long weeks and something to look forward to on the calendar. I spent time preparing my students for guests, and told them they would have a chance to write thank-you notes. This was an opportunity for the men to write something that was real, connecting them to the outside. The letters were lovely—honest and heartfelt. I never corrected anything. They had their own format, often starting letters with, "I hope this finds you in the best of health and spirits." They ended them in their own way, saying "I am grateful with all my heart and soul" and "Thank you dearly" and many with "God bless you." One man ended his note with, "I know there is a place in heaven all ready for you."

A deep humility imbued their thank-you's to guests and to me. When writing at the end of the semester, they would often express their academic insecurities. Mr. Gates wrote, "When I first came into your class, I didn't know anything and my eyes got opened to many different things. It was real hard but I was real glad. Next time when I'm in your class, I will do a lot better because I know I can. I would like to thank you very much for accommodating me in your class." I never asked him, but I wondered how much school Mr. Gates ever really had.

He also wrote to a guest, "Thank you for coming to see a bunch of convicts and letting us know we are important."

Mr. Ford wrote, "I lost my zeal for school a long time ago, and you helped me get it back."

Over and over I marveled about the joy of teaching adult returning students. I started my career there in my early forties and left in my mid-sixties. As I became a mother and then a grandmother figure, I got some Mother's Day cards. They would reference their own mothers and how much they were missed. As I got better at raising my expectations and making them work harder, they would thank me for that—at the *end* of the semester, afraid I would add more work if they said it before. "Thank you for believing in me," was a common refrain.

Their letters gave me a rare glimpse into how they saw themselves, and I read them over and over. In a two-page letter attached to a class evaluation, Mr. Hopwood gave me valuable feedback when he wrote:

"Don't give up on discussions. Although there are many complex issues that can't be readily discerned or internalized, just talking openly brings crucial points into focus for us. We need our intellects awakened. Honest and forthright discussions do that and add greatly to the tools we use every day as we interact with each other in here.

"It has been inspirational and gratifying to see guests come in here and teachers come every day to share their wisdom with us and give so freely of their precious time and energy to help us. I am so thankful to be part of this program. It restores my faith in people and lets me know that all is not lost and that there is still hope in the future. I am so thankful for a reciprocal exchange of opinions, an atmosphere of mutual respect

and tolerance for differences. Everybody has something to offer and this program gives us a chance to say it."

Mr. Engling was in one of my first history classes and played the role of the grandfather in our play. He had been in prison for decades and was delighted to be part of the program. I was new to having guests, but I could not have asked for more grateful students in a class. Mr. Engling told me how honored he felt to meet David Bassett, our Quaker friend and frequent visitor. In a letter to him, Mr. Engling wrote:

"Your presence, your knowledge, your interests and your compassion bring us a calm that dispels the tension in the air. You made a comment that I've been thinking about when you said that you are just an ordinary man. Many times, we cannot see the extraordinary because we focus on the ordinary in ourselves. Your own evaluations of your stature or impact among fellow men are not a good measuring rod as to the truth or totality of that impact. It is what stays behind when you leave that makes a much better gauge to measure by. Please don't let your humility rob you of the heart of the joy that comes from knowing how much you have helped us."

It was not unusual for a student to type two pages as a thank-you, needing to reaffirm their gratitude and I think, keep the connection real. Men struggling with English were no less sincere. Mr. Alanos wrote, "Thank you for visita and take time to come this place where everyone forgeter us as a person. Your visita change my mind about the gringos. They good people too."

Mr. Cabana wrote, "It was good experience for me to know some very important caring person like you."

One of the letters in my folder has a remarkably good pencil drawing of my friend who visited. Around her portrait he wrote, "Thank you for being so comfortable and not afraid of all of us convicts. That sure felt good!"

Another letter to the same guest asked, "Why is it that truly beautiful, wonderful, creative people like you are *never* in any position of power in the government??"

Part of the joy of these wondrous missives was that I could deliver them to the people who so generously gave us their time. No one seemed to expect them. Asking me to stay for tea one day, a friend couldn't wait to look at them. Before she'd read too many she was in tears, but she was not the only person with that reaction.

On occasion, when guests would come back for more visits, the guests would write back—to every student individually. One of our school superintendents did that, making my students speechless when they opened them.

One of my favorites from Mr. Tamif, who came from Turkey, was written to a violinist. "P.S." he added at the end of his letter, "I thought your outfit that night was in extremely good taste."

Mr. Mason was from Jamaica and came to us with reading and writing skills below fourth grade. He worked for years in our program, taking reading and language classes so that he could finally take the classes he needed to graduate. He rarely said a word—he was too busy working. I can easily remember him in the back row quietly bent over his work, his dreadlocks falling forward around his face. He wrote a guest, "Sir, you bring us grace."

Mr. Carmel, our resident philosopher, wrote, *"We are so blessed no matter what. We need to look hard to find the gifts we receive. Very often the gifts come wrapped in packages of pain, with loss, hurt and disappointments. These are valuable gifts because they say we can survive pain. It isn't those with the biggest names who make the biggest differences in our lives. It is those with the biggest hearts. You all will be my teachers for life."*

I cannot count the number of careful letters of gratitude and specific appreciation that Mr. C wrote over the years, all of them appreciated in return.

I've saved a small note from Mr. Ramsey and keep it near my computer where I can see it easily. It's in red ink and pasted on black paper, our school colors. I think of him when I read his note, see his ready smile and his long blond hair. I think of how hard he worked, how patient and loving he was to everyone every day. The note says, "Being in school not only changed my view of the world, but it changed my heart as well. Now that I see what is truly in my soul, I long to help other people out in the world. I will be forever in your debt. You were a guide that led me to my true self."

It is a cold, cold world, and prison is a cold place. But, like so many upside-down things, these men were able to warm it up in such loving ways. The gratitude—going in all directions across the fence—was such a lovely, loving connection, warming up a little part of the world. Their gratitude was an expression of God's grace. I was warmed then, I am warmed now and my folder, available when I need it, will warm me for the rest of my life.

CARING IS THE GREATEST THING, CARING MATTERS MOST
—Friedrich von Hügel

When I told people how kind and compassionate my students were, I heard variations on, "Ya, right. But what did he do?"

I even heard people say that anyone who sold drugs should get the death penalty.

What we learned in my classroom after years and years of rich arguments and helpful dialectics was this: Finding truth is hard and how people think is very interesting. We talked a lot about the difference between "little t truth," usually a collection of facts, and "big T Truth," the kind that embodies wisdom and larger kinds of understanding.

I see a very human impulse to believe things from people we know and trust—and to disbelieve people we don't like, disagree with or who push our buttons about what we care about. We see things through our own perceptions, often holding tight to our own version of the truth.

A presumptive truth surrounds us when people with authority, experience and power talk about the same thing over and over until it takes on a patina of truth—even if there's no basis in reality. If what is being told conveys fear, we believe the stereotypes to protect ourselves. Sometimes that means we deny what is right in front of us. If we've held a stereotype about another group and that idea is challenged, I think it often takes a while and often firsthand experience to admit we've been wrong. Within our politics of fear, finger-pointing and anger, I know of no more presumptive truth than the prison fence, a powerful symbol of good people being on the outside and bad people living on the inside. Once people are behind bars, the label of *bad* is hard to disprove and remove. When people are incarcerated, their mistakes, unfortunately, define them more than all the rest of their personalities and behavior.

Seeing them as bad people was never my experience. I had, over the span of 25 years, *the privilege of proximity*, the opportunity to know hundreds of men well. I saw a prison culture of caring, unlike what is shown on television. What I witnessed over and over, my "big T truth," were expressions of caring: condolences about losses, attendance to all kinds of suffering, compassion for all kinds of victims my students knew were far worse off than they were and ordinary hands-on help. What I saw every day was ordinary, everyday kindness. It never failed to move me.

Every assignment Mr. Carmel handed in ended with his philosophical thoughts for the day, such as, "Let us look into people's hearts. Let us find out where they hurt." I looked forward to every one of his papers, keeping many of them in a special folder. I saw tenderness and I saw wisdom in many people—all the time. Prisons aren't set up to be places of kindness and caring. It took courage and maturity for inmates to show their tenderness. It was not easy for staff either—to break the rules and respond with sensitivity and caring when it was needed.

Because they were not always treated kindly, the men I knew developed a hypersensitive awareness of kindness when they did receive it. Mr. C had to be taken out to a local hospital for a CAT scan. In spite of his sterling reputation, the two officers, both rookies, were required to follow the rules and put him in an orange jump suit and shackles. When they got to the hospital and were sitting in the waiting room, the technician on duty demanded they take the shackles off—or she would not take him inside for the test. When the officers hesitated, just doing their jobs and following the rules, she informed them they could simply take him back. They relented. When the doors were closed, she treated him like he was on a special outing that would be nothing but fun. "The first thing we need to do is to get you some ice cream," she announced. When he thanked her, she said she was just doing her job. Mr. C talked about the incident a lot after it happened.

"I was nervous about the test, and that woman made me feel relaxed and important. It helped a whole lot," Mr. C said.

Being kind took attention and courage to get above the institutional guidelines, and it was risky to break the rules. "Rules are meant to serve people," noted Amy, our minister friend. "But when people serve rules, we lose a chunk of our humanity."

Prisons are places of loss and grief. In an English class, there was a unit on letter writing in an easy-to-follow booklet with all kinds of examples. One was about writing a condolence note. Mr. Danson, a soft-spoken, shy young black man, sat in the back and said almost nothing in class, but his condolence note was so completely loving that I made a copy for myself.

"I will do anything I can to help you, and here is a list of things I can do," he wrote. "I will call you to see if you think of anything else."

In our own hard situations, how many empty promises have we all heard—and made? Mr. Danson's list went beyond the usual platitudes.

Mr. Sullivan lived on the snarky side of the street most of the time and put up a fuss about writing a condolence card. "Do you have any idea what I've been through?" he asked. I tried to make light of the assignment, asking how long it would take him and if he really wanted a zero. He did the assignment, later telling me that it had pushed him to think about a sister who had recently lost her husband. "It was late, but I finally wrote her a letter," he said. "And I feel better."

Before I knew my students well, Mr. Sullivan's snarky reaction was what I would have expected from most of them, but I discovered that attitude was rare. Their daily kindness and caring knocked me over. We talked about courage as I suggested they see courage as something beyond physical daring. These are people who dodged bullets in the streets, some of them for their whole lives. Prison forces an awareness of physical power if there are threats around—or until they learn there are not. Many men used the gym and pumped iron, were proud of their athletic and physical prowess. Another kind of courage is the effort to develop sensitivity and not worry if it is seen as "manly" or not. Prison is a classroom for that.

Kindness begets more kindness, and I watched these men build on their natural capacity for caring. Any story from the developing world traveled directly to their hearts.

"It makes me hurt to hear about people not having enough food or a decent place to live, so we really have nothing to complain about," Mr. Carroll said.

Mr. Mack, who was in the program for years, starting out as a nonreader, had an article for the Round Table about Michigan's Governor John Engler shutting down mental institutions.

"This bothers me so much that I couldn't sleep last night," he told the group. "Where are these poor people going to go? Where will they live? What will their families do?"

Having students in wheelchairs was not uncommon. I remember a very affable white student who was pushed into my room every day without ever having to do it himself. His classmates found a small table somewhere in the Complex and made a space for his chair and his table every day. When lunch was called, it wasn't unusual for men to argue about who would push him over to the chow hall. I saw this with people in wheelchairs all the time.

In 2009 and 2010, I taught a class about higher education and employment after they were released. The kindness they extended to each other warmed the room. Even when a student did a poor job in practice interviews with questions or conducted himself inappropriately, his fellow students would gently inform him how he could improve. One very young man was out in the hall nervously waiting for his final interview, the staff person ready at the table.

He finally came in, red-faced and flustered, saying, "I just can't get this knot on my tie right!"

Three men jumped up to rescue him.

I did not totally connect with every student. It bothered me sometimes, but I had to keep reminding myself about personalities and how sometimes they just don't click. Though Mr. Tellis was close to another teacher, he and I did not have a relationship. He walked in and out of my class as an excellent, straight-A student, but he said little and I didn't know him at all. He handed in a term paper at the end of the semester that was four pages, typed and double-spaced with no errors at all. It was very hard for them to type anything with just a few typewriters in the library and all of them in use all day. His essay went into my "Keep!" file immediately, one that I could bring out when I needed to be propped up.

He wrote about his time in another prison where the chaplain had a program for hospitalized inmates to make them feel wanted and to give them hope. Mr. Tellis looked for fellow inmates who could help, and before long found himself director of the program. He wrote that they all needed more training, and together with the chaplain set up sessions with someone from the outside. The work expanded to include a hospice program, and he wrote about how the men in his group had to learn to listen. This was at the beginning of the AIDS crisis, so with training they learned to not be afraid to touch their patients. They did it all—wrote letters, helped them shower, helped them eat—and got attached. "If everyone would spend more time helping other people out, this world would be so much better," he wrote. I wondered how many other men had experiences like this. If Mr. Tellis hadn't written this paper, he would have faded from my memory entirely.

———

My students' loving-kindness to me will stay with me for the rest of my life. My dad was an exemplary citizen, and I talked about him in civics classes. In the last months of my dad's life, I was often flying to see him. When I walked into the Complex after his funeral, current and former students were standing in a small group. When one of them called me over, they formed a tight-knit circle around me.

"We're SO sorry about your dad, Mrs. Wenzel. We've been praying for you since we heard, and we want you to know we've got your back." Then they presented me with a large envelope. Mr. C cautioned that I wait until I got home to open it. I was so glad I did.

It had a large, creative card they'd made with enough space to have people write notes and then passed it around so that men I'd had in class could sign it. It was filled with expressions of sympathy, care, concern and overwhelming human kindness. I dissolved in tears, and it remains one of my most precious possessions.

Early in January of 2008, I walked across my snowy driveway, hit a patch of black ice, fell and broke several bones in my ankle and leg. I needed surgery and a convalescence of several months. The warden, concerned about security, said I could not return to work until I could walk unaided. So, I could not go back to work until early March. By that time, I was fairly sick of sitting around all day and eager to get them back to work. Again, my students flocked around me. I explained that the best thing they could do for me was to work really hard. They did. I did not have to ask them to help with books and materials—they came in early and made a huge effort to clean up at the end of the day. Teaching while sitting down was not my style, so it didn't take me long to overdo it, yet I was miserable if I did not stay off my feet. The men watched me closely and devised all kinds of ways to make things easy for me. When I got there, they would have arranged the chairs so that I could put my foot up—with a cup of tea nearby. In a walking boot, I was limping fairly badly, so they would flank me going down the hall. Get well cards appeared on my desk every week, as did little notes saying, "Take it easy, Mrs. Wenzel. We want you to get well. We're praying for you." I could not have conjured up a more caring community.

Our friend April, a frequent visitor, said, "I sometimes forget that I am the one who gets ministered to when I visit. Just when I need it, one of them will say exactly the right thing."

Compassion is at the heart of world religions; and so many of the men I knew demonstrated that compassion was at the core of who they were.

Caring is the greatest thing. Caring matters most.

THE CHARM OF FLEETING MOMENTS

In spite of pain and loss, sorrow and grief, for the most part, my students got up in the morning, came to class, went to work and persevered. I spent 25 years wondering what got them up and what fed their spirits. Two stories of men enduring extreme conditions were helpful in answering the question. I read the story of Sir Ernest Shackleton's voyage to Antarctica and watched an amazing film of the crew's long ordeal after their ship was destroyed by ice. The whole crew survived, reporting the importance of *morale*. As long as they were hopeful and cheerful, they could deal with the ice and their wretched conditions. The other story comes from Laura Hillenbrand's *Unbroken*, an account of American airmen shot down over the Pacific in World War II, who were then held in a Japanese POW camp. They could deal with all kinds of brutality as long as they maintained their *dignity*. There is a link between finding beauty in the midst of ugliness to feed one's morale and enhancing a sense of dignity. My students often talked about needing dignity, and their caring for each other boosted their morale.

People behind bars miss the world beyond the fence. I heard them miss beds they could stretch out in, taking a bath, swimming, good food and home cooking, walks in the woods, seeing the stars at night. Mr. C told me one day that he would give anything to hold and play with a baby. The prison compound is monochromatic, and they miss color. Beautiful things matter to them in a different way; beauty pulls them out of the present ugly reality. People in prisons have a lot of monotonous time to fill. Mr. C told me once that daydreams were essential to surviving prison for him. The empty time stretched their imaginations to draw, paint, write poetry and letters, and occasionally—their life stories. They imagined beauty.

Mr. Garza was a middle-aged man from the Southwest, who wore a handlebar mustache and a huge smile all the time. He loved his art class and wrote, "Men and women have given us their dreams, their visions of beauty, their responses to good and evil, love and happiness, the great truths of existence. They have shown us that the human imagination has no limits and *the charm of fleeting moments* can be valuable forever."

I wanted to stimulate their imaginations. Playing music helped them write. Looking at art books gave them ideas. Paying attention to sunrises and watching the sky helped them put images on paper, and most of them loved trying to write creatively. There were always a few who rolled their eyes and fussed about not having any talent nor any creativity. The fussing led to discussions about what it means to be creative, what it means to be an artist. One day someone decided that *appreciating* beautiful things is part of being an artist too. We made a "poster in progress" and hung it up so that anyone could add to the list.

It started with: "An artist is anyone who" and they added the following: *"learns to love a poem he hasn't heard before;" "listens to new music and loves it;" "learns about a famous artist;" "watches the sky change;" "listens to birds sing and watches them fly;" "loves a big blizzard;" "makes a new friend."*

Thanking a musician who visited and played his harpsichord, they wrote: *"You moved my heart." "Music is the soul's language." "Your music brings peace to our lives." "Life without music would be like a tree without leaves."*

In such a deadening environment, being creative, no matter if you are the creator or the person appreciating art, not only wakes people up and uses all the senses, but it makes people feel more alive. In a place where your identity is a number, creating anything says, "I count, I matter." Being back in school was a creative process of re-creating and re-imagining themselves.

I decided to build on their love and need for beautiful things. Parker J. Palmer, author, educator, philosopher and activist, wrote several books on education. His writing and wisdom became a beacon for me. He wrote about *the grace of great things*. Fridays were the hardest part of the week for me. The afternoons could be chaotic in the competition with religious services, men extending breaks, and the every-student, every-teacher desire for the weekend. One semester I was at the end of my rope, especially dreading the last two hours of the week. I had to figure something out.

I knew that my students loved looking through books and that they responded positively to the arts. Knowing how much they loved rituals and something to look forward to every week, I borrowed Palmer's idea of great things and decided to try what we named Gather Around Great Things in the last hours of the week. I put them in the smallest circle of chairs I could manage, and one by one around the circle, they had to share something they found beautiful from the previous week.

I had a nice, easy group of men that I knew well, but I still approached new activities nervously. Men who had come around and learned how to behave well could regress into old habits when they felt threatened by something new, often making me a little wary about changing routines and trying something different. I knew that it would work only if they could see each other in a circle, and predictably, a few people balked at first. Generally, the men had all kinds of tools to thwart new plans. They left the room—or resisted moving their seats when they felt threatened or uncomfortable. Forcing any kind of intimacy could and did backfire on occasion. After all, they were *men*, living in a most inhospitable place. They had to learn to trust the process, trust each other and trust me.

It took a while for all of us to figure out some rules and get it right. We started small. This was an English class, and I'd learned that using the arts to stimulate creative writing worked. Gather Around had its own organic process as the weeks went along. I wanted them to search, so the rules were that they could bring a picture of their child or their girlfriend, but they also had to have a poem or something else to share. I said they could look through art and photography books, bring in or play a short piece of music or read whatever they found that really moved them. Most men found poems they loved.

Mr. Sinclair had a face full of freckles and a shock of thick, light brown hair. He was tall, lanky and laconic, never known for having any excess energy. We learned to expect him to come into the room on Fridays, usually at the last minute, see the chairs in a circle and say with a groan, "Ah no. Not again." Then he would rush into the closet, grab the same book of poetry every week and flip to the shortest poem he could find. Even Mr. Sinclair became part of the group as the other men teased him, patted him on the back after he read whatever page he'd found and said, "Wow! Just great man!" He would grin and his mumbling few words became part of the ritual.

I first thought I had to work on getting them into it. In one of the first few weeks, I brought in some flowers and set them in the middle of the circle. I tried to help them find things. I knew that my African American students loved the paintings of Jacob Lawrence, the poetry of Paul Laurence Dunbar and the photography of Gordon Parks; Hispanic men loved the murals of Diego Rivera and the poetry of Pablo Neruda; Native Americans loved books with photos by Edward Curtis and poems by Joy Harjo. But, they did not need me. I was continually fascinated by what they fell in love with and were eager to share—a piece of music played on a lute or a poem by Edna St. Vincent Millay or the determination of Eleanor Roosevelt. Every week someone shared something from a culture different from his own. Several of them found heartwarming news stories and shared those. None of my extra help was necessary, and they politely resisted me when my efforts were inappropriate. They were just fine on their own. These men knew all about what is beautiful.

Now, from a distance, I can see how much their resistance to my help affected me. I had to learn to respect them, give them lots of materials and a safe place to express themselves, but interfering or trying to *fix* people does not work. I learned to see the great complexity of who they were, not just as black students or Mexican students. Now I see that the search was about finding beauty—and at the same time, finding beauty in themselves. They were feeding their morale and enhancing a sense of dignity.

Gather Around evolved from semester to semester. Like the

Round Table, I was hesitant to join the group. Usually they simply went around the circle without a leader, but in one of the last classes before I retired, things changed.

I had Mr. Jacobs for several classes in which he did well, but he really struggled with both reading and writing in English class. He had a head full of braids, a pointy beard and soft, kind eyes — I love remembering him. He wrote about being a gang banger in California and how he'd been incarcerated as a teenager.

One Thursday, he said he needed to see me in the hall. "This Friday thing just ain't goin' right. I gotta take it over—and I don't really care what you say—you gotta be in the circle too."

Surprised, I agreed.

The next day he perched on top of his desk and in the gentlest of ways, led us around the circle. In a soft voice, he insisted that everyone pay strict attention and that everyone have as much time as needed. When it was Mr. Preston's turn, he said he didn't have anything—that he'd had a bad week. Mr. Jacobs asked him if he could tell us, and Mr. Preston shared that his mother was dying. Mr. Jacobs put his hand up when the next man began to share. "We need to hear more about that, brother," he said to the man whose mother was dying. They all listened as Mr. Preston told us more. The room fell silent when he finished and Mr. Jacobs let the quiet linger a little before he asked the next man to take his turn. I could not have managed to be so graceful.

Mr. Boyle, a middle-aged, very mature and charming man, hated being in prison and could not wait to get out. He kept reminding us of his out date as it came closer. Toward the end of the semester after a particularly beautiful round of sharing in Gather Around, he asked us, "What will I do when I go home and don't have this every week?"

Looking and thinking about beauty helped them find beauty in themselves. Mr. Kirkland, not yet 30, said, "Beauty is what motivates us to new life."

I loved Gather Around Great Things too, and it ended the week on such a high note.

A DINNER PARTY

Mr. Zeller was in his mid-seventies when, as a student, he had participated in one of our plays, immensely enjoying playing an old man. When it was over, he walked with me slowly down the hall. "Do you have a favorite restaurant?" he asked. When I said I did, he wanted me to imagine that he would take me to dinner there as a thank you. "I want you to think about ordering anything on the menu that you want, and I'm just real sorry I can't be the one to take you."

I thought about my own dinner party, how much I would love to have so many of these men around my own table. I started to imagine taking them home and making them dinner. I love dinner parties that create a space for people to express their inner voices about what matters deep in their hearts, of their ultimate concerns, of their biggest joys and largest sorrows. How honored I would have been to invite my friends and family—all of our voices blending together.

"The most substantial growth occurs in response to pain and disappointment. How we transform pain into growth defines who we are. Usually it's not the major crises that make us wonder if we are maturing spiritually, but the repetitive day-to-day aggravations that make us wonder about God's care," Mr. C wrote.

Prison certainly provides day-to-day aggravations, but men were expressing their inner voices all the time. Mr. Carson, our resident poet and the man who had defined prison as a village, was seeing himself close to the end of his life. He wrote that he had three jobs: *"1) to see God in everyone who crosses my path 2) to ask the right questions and 3) to die well."*

Mr. Ellison, a quietly thoughtful young black man, wrote: *"So many people are lost about who God is. We get stuck on labels and titles, instead of having a true understanding of what God represents. God is*

275

*not a label, and we are made in his image. God is love. He is humble,
understanding and patient."*

Mr. Jamieson was never enrolled in the program, but he worked
in the Complex and provided ever-present help. One semester he
often sat in on small group discussions and after one of them,
dropped a 3-by-5 card on my desk the next day. He wrote:

*"Through a series of troubles unwilled by me, I was faced with at
least three spiritual challenges. One is to forgive my enemies. Another
was to not live totally out of my guilt, and the last is to dampen the
invasive doubt that God loves me."*

All of the above men were bright and capable, had sufficient
language skills to describe their inner journeys. But, even when men
did not have the same verbal or writing skills, I saw the same
yearning toward being more spiritual and more whole.

I was warned about Mr. Koch before he began my civics class.
His test scores were miserable and his other teachers described him
as trying very hard, but tending to be disruptive in the process. "He's
very needy," another teacher said.

Since he lacked adequate writing skills, I had a hard time even
reading what he attempted to write, but he came alive in discussions.
When we talked about integrity one day, he said, "I don't know that
word!" Then he jumped up to cross the room and look it up. As we
filled out the meaning with examples, he said, "Oh! Doin' what's
right! *Now* I know. I think hard on that all the time!" Then as the
weeks went on, he was able to give the group all kinds of insights on
very complicated ethical situations. The strength of his inner voice
began to carry on the outside.

I know that having these men around my table would have been
a mystical experience, exhilarating and addictive. What a privilege it
was to see how the men yearned to make their lives better, listened
to each other and their inner voices, and found meaning and joy in
an ugly, lonely place.

I did not know that our village would be like a monastery. Nor
did I know that the long years spent with hundreds of men would be
a kind of pilgrimage we would take together. My students were

learning about and validating their basic goodness, discovering ways to make their lives more whole. I was learning to be a better teacher by listening and learning from them. I was discovering the richness and wholeness in my country's history and culture. I was on holy ground and in the company of holy men. On so many days, they enlarged and sharpened my experiences of who God is.

V. 'Make of yourself a light,'

said the Buddha before he died.
—Mary Oliver, *The Buddha's Last Instruction*

IN THE LAST few years of my prison classroom, I was experiencing a range of emotions. Like many teachers as they reach 30 years of teaching, I was feeling some burnout. My patience, which had always been fairly long, was waning. Mr. C's long sentence, then past the 20-year mark, still stretched on another six or seven years. The long years already behind him had taught him to pay attention to energy over time. When I would point out that an important worksheet needed a little revision, he would say, "Use your energy wisely. This lesson has worked for many years, and you need to think carefully about how you expend your energy." He was losing patience too, and I was worried about how he would endure even more years. We were both losing steam.

After so many years, and even though I was still being challenged by new students, I knew my students far better. My eyes and ears were sharper, and I understood some of the problems they would be facing when they were released. I still loved teaching English, U.S. history and civics, but it felt good to be teaching the course that addressed life skills like going on to school, developing job skills and learning how to manage money. By then, I had learned about the stress and trauma that men experienced in the few months before they got out, and I wanted to pull students together to talk about it. I could see how badly they needed to move beyond the identity of *felon* and feel like they had a secure and useful place out in the world. They'd had a lot of time to dwell on their mistakes, and I wanted them to approach the outside world with healthy attitudes about the good they could create outside the fence. I wanted them to *make of themselves a light.*

MISTAKES

After seeing something on television, my grandson Cameron, an old soul at age 4, wanted to know about prisons. Carefully, I tried to explain as he sat back in his car seat, one leg crossed over the other.

"Well, when people do bad things, sometimes we put them in places where they can't get out and do more bad things," I said tentatively.

"We lock them *up*?" he wanted to know, alarmed and now leaning forward.

"Sometimes we do," I answered.

"You *gotta* be kidding," he said. "I don't know anybody in the whole wide world who doesn't make a lot of mistakes." Out of the mouths of babes.

I attended an adult education program at the end of a school year and heard the speaker suggest this question to students: *Who has made a good mistake?*

My students and I talked a lot about mistakes because this was a group of people who understood them intimately. I used the question a lot, and discussions about what they would do differently the next time were always heartening to hear. When I think back on my prison teaching career, I know now that it was my many, small and large, sometimes embarrassing mistakes that made me a better teacher. Without them, I would not have reached my students in the most important ways. I would not have been able to hear what they really needed: to be given enough challenges, to have the support to work as hard as they could, to learn about their cultural heritage and the painful lessons of history and to learn to work together. The most important lesson I learned was to *listen* to them—and to put them in charge whenever I could.

We all make mistakes—it is the nature of being human. For me, there are many unanswered questions at the heart of prison reform.

We spend a lot of time looking at criminal behavior, but not nearly enough at the reasons the United States locks so many people up in the first place. We need to understand the origins and cultural beliefs surrounding our prison policies and why we've relied so much on punishment. We need to carefully examine our punitive policies. We need to examine the persistent racism that puts so many people of color behind bars.

The focus on punishment obscures the questions about whether or not people can change and improve. Larger philosophical questions lie underneath the beliefs about whether human beings are basically bad or basically good, basically important or really not valued at all. If we believe that human beings are basically bad, then we favor punishment over rehabilitation and have little faith that people can change and improve their lives. Punitive policies can also obscure our own behavior—and our own sordid history of racism in the United States. If we believe that people are basically good and we realize that we all make mistakes—and occasionally break the law—then we could reduce our prison population dramatically. We could try to understand that people behind bars are like the rest of us—and not project our own failings on people inside. We could make sure that all students are getting a good and comprehensive education—*before* they drop out and turn to criminal behavior.

If we want prison to be restorative, a high school education is a good start. Over and over, I watched as my students changed their identity from *drop-out* and *felon* to *graduate* and *successful person*. For decades, I saw examples of men who were transformed when given a chance to examine who they really were, a chance to find their inner light—and not just the darkness and brokenness that exists in all of us.

It's painful to look at our mistakes. I don't think any of us likes to look at what we have not done to make the world a better place, nor do we like to examine the dark corners that lurk in each of us, the potential each of us has for bad or even evil behavior in the right context or circumstances. We don't like to remember when we have stood silent or been complicit in wrongdoing. It has been painful for white Americans to look at the harm we've done and are doing to people of color. That doesn't mean we shouldn't do the hard, inner work.

I saw and knew people who needed time to think about how they'd hurt other people and make some serious course corrections. If people are a danger to society, then they need to be incarcerated so that the rest of us are safe. I want to be quick to say that owning our behavior, making amends to people that we've hurt is the first step in healing. In order to function in this society, we must learn to be responsible for our actions, to participate as responsible citizens, and if we are part of a family and or a community, we need to be responsible members of those groups. I think we also need to see that none of us gets it all right every day—these are daily, lifelong lessons for all of us.

Progress toward rehabilitation and restoration can be made behind bars, but we need to look at the larger picture. Our finger-pointing and pervasive, punitive attitudes define so much of our culture. My students responded so well to high standards that were set for them, to being treated with respect, to an expectation that they would behave honorably—and to being treated with compassion. We need to look at whether we are helping—or hindering the people shut away from the world they must eventually learn to function in. If people are assumed to be bad and in need of harsh punishment, what are their incentives to change and be better? Why would we believe our returning citizens would get out of jail and automatically turn into good people if they've been told and treated as if they were bad for years and years? How do they become responsible when so much responsibility is taken away from them as inmates? How do people function well in a world they haven't seen for years or decades? How do they possibly make it in the world without at least a high school education? How do they leave prison without crippling anger and resentment about so many years wasted and lost? How do they succeed in a world where so many doors are closed to them upon release?

Mr. Knox makes the case for looking carefully at people serving time for violent crimes to see whether they could be released. The Posted Picture File (PPF), a black-ringed binder containing the photos of supposedly dangerous inmates, was brought around only once in a while, dependent on the policies of the current administration. Lieutenants would call me out in the hall so that I could look through it and be duly warned. Federal staff people were simply watching out for us, but I hated looking through it. It felt like looking in their files to figure out what their crimes were—perusing the PPF was like the mistake I made in looking up a student's crime. Knowing they were perceived as dangerous did nothing to enhance our relationship, nor did I need the information in any way.

One day, I was called out in the hall to look through the PPF. I came back in after seeing Mr. Knox's mug shot in the PPF, and then I looked at him sitting in the front row working hard on an assignment. His photo exactly matched his long, messy hair, missing teeth, tattoos and dirty clothes. If seen in a dark alley, he would probably scare people.

Mr. Knox exuded all kinds of positive energy, coming into the room with a smile and a friendly greeting every day. He would often stop and tell me that he'd pondered a question or an issue from the day before. He wasted no time in class, working hard the whole time. Popular among his fellow students, he smiled and laughed all the time. When he discovered poetry, he fell over the cliff in love with both reading and writing it—acting like he had just been given the best gift of his life. He came bouncing in one morning with a big grin and said, "Mrs. Wenzel, you need to know you kept me up almost all night with this!" He was holding a beautiful poem he had written, reworked and tweaked for hours. It was called *Wild Grace.* I wish I'd asked him for a copy.

A favorite image of Mr. Knox stays with me. Our friend David Bassett came in as often as I thought I could ask him. At the time, he was a cardiac research physician and had been a Quaker for a long time. His many friends and acquaintances don't hesitate to call him "saintly." For one of his visits, I asked him to talk about the values that directed his life and the people who helped him articulate them. He told us about people like Quaker founder George Fox and how Quakers try to see "that of God in every person;" about each person being equal to every other person; about equality for women; about Lucretia Mott, another Quaker, who worked for the abolition of slavery and for women's rights. He mentioned Albert Schweitzer, a philosopher and physician in Africa. David talked about his own pacifism, his refusal to inflict suffering on any human being, and he talked about his efforts to prevent disease. He talked about the basic goodness of people and that what is right is always stronger than evil.

I can still see Mr. Knox pulling his chair as close to our honored guest as he could. He hung on every word, as if David was waking something in him. I remember the radiance in this student's face, as if there was a light shining on his essential goodness and all of his goodness was coming to life. I think about how many men told me that their biggest mistake was not the crimes they committed, but dropping out of school. After knowing how many people "woke up" to their goodness and light like Mr. Knox, I wonder what happens to the thousands of people behind bars who don't have the opportunity for comprehensive, challenging educational opportunities.

The other thing I remember about Mr. Knox is his relationship with his 18-year-old daughter. He had a pact with her about doing well in school as they would both graduate the same year. He would bring his daughter's report cards in to share with us, obvious pride showing all over his face. I got into it too—keeping track of her good grades. I was happy to write comments on his papers that he could send home. They did it; they both graduated the same spring! Shame and stigma attach to family members of people who are incarcerated too, but graduating from high school can ripple out and shore up people at home. Mr. Knox, as I knew him, was not the person the PPF portrayed. Looks—and a criminal history—are deceiving, and when given challenging opportunities to better their lives, most people will take them. When treated with respect and caring, most people treat others the same way.

My years in prison shone a light on truths I had not known at all. I learned many hard lessons and got many of my notions tipped upside down. The men I worked with taught me that it is impossible to draw a line and put good people on one side and bad people on the other. We are all far more complex—and more whole than that. There is good and bad in each of us, but what my students also taught me was that we are essentially good. For a long time in human history, great truths have come from outcasts. The men I worked with showed me, with gentleness and patience, that the truth is found in listening closely to people whose lives and views are most different from my own. And, they taught me that love can fill the distance between us.

As a country, we need to be accountable and admit the many mistakes we've made too, and it seems to me that the least we could do with people in prison is provide them with the chance to earn their high school diploma—and a way to get college credits too. Costs could be offset by reducing recidivism and the payments for social services when they are released. A good education supports self-knowledge. It's all part of a whole. Within prison settings, I can't think of a better way to restore goodness by giving people a way to correct their mistakes, a better way to spend money on rehabilitation, than to provide more education behind bars.

My students said it all the time. Mr. Rodriguez wrote: *"I have learned and discovered much about myself. I listen harder and pay attention better. School has lured me with its contagious magic, and I have discovered how to love in a way I never knew existed."*

Mr. West, with his long ponytail and newfound love of poetry, said he was writing poems for his granddaughters. In one of his own poems, he wrote, "Open a light for my darkness."

SHORT

Many men were distracted when they were *short*, close to the day they would be released, their *out dates*. They struggled with sleep problems and worried about how the outside world had changed. They wondered how they would be able to cope with myriad challenges before them: reconnecting to families, especially their children; finding housing; getting adequate health care, and learning technical skills with things like computers and cell phones. What I heard most was their worry about getting a job, now that they were marked as ex-felons or ex-offenders in many places. Progress has been made with language, however, as people familiar with the issues are now insisting on calling people who have done time *formerly incarcerated* and *returning citizens*.

Mr. C often talked about the damage from very long sentences. The world—and families—change very fast, and he would say that the longer the sentence, the harder it was to re-enter the world. When asked what is the most difficult day to be in prison, I heard many fathers say it was on their children's birthdays. No wonder. I don't know any parents who don't regard their kids' birthdays as special, even momentous days. In prison, a child's birthday means not being there and it means another year missed and forever gone. I watched Mr. C endure so much heartache about his children growing up without his presence and guidance, and I watched him miss his children all the time. Many of the men I knew missed everything about their children growing up. There is no way to imagine or calculate what the children missed without their fathers.

I watched prison make parenting so hard. My students had fathers who were also incarcerated, making incarceration generationally even more complicated and challenging for families. Telephones were a constant hassle. People had to be aware of time zone differences and stand in line. Calls were expensive, limited to fifteen minutes, and could be monitored by the institution. They could send letters home, of course, and many of them did, but letters are no substitute for being able to spend time with someone. An e-mail program was introduced with computers in the hall of the Complex where our classes were held, and that helped. Not every family in poor communities has a computer, however. The harsh and damaging realities of separation remain.

The Bureau of Prisons tries to place an inmate close to his family, but that doesn't always happen. It was heartbreaking to hear about family members too far away to visit. In many instances, people could not afford the bus fare—or the motel bills once they got there. We were amazed during a graduation to meet one of our graduate's mothers, who had never been away from her reservation in the Southwest but had saved her money for a long time in order to take the bus across the country to be there at the ceremony.

That men were nervous while short was no surprise. I knew a lot of men who didn't have the first idea of what to do when they were released. They were handed a small amount of cash and given a bus ticket. Some went to half-way houses with many restrictions.

Mr. Baker was in his fifties and in one of my early humanities classes. He had a gentle smile and rarely said anything. He was short after a sentence of several decades. Naïve and lacking experience, I stopped by his desk one night to sit next to him and ask if he was excited about going home.

"I've been down 30 years, and I don't have any family left. I have a daughter somewhere, but I've never met her. I have no idea what I will do or where I will go when I leave," he told me. I can still see his deadened face and the tired look in his eyes.

Many things would be forever changed when men went home. While serving their sentences, men feared being called to the chaplain's office because it usually meant bad news about a loved one. It was hard enough to endure the loss of loved ones in any place, but when they heard of a death at home, I could see them drift around the compound like they did not know where to go or what to do with themselves. Missing funerals was very hard.

My employment and educational opportunities class had its challenges. Even without a prison record, many of my students were people who would not have an easy time securing employment—let alone a job that would support them adequately. The number of my students who had never held a job was staggering—really no surprise when they had grown up in impoverished inner cities. Most of the schools, teachers and programs in their community had been compromised by a lack of support and had been underfunded for decades. Jobs are not plentiful in these communities.

When asked, "What have you done that you never thought you could do?"

Mr. Hoover answered by saying, "I got a job in the unit as I was starting school, and I'm holding it down and doing a good job. I never thought I could do that."

We worked on résumés, but with no experience out in the world of work, they had to figure out how to sell their prison job experience to an employer. It took weeks for most men to write a decent résumé—often because the student did not think he had anything to offer. Luckily, I had computer assistance in a federal computer lab and from other inmates who were happy to be creative, encouraging and helpful. The big, scary, elephant-in-the-room issue they dreaded talking about with employers was about being labeled an ex-felon. No matter how much they practiced talking about it, it was never easy. My brother Eric visited and helped us figure out the difference between *qualities* like being honest, hard-working and reliable and *qualifications,* such as their education and experience. He told them to establish their integrity immediately by being straightforward and honest in the interview and to talk about the positive ways they had learned to cope inside prison walls. But, it was still a tall order. Helping them think about the qualities they had developed as inmates like being eager to learn, eager for challenges and being able to get along with people in difficult situations, was helpful to balance the reality of no job experience outside prison walls. They could and did include having a high school diploma and some training in building trades, auto mechanics and janitorial work that the federal system provided.

Still, I was always struck by how potent the identity of ex-felon was—even as they practiced in interviews with fellow students. They needed all the confidence they could round up. I loved watching them grow in the interview process, and we all delighted in seeing someone do really well, but the subject of prison time made almost all of them nervous and tongue-tied.

I found it hard to tell students just how difficult the real world would be. They had every reason to feel nervous and scared. The problem is that even getting an interview is very difficult if the employer discovers the person has a record. Even if they have their record expunged or they live where they "ban the box," the question of whether or not an applicant has been convicted of a felony is not on a job application, the gaps in the résumés become huge red flags. Many of my students wanted to start their own businesses, which in the current job market is a good direction, but small businesses are difficult with little business training or experience. Visitors from two- and four-year colleges came in and told them that high school is really not enough for good paying jobs and that two years of community college or technical training were far better. In my first few years, a college program provided classes toward an associate's degree. When Congress cut funding for Pell grants in 1994, the college program vanished. There were a few college correspondence classes, but no real comprehensive programs.

When I talked to a particularly bright and eager student about college, he told me that he knew no one from home who had even attended college classes. I wondered how my students would fare in college classes if they had no mentors to provide direction and support. I talked a lot about the value of community colleges, but the reality of going home and facing the challenges of supporting themselves and their families does not give them much energy for adding the logistical and financial stress of even taking a few courses. It sounds good to those of us who take college for granted, but it represents a far dream for people who don't have a car and have trouble with rent and groceries.

Still, a high school diploma in hand makes a huge difference. It was not just the piece of paper, but the "soft skills" and confidence that people gain when they've been able to figure it out, do the work and accomplish something difficult.

Mr. Walls wrote this when he was short:

"My personal experience with the educational system since I've been incarcerated leaves no doubt in my mind that it is the No. 1 rehabilitation tool. I haven't been free for 25 years. I was an 18-year-old high school dropout and took my education for granted, so much so that I could barely read or write at the time of my imprisonment. Since getting involved with education, I've been able to grow as a human being and understand the wrongfulness of my conduct, which created my lengthy stay in prison. The pursuit of education is a discipline. Not only did I have to learn the lessons being taught but I had to be conditioned to work hard and constantly to achieve my goals. I was living in darkness. Education has been the bulb that has lit up my mind and world. It has given me hope."

I couldn't imagine him not being able to read or write. His written work was done with thought and care until it was perfect. He aced every test, and he was engaged in every discussion we had. I wondered what would have happened to him out in the world, if it hadn't been for the years of school he had in prison.

Being a serious student taught them to be punctual, to be reliable and accountable not only to assignments, but to other members of a group. The wide diversity in cultures, age, life experience and nationality taught them how to get along and appreciate people who were different. Important in a setting like the rule-bound prison, school taught them to make good decisions. It taught them to look at the other side of an issue, that sometimes there is more than one answer or solution. Getting encouragement and help from their fellow students helped them try and try again.

"The most important thing I've learned is to pick myself up and go on after failure," Mr. Lott said.

I hoped that when employment doors would close in their faces, they would keep trying.

For inmates who are short and don't have time to graduate, a GED was a chance to have high school equivalency. Some inmates wanted only a GED and were not interested in getting a diploma, and I knew many men who wanted both. Every inmate faces a different set of circumstances, of course. If there is a big network of support, they can do well. Men going back to reservations have a hard time. There weren't many jobs when they were arrested, and little has improved on most reservations. In some parts of the country, Hispanic men leave prison and face the growing oppression and harassment experienced by immigrants in the United States. Some of them are fearful of being deported to face even more disconnection from their families.

Mr. C used to tell me that prison gave people lots of time to daydream. To get started on a writing project, I asked them to make a list and finish the sentence, "Someday I would like to ..."

Here is some of what they wrote:

"... erase my childhood"

"... just hold my baby girl"

"... hug my family whenever I want"

"... be a good father"

"... go home and finally appreciate my family"

"... be successful at selling real estate so that I could find a good woman"

"... eat whatever I want"

"... never hurt anyone again"

In civics classes when we talked about our inalienable rights and their corresponding responsibilities, they said "freedom" is:

"... not having your wants bigger than your wallet"

"... not being restrained or restricted from society after my time is served"

"... applying for a job and not have anything about felons on the application"

"... having a good job and being paid enough to support my kids"

We spent a lot of time talking, brainstorming and dreaming about what kind of job they would like. It sometimes broke my heart to hear them talk about wanting to be physical therapists, nurses, kindergarten teachers, high school math teachers, day care and elder care workers. We have created such a culture of fear around the word "drugs" that any job requiring a license is a barrier in most states. I had a lot of nervousness about the harsh world they would face, but I wanted them to dream big too. When I heard them talk as if they wanted to be architects and doctors, accountants and professors, I encouraged them.

We were asked to leave our room one Friday afternoon, and a number of people were missing from class. Without access to our books and materials, I decided to do something fun. We had been talking about the rise of cities in history class, so I suggested they plan the Perfect City. I gave them large pieces of paper and all kinds of markers, pens and crayons. They put their heads together and came up with the most imaginative city plan I have ever seen, which turned into a 3D model in many colors. They had experienced cities that do not work, so they drew large green spaces, green transportation, neighborhood gardens, bike trails, futuristic modes of getting around, open schools connected to the community, fresh air markets and all kinds of spaces and structures where children could play. One very bright student interested in architecture was on fire that day.

Who is to say that they could not be urban planners too? If we cared enough about them and what happens to their futures to put enough money, creativity and training to get them back on their feet, they do have their own answers—and many for the rest of us too.

OUR BEST STUFF

I think Americans are basically good people, kind and generous, which doesn't square with what I heard from many students: *Nobody cares about us.* The problem is our disconnections from each other and how we misunderstand people we don't know. With over 2 million people locked up in this country, more than in any other country in the world, it is not hard to understand why people inside prison walls would feel forgotten and erased. These ugly realities represent huge fractures in our common American life, and our *united* states don't feel that way anymore. It's as if we live in different countries within our national boundaries, and mass incarceration does not represent our best stuff. Instead, it characterizes our deep divisions. The prison fence is a powerful tool to keep us divided.

Even in the same community, it's as if different groups live in separate circles, segregated by income, by race, by educational levels and by ethnicity. Different groups relate to each other like foreign countries who do not speak the same language or have the same currency, and the gaps between the groups continue to widen. Without thinking very much about it, people with privilege accept the hierarchal structures America has forged. Citizens accept that people with money and power get more privileges. We accept the assumptions that people with money—and their children—matter more. We accept the assumption that "successful" people, the ones with power and money, *know* more. In many instances, paternalistic policies are inevitable.

Over and over again, I was struck by the deep divide between privilege and poverty. My experience growing up comfortably with expectations of security and prosperity was worlds apart from the kind of confused murkiness my students experienced about their futures. As I grew up, I had no doubt whatsoever about being able to settle comfortably in the middle class. My students helped me open up other perspectives, and I continue to realize how much I take for granted, how judgmental I can be, how much my life experiences blind me. When I examine the wealth divide and understand the head start my siblings and I had growing up, it creates feelings of both gratitude and embarrassment. Looking at my automatic expectations of a good job and a good salary along with attaching entitlements, like being able to be buy a home in a neighborhood I choose, makes me uncomfortable. Our parents expected all of us to get a college education. Though we moved a lot, my family *owned* our houses. We took getting help for college and on down payments on mortgages for granted. It was like hearing about another world when my students talked about "comin' up," of what they could neither expect nor even envision. Even after 25 years of listening, reading and trying to understand, I still don't know what it feels like to be traumatized by poverty, racism and violence.

We may espouse our "rugged individualism," but it is our family backgrounds going back decades, our inherited savvy about negotiating the world, our stable communities, our good schools and some government perks all working together that gets our kids in college and ahead in the game. It will require much effort, risk-taking and painful personal realizations for more affluent, white people to understand, to not expect poor people and people of color to be "financially responsible" or to "make good decisions" when their realities are so drastically different.

Our prison problems reflect the huge divide and present huge complexities and misunderstandings. I began to see that my frustration with my students about not being able to set goals or think about their future came from their experience growing up and feeling overwhelmed about *today*. Those of us who own homes, have savings accounts, investments and some financial savvy, an education and marketable skills, have the luxury of looking ahead.

I participated in a national forum about private prisons and talked to a black community organizer, who was a grandparent.

"The system is so stacked against us that I worry constantly about the young men in my family going to prison," he said.

As a parent, the idea that any of my children might go to prison has never crossed my mind. Too many of my students told me that they simply assumed while growing up that they were going to spend some time in jail.

The drug problem presents another complexity. Language is powerful. The *War* on Drugs speaks volumes, though the grim realities of the drug wars elude most of us who live in nice neighborhoods. Our middle-class denials of our advantages spill over into the issues of drug use. "Just Say No" is still with us decades after Nancy Reagan coined the phrase. We've made little progress treating drug use as a health problem instead of a criminal or moral one. We focus on people making "bad choices." Selling drugs in order to survive is an alien concept for people who derive their income from sustainable employment.

De-facto segregation exists everywhere. We have a racial divide from north to south in Michigan, which creates all kinds of separation and misunderstandings. Many people don't know anyone who doesn't look like them, and fears seep in. White people are often unaware of how afraid black people are, how intimidated they feel about being outside of their own safety zones. Going to all-white communities, in spite of our warm invitations and hospitality, can make them feel nervous—sometimes even frightened. I don't think we begin to understand how marginalized, nervous, intimidated, frightened and bullied black, Hispanic, Native American, immigrant and Islamic students feel in our schools across the country. We should not be surprised by gaps in achievement or dropout rates.

It saddens and frustrates me that we are so divided, as our fears about safety and security creep in, and we get paralyzed into political inaction. It's painful to realize how seldom we really try to understand another reality and put ourselves in other people's shoes. We don't know each other, hear each other's stories, listen hard to understand how differently people see the country we all live in.

Powerful media narratives, which report far more frightening news than anything that would make us feel sympathetic and secure, feed the problem. To be tough on crime has worked well for politicians, winning elections. A sense that the criminal justice system is *American*, therefore impartial and fair, pervades the culture. Many Americans still resist talking about and examining racism and classism, still have few real tools to discuss and understand the structural complexities in a constructive way. So, what we hear is "three strikes" language and talk about throwing away the keys. Television, with its increasing reporting of crime, despite the fact that violent crime rates continue to fall, does an excellent job of telling us how afraid we need to be, its racist elements alive and well.

Mr. Walls was my student after having served 25 years. He was short when he wrote this: *"I have thought a lot about this in the quarter of a century I've been locked up. When it is their loved one who is charged with a crime and convicted, they always want leniency, mercy and humane treatment for their loved one. But, when it happens to people you feel no connection with, it is common to hear cries of, 'Execute him!'"*

Exactly. It is our disconnections that form the basis of the problem, and people pay dearly for our fears. It is my hope that these stories at least begin to open people's minds to our citizens behind bars.

Mr. Walls is a good example of another potent problem: the idea that people who've committed violent crimes need to *stay* in prison. I need to be clear. Many people are too dangerous to be on the outside. But, I knew many men who talked about outgrowing the violent tendencies of their youth. Mr. Walls was one of them. He was very open about committing murder as a teenager, and about how his thinking and behavior had changed.

"I grew up in a terrible neighborhood where violence was a given. I had a gun, and in a bad situation, I used it to kill another person. I will never get over my guilt about that, but I can make my life count in positive ways."

Mr. Walls worked tirelessly against the death penalty, writing letters and speaking to any group he could. He provided rich discussions on the topic in my civics classes.

In many ways, prisons are a failure of community. Two factors sustain a community: All people are cared for and valued, and people are held accountable for their behavior. The mere removal from society and putting people behind the prison fence does not lead to automatic accountability. My students talked about feeling *warehoused,* feeling locked up and forgotten without adequate skills to succeed on the outside. Exiling people away from society takes away the very skills they need to survive: how to get and manage training and education, how to manage work in the world, how to build community and community support, and how to be good parents and partners. Prison is reductive. At a time in their lives, especially for young men, when they need to be growing and learning, inmates are diminished, becoming a federal number they are assigned and taking on the label of *felon* and then *ex-felon,* which makes getting a job even more difficult when they are released.

It is heartening to hear interest in prison reform from both liberals and conservatives. We cannot continue to wage the drug war and lock people up, nor build more prisons. It will not make us safer when so many communities are ravaged. Our disconnections are breaking and overshadowing our old, courageous abilities to love and care for each other, and we are turning on each other. We are allowing our fears and greed to accentuate our differences instead of reaching out to include, befriend and accept all of us as part of a whole. We are a better people than that, and there are solutions if we care enough.

I knew of many people who volunteered in this prison in religious groups particularly. I know a woman who has visited one man once a month faithfully for years and years, and I heard men say that they had a pen pal to correspond with them. I know of a program in which volunteers collect children's books, and then they help men read and record them for their children. A letter from dad, the recording and a copy of the book goes home to the child.

If I could wave a magic wand, I would have Truth and Reconciliation Commissions all across the country to heal our old and potent misunderstandings around race: the ugly legacies of slavery, Jim Crow and the subsequent, powerful, hierarchal structures that so successfully keep people of color in inferior schools, hinder fair housing and hiring, widen the wealth gap, limit access to good health care and have given us such realities as racial profiling and many black people killed by police, mass incarceration and prisons for profit. I wish we could see drug use as a health issue and not a criminal one. I wish we could see prisons as places of healing and rehabilitation instead of punishment and warehousing. I wish more and more restorative justice practices would provide great hope as both victims and perpetrators meet each other in carefully monitored sessions to heal the hurt and damage experienced on both sides —and, in the process, to build community.

Hopefully, we will be able to summon our best stuff. The men and women wasting their lives behind the fence are not irrelevant. We are *all* diminished if we allow the destructive policies that create bad and failing schools to continue, if we continue to allow racist policing procedures, if we turn away from the number of people of color behind bars in the United States—and if we fail to understand how punitive attitudes and policies only make things worse. So many of the men I was privileged to teach spent years of their lives languishing behind bars because they made the first mistake of dropping out of school. We need to look at our many failing schools and see that *all* children need to be nurtured and challenged.

Those of us on the outside are not served in any way by not knowing—or caring about—our fellow citizens behind bars. I grew up with the notion that the opposite of love is not hate, but indifference. Prisons, by their very secretive nature, create indifference. This is not our best stuff. No one's life is served without an education—or an inadequate one, and we can all work to promote good schools for all children. We can write to legislators and support educational programs behind bars. Education extends their reach in the world— beyond the fence. Education is the beacon, like a lighthouse that guards against danger and provides a reassuring light in the darkness. It helps them grow and it leads them into a deeper way of living— just what they need to put meaning into their lives.

OUT DATES

When I arrived one Monday morning in the fall of 2009, Mr. C looked like he hadn't slept in days. When I asked if he was sick, he confirmed that he'd barely slept all weekend. At the end of the day, he said there was a note for me in my bag. I went home, went for a walk and forgot about it for an hour or so. He had been chiding me about taking better care of myself, and I'd put it off. When I opened the note, he had written that he was going home. I didn't see that it could possibly be true, even though he had waited patiently for about a year to hear from a court after Congress passed some legislation to shorten sentences. Then, I could hardly sleep. He had looked beaten down by the years for a long time, and I was amazed that finally, he would be free. I got there early the next morning—and was shocked to hear him say, "I don't have an out date yet, but I'm hoping there's more time before I go. I'm not ready to go home yet—and my family isn't ready either." He wanted to be there for graduation and be able to set things up in Jamaica. He hadn't counted on eight more months until he was released.

The first years were very hard for him "back home" in Kingston, a place plagued by poverty for decades. I talked to him often on the phone when he went home to Jamaica. He talked about being overwhelmed by the size and choices in a supermarket and had to ease back into grocery shopping in small, manageable doses. He hadn't driven a car in over 20 years, so he talked about his fears about that, again taking it slowly. He found a very helpful young man in a bank and was very grateful to have him slowly explain banking procedures and obstacles like cash machines, radically different from what they had been before his incarceration. He had a very hard time finding work.

But, after a course in business management and some connections to foundations and organizations with grant money, he planned and supervised the construction of a community center on the street where he grew up. Named after his neighborhood, it is called *The Waterhouse Center for Excellence,* and he describes a music studio, after-school programs, computers donated by a corporation and computer classes. He has partnered with a university for student teachers to hold classes in the arts and has planned soccer teams and community gardens. It is exactly what I always expected of him. Talented and open-hearted, he knows the value of *connections* and how people have a huge need to take care of each other. He also insisted, "I'm doing this for *me.*" So many of the men I knew had a huge need to give back to their communities.

———

Mr. Urban, an orderly, worked very hard as he cleaned every day, and though he could not read at much more than a third-grade level, he loved being in school. I struggled to understand his speech, mumbled and exacerbated by not having any teeth. He was in his sixties, smiled all the time and was the first one there to open the door, straighten desks and greet everyone.

During one cold and flu season, I decided to do a quick cleaning in our classroom, gathering pails of hot soapy water and some rags. I had no clear plans for this activity, but I wasn't needed. Mr. Urban took over. This was his turf as he blocked the room into sections, put men on teams, showed them the best way to work and then moved across the hall to another empty classroom. The place sparkled when we were finished. He grinned from ear to ear, bowing to the applause from his classmates. I remember learning in college education classes that a teacher's best friend in the building was the custodian. This was no less true in a prison school, and any workplace would be brightened by the likes of Mr. Urban.

Not every single one of them, but most of them can be custodians and theologians, businessmen and job creators. They can be drug counselors and mentors of at-risk kids. They can be imams, priests and preachers, personal trainers and computer experts, artists and craftsmen. They can be cooks and chefs. With help and support, they can go to college, work hard and shine brightly. All of them could make us richer in spirit as a people. They can become the people they were born to be, use their gifts, take their rightful places on the American stage.

In one of his Round Table comments, Mr. Lara wrote: *"All I hear and see in the news is talk about gas prices, the rising prices of everything, the sliding economy and how the American people can make a better living. But, I truly believe that there is something infinitely better than making a living and it is making a noble life."*

Mr. Lara went home. Hopefully, the way ahead is clear enough for him to live his noble and honorable life. Many of the men I taught reached their out dates and went home, but I often think about many others I knew who continue to serve their sentences year after year and decade after decade. They will never get those years back. Under President Obama, Congress did shorten sentences that affected many inmates who went home before their long sentences were totally over. Congress and state legislatures could do far more. Many men outgrow their youthful, violent tendencies and need to be released. Legislators need to hear from their constituents about prison reform in its many iterations.

One (very hot) day in summer school, I had piled the work on. Mr. Durham had been my student for many semesters and worked very hard every day. But, I could tell on many days that he was getting sick of school—and sick of me.

Watching in dismay as I put one more assignment on the board, he said, "Miz Wenzel, when you gonna retire?"

"When I can no longer make you work hard," I replied.

Turning to the man next to him, he noted, "She ain't there yet."

Continually challenged by new material, new ways to approach a lesson and new men in my classroom, I was a happy teacher. I wondered how in the world I would live without the joys of working with these men, and I worried that I would not know when to leave—leaving anything at the right time had never been one of my strengths. But, in 2010, my last school year, my energy was fading. I was there, facing my own out date. Leaving was hard and I had to do it slowly, but I knew my time was up.

I had reached the end of this remarkable journey.

Epilogue

Retirement is filled with sweet memories that come unbidden all the time. My decision to be a teacher felt like the only one open to me when I was in college, but I was so lucky—education was the right place for me—and the forces that put me in this particular classroom will astound me for the rest of my life.

The faces of so many men, smiling, leaning intensely over their work for hours, days, weeks and years, come to me often and give me courage and hope about the world and the country I live in. I feel so fortunate to have known these men and their intense desires to make something better of their lives. I wish all that life-giving energy I received over so many years could be bottled up and marketed. When I feel down or discouraged, I think of their loving-kindness, their humor and their wisdom. Their uncommon grace. I remember this lesson especially: that loving-kindness is our greatest strength as a nation.

My men lovingly chipped away at my white, middle-class privilege and opened my eyes to other stories that make us Americans. I now see my country as far more complex, and though it was painful to hear so many heart-rending stories, my students opened both my eyes and my heart to realities I would never have known otherwise.

For 25 years, they were patient and loving about my wrongheaded-ness. They let me know how bright and wise they were, that they deserved my hardest work. They let me make mistakes and develop the humility I needed to nurture the very best of who they were. They helped me see my country whole. They made me more whole.

They were among the finest people I have ever known.

Acknowledgments

Writing *Light from the Cage* spanned many years. I could not have completed it without people's consistent presence, patience, and encouragement along the way. So many people listened to the stories from my classroom and to my angst in hard times. They not only provided hospitality and comfort, but good direction. They visited our classroom, read parts of this book, helped with technology, opened their homes, set up places for me to speak and came to hear me. They accompanied me, commiserating with disappointments and celebrating successes. I owe all of these fellow travelers my immense gratitude.

In alphabetical order they are: Mary and Harvey Amoe, Doris Bernlohr, Sarah Beuker, Pat Bova, Jan Brimacombe, Nancy Bristol, Brenda Brown, Denise Campbell, Pat Chapman, Sacha Coupet, Martha and Tom Daniels, Phyllis Ford, Marijo Grogan, Fred Fuller, Eileen Hatch, Nancy Heers, Amy and Rob Heinrich, Sandy and Tom Hines, Marie and Kent Imai, Erika and Kenny Ingle, Greg and Jennifer Lamb-Taylor, Wiete Liebner, Peg Lourie, Vivian and Dennis Low, Milli Maddux, Mary Anne Perrone, Dal-Mar Roquemore, Ron Simpson-Bey, Elsa Stuber, Lisa and Mark Stucky, Jane and Joe Swallow, Ginny and Keith Titus, Sue VanAppledorn, Linda Wan, Sheri Wander, Nancy Wessinger and La'Ron Williams.

I also owe some wonderful readers and editors my gratitude for their finely-tuned efforts in helping me shape and polish this story. Betty Damren read the early drafts and has been a cheerleader since the beginning. Cathy Chiappe, Patti LaLonde, Sarah Mahoney and Betty Werth Westrope read another draft, responding with careful edits, good cheer and valuable advice. Amber Hughson provided her expert editing—and her friendship. Stephanie Mills read the manuscript, offering her unique vision and her experienced inspiration. Sonya Vann DeLoach, with extraordinary patience and expertise, provided final and copy edits. Their commitment and their big hearts mean everything.

My Patterson siblings, Mary Beall, Mark Patterson and Patty Barrowman, Madeleine Langlois and John Patterson, have listened, read, provided technical help and provided their own special brands of hospitality. My Wenzel family is: Stefan and Gina Wenzel, Seth Wenzel and Marc Watson, Natalia and Pete Raftis, Zoe and William, Cynthia Wenzel Cole and Cameron Cole. They all provide constant joy and love in my life and are steadfast with their support

Fifth Avenue Press at the Ann Arbor District Library came along at just the right time with just the right help. My heartfelt thanks to all the members of the team.

About the Author

Judy Patterson Wenzel has been engaged in prison reform as a teacher, speaker and writer for more than thirty years.

She lives in Ann Arbor, Michigan.